IF YOU LIVED HERE YOU'D BE FAMOUS BY NOW

IF YOU LIVED HERE YOU'D BE FAMOUS BY NOW

TRUE STORIES FROM CALABASAS

Via Bleidner

FLATIRON
BOOKS
NEW YORK

IF YOU LIVED HERE YOU'D BE FAMOUS BY NOW. Copyright © 2021 by Via Bleidner. All rights reserved. Printed in the United States of America. For information, address Flatiron Books, 120 Broadway, New York, NY 10271.

www.flatironbooks.com

Designed by Omar Chapa

The Library of Congress Cataloging-in-Publication Data is available upon request.

ISBN 978-1-250-75393-9 (hardcover)
ISBN 978-1-250-75392-2 (ebook)

Our books may be purchased in bulk for promotional, educational, or business use. Please contact your local bookseller or the Macmillan Corporate and Premium Sales Department at 1-800-221-7945, extension 5442, or by email at MacmillanSpecialMarkets@macmillan.com.

First Edition: 2021

10 9 8 7 6 5 4 3 2 1

To my mom

Contents

Abstinence and Adderall

It's mid-September. But in Los Angeles, autumn waits. Autumn sits back and lets summer overstay her welcome while we settle in our desks and listen to the rhythm of an old air conditioner chugging through a dense heat. It never gets cool enough. The archdiocese regulates room temperature from Wilshire Boulevard, but they never account for the special kind of heat that lives in the Valley—specifically, Woodland Hills. The sauna suburb. It's often a good ten degrees hotter than anywhere else. Right on the edge of severe drought, the city has just recently turned to regulation gravel yards and potted cacti. Chapped soil crunches under our uniform sneakers. At home, neighbors are encouraged to alert the city about any houses watering their plants more than once a week. We grow suspicious. Sprinklers turn on only in the loneliest hours of the morning. Some nights I lie awake, tuned in to the gentle chirping of irrigation systems activating in secret. Where is El Niño, we wonder? Does he watch us while we brush our teeth? Each time I open the faucet for a drink of water, I feel a pang of guilt, imagining the Valley a year into the future: a concrete, postapocalyptic wasteland, strangers divining the LA River for one last drop of septic muddle.

Woodland Hills is the purgatory of the San Fernando Valley. It's the middle child, nestled between Calabasas and Tarzana, the quiet, declining byproduct of a wilting porn industry. There is at least one Porn House in every neighborhood. Block parties and cul-de-sac kickball games are soundtracked by the coital groans of invisible porn stars, as predictably suburban as the drone of a lawnmower or clack of an ice machine. We accept it into our humdrums. Every middle school parent knows that no matter how high you crank the volume on Owl City's "Fireflies" at the sixth-grade pool party, it just can't seem to drown out next door's in-production *Avatar* porn parody. Grape Capri Sun will forever have a synesthetic association with the fleshy smack of Na'vi braid-mating.

Zombified and heavy-footed, Woodland Hills trudges into early fall. The air stays sweltering and stagnant. No humidity. Just plain heat. Sometimes, in the morning, the temperature lifts, and we'll be shivering in a surprising seventy degrees. But the San Fernando Valley is tricky; come one o'clock and you'll be shedding layers of clothing like onion skin. By the end of the morning, the heat presses through our classroom's plaster walls, and we resort to prehistoric cooling mechanisms like fanning study guide packets and three-ring binders.

Morning prayer is at 8:05. The Pledge of Allegiance is sandwiched between an Our Father and a Hail Mary. On one side of the room, there is a flag, and on the other side, a cross. We flip back and forth until a message from the principal releases us to our chairs. We start the day.

A teacher calls roll. There are usually thirty-one of us. But today, there are two absences. One is Owen Mason (who has head lice) and the other is Bridget Penderman, who usually sits right in front of me.

Her empty desk leaves a window between Marcus Brown and me. He's got dark hair and green eyes and we're all in love with him. During social studies he turns around and asks: "Where's Bridget?"

I shrug and he turns back to the front.

Wait, shoot, I think to myself. I reach forward and tap him on the shoulder. "She's probably sick or something," I say. I'm grasping for straws here.

He nods. "Probably."

But a week passes, and Bridget is still gone, apparently in the throes of the swine flu. Each day I talk a little more to Marcus—short conversations about art class, or recess kickball. Bridget even misses Sex Ed Day. Our teacher passes out virginity contracts and puts the extra on top of her absent-work pile.

They separate us. Boys in one room, girls in the other. We watch an ultrasound of a fetus at six weeks while an old lady from the church barks about vacuums and murder and mortal sins. Gracie Knibbs, three desks over, is so scared that she whimpers big, shaky tears. We pass around pamphlets with "chlamydia" and "syphilis" printed in the *Goosebumps* font. The woman then warns us about the dangers of SEX and TEENAGE BOYS.

"Many only want one thing," she says. "They might not even care about you. They might lie. They might say whatever it takes to get what they want. They could tell you they love you just to get you in bed. TEENAGE BOYS are not like us." She scans the room until she spots Emma Hawthorne falling asleep in the back of the class. "You, there. What did I just say?"

"Boys just want sex."

"Alright," the lady says. She stares us down. "Good."

We still have our virginity contracts on our desks. In a pretty cursive scrawl, the words leer up at me: *I make a commitment to God, myself, my family, my friends, my future mate, and my future children to a lifetime of purity including sexual abstinence from this day until the day I enter a Biblical marriage relationship.*

I flash on a deeply disturbing montage of myself padding around the desert with some old bearded dude, eating mustard seeds and whining over lost sons.

"These are a promise to God to save yourselves for holy matrimony," the teacher says. "Raise your hand once you have signed yours."

Slowly the whole room has their arms raised, all except for Ruby Smith. Her hands stay folded. When the teacher asks, she says she doesn't feel like making any promises to God. From now on, Ruby is the official whore of the eighth-grade class.

The boys come back. It's awkward. Our minds reel with words like *sin* and *pubic crabs*. The presentation is over, but we haven't forgotten the lady's warnings. Sex must be the most awful thing in the world. I decide that I will definitely never have it.

Marcus sits down. I look at him, curious. I wonder if our little chats have some ulterior motive. I lean forward, the first to break the silence that the church lady has dropped on us. "What did they say to you guys?" I whisper.

"All girls just want sex," he says. "Basically."

School lets out. I hold my contract close to me because I'm scared of seeming like Ruby.

I see her throw away her contract and get into her mom's minivan. Her dog is sitting in the front seat. It's cute. A floppy yellow Labrador. She laughs and scratches its ears and her mom leans over to kiss her on the forehead. They're playing the new One Direction album.

Annie Kostov shoulders her backpack and calls Ruby a slut— just loud enough for us to hear.

Three times a year, my class goes to church to receive the sacrament of reconciliation. We line up in our formal uniform. The monsignor hands out orange cards printed with the Ten Commandments and we're supposed to reflect on what we've done wrong, what sins we've committed, and how we've disrespected God. Most confessionals last five, maybe ten minutes, because nobody tells real sins, just generic easy ones. Sip of wine at Thanksgiving. Wandering eyes during a spelling test.

If we were honest, reconciliation would take hours. Twelve-year-olds are sinners by nature. "I stole my dad's credit card to pay for extra lives in Clash of Clans." "I drew dicks all over the class test folders." "I tried to get high off the auditorium's fog machine, and I also had sex with a vacuum cleaner and every object with a hole in it that I could find in my house." Confession doesn't mean much to us, besides the fact that it is a substitute for religion class. I would rather lie to a priest than spend an hour memorizing a list of good and merciful popes who most definitely were not guilty of rape and murder.

Bridget Penderman comes back to school just in time for fall confession. But something's different. She seems like she's operating on autopilot. At lunch, she just sits there and picks the crust off her peanut-butter-and-jelly sandwich. When we walk to the parish as a class, Bridget doesn't break eye contact with her *iCarly* folder, not even for a second.

Once inside, we all rush to Father Mancini's confessional— he's known to give the most lenient penances of all the priests. But I'm too late. Instead, I'm sent to Monsignor Fernsby, our parish's number one source of tradwife propaganda. Once, when I confessed I'd fought with my mother, he embarked on a fifteen-minute lecture about how two adult females cannot coexist in a home without experiencing domestic struggle. "You're both battling for your father's approval," he said. "It's normal for your age."

I kneel in the pew, waiting for my turn to receive the sacrament. I press my forehead to my prayer hands and focus on shifting my weight from one knee to the other. A roaming nun nods in approval. I look ahead ten or so rows to watch Bridget. She flips a Commandment card over and over in her hands. "She didn't have swine flu," Della McHenrie whispers in my ear.

"Huh?" I say, and Della tells me what really happened, that Bridget raided her parents' medicine cabinet and stuffed pills into her mouth like they were Skittles. Her mother had found her on the floor, scraping at the bathroom tile. After that, they kept her in the hospital, and that's where she was for the whole two weeks. I ask Della if she's sure about this and she says yeah, pretty much.

Back in class, after lunch, the teacher asks for a volunteer to take some photocopies to the main office. The kiss-ups wave their arms like the wind balloons in front of a car dealership. But she calls on Bridget.

As soon as the door shuts behind her, the principal pops in from the opposite entrance, clears her throat, and embarks on what could possibly be the vaguest speech of all time:

"I know that there is a thing that has happened. If you know what I'm talking about, that's great, keep it to yourself. If you do not know what I am talking about, I would ask that you do not ask anyone about what I'm talking about. Please do not hesitate to ever come to me if you have anything to tell me."

In the spring, the mathlete kids poll eighth graders to find out which high school is the most popular with the graduating class. They organize the data into a pie chart, and the chart's then put on the cover of the monthly parent newsletter. The pie is split mostly between the two single-gender schools, Crespi Carmelite Men's High School (blue slice) and Louisville School for Girls (pink slice). And then there's a medium-size purple slice, which represents the six kids going to the co-ed Christian school. And finally, there's a yellow slice, so narrow it could be a printing error: OTHER. The word can't even fit on the slice. They had to type OTHER out all separate and then draw a little line to that stupid flash of yellow. OTHER (2). That's me and Samuel. Samuel is moving to Texas. I'm going to Calabasas High School.

My only connection to Calabasas, prior to my enrollment, is Connor Nesbitt, the class dickhead. On the last day of school, Connor tells me I'm ugly and weird and that I read too much. I laugh it off, because that is what you are supposed to do, according to grown-ups. "Stop laughing," he says. "I'm making fun of you. It's funny to me, not to you." And with that, he slams his locker. "This is why nobody invites you to parties."

Connor Nesbitt is the son of a television reporter. He lives in a gated community in Calabasas, and his neighbors are A-list celebrities. He is the first to smoke weed, the first to drink beer, but only the third to cut holes in his shorts pockets so he can jack off during class showings of *The Prince of Egypt*.

He turns to the pick-up line, where his brother awaits behind the wheel of a Range Rover. Wiz Khalifa's "Black and Yellow" is on full blast through the speakers. Connor tosses his JanSport in the back seat and kicks off his sneakers. I watch them peel off, join the stream of other cars headed into Calabasas and away from Catholic school hell. Contrary to Woodland Hills's majority of single-family houses, Calabasas' streets are lined with McMansions—sky-high concrete boxes with marble fountains strewn across Astroturf like discarded toys. The kids who live in them don't have parent chaperones at their birthday parties. They wear brand names and swim at the fanciest country club in the Valley. Calabasas kids don't maneuver drug deals through late-night texts and parking lot meetups—instead, their parents buy them bourgeois, medical-grade kush from celebrity suppliers. But Calabasas High School has one of the best music and theater programs in the Los Angeles area. I've been participating in plays for as long as I've been able (yes, I apprehensively report that I am a theater kid) and the other high schools in the area don't offer theater classes of the same caliber. And as someone who's grown tired of the same old plaids and navy blues and bleeding

Jesus statues, that's enough to outweigh the negatives. I will take the possibility of many more Connor Nesbitts if it means music classes and a Confirmation workshop exit strategy.

"I have a connection with the counselors over at Louisville, if you need to get her in last minute," a PTA mom tells my mother after the big church send-off. "I've heard there's a lot of troubled kids where you're going."

"There are troubled kids everywhere," my mom says. My mother had sent me to St. Mel when she was still new to Los Angeles; she'd fallen in love with the flowerbeds, the blue-tiled drinking fountains, the first-grade artwork pasted on the walls. She'd gone to Catholic school as a little girl, too. But my family's relationship with religion has always come in waves. We'd flirt with piety, though our bouts of regular church attendance always seemed to coincide with external factors. The year 2008, for example, was big for the Bleidner family Eucharist. But as I've gotten older, I've noticed my parents growing more and more exasperated by the Catholic school milieu. The church wants to raise a quarter of a million dollars for new halogen lights. A PTA mother calls CPS to unjustly accuse a set of second-grade siblings of incest. A priest is sent to another district far away for suspicious reasons. After posting an old-school meme of Bob from *The Suite Life of Zack & Cody* on Facebook, I'm sent to the principal's office for discriminating against gingers. So. Change is good.

After my eighth-grade graduation, I make my mother drive me to my new school. It looms in the hills, a splotch of boxy modern gray cement playing neighbor to a Gelson's Market (grocery store that sells bottles of minty water for six dollars) and an M.Fredric (owned by Adam Levine's family, sells fifty-dollar leggings for *babies*). All the kids seem so much older than me. I try to imagine myself interacting with them, laughing at their jokes, wearing American Apparel tennis skirts. They look like stock-photo models.

On Urban Dictionary, someone had nicknamed Calabasas High "the MILF warehouse."

I kick at a little orange canister rolling around the school parking lot. "I don't know if this'll work out."

"Why?"

"I don't know why," I say. And that's the truth—I don't. There's just a *feeling,* but how is a fourteen-year-old girl supposed to explain *feelings* to a mother? (Blame it on our domestic struggle, I guess.) I catch the rolling canister under my shoe and push it around a little. "Someone on Urban Dictionary said this place is a total MILF warehouse," I say offhandedly. (I'm in the worst kind of adolescent limbo: testing the boundaries of grown-up talk with my parents. Today: Urban Dictionary. Tomorrow: the word *shit.* Someday: *Harold and Maude* without pretending I received an urgent text during the sex parts.)

"You know what a MILF is?"

I pick the canister up from the ground. It's someone's empty Adderall prescription bottle. Valley ornaments. My own face peers back at me in the plastic reflection. I am a sum of different parts, none of which I feel comfortable in. Freckles, braces, the beginnings of a unibrow. Pimples and unkempt brown hair. In the bottle, I look orange and sickly and small. "That's why I'm freaked out, kind of," I say. "I don't."

Family dinner, one week before the first day of school. "I'm changing my name," I say, staring down a glass of water.

"To what?" my dad says.

"From Olivia to Via, I think." I say this casually, as if I haven't spent nights chopping up my name and rearranging it, mouthing the syllables to my reflection.

"Via," he says. "Well. Okay."

On the first day of school, I write it out on the tops of my registration papers. Four lifts of a pencil. I stare my new identity in the face. This Via has never held a Commandment card. This Via could get drunk on the idea of Being Known. This Via will scour eBay for knockoff designer bags and will make wonderfully average grades. This Via will breathe the same air as Kylie Jenner and *love it*.

"Drug dogs come regularly but you won't know when," a counselor tells us. I'm in a classroom with thirty other freshmen, although it seems like everybody here already knows each other from the district middle school, A. C. Stelle. And even though I've left Catholic school behind, it's evident that there's still an unspoken dress code—almost every girl in the room is wearing the same sunflower print from Brandy Melville. "And if you're caught with illegal substances you'll be punished accordingly."

Someone's phone goes off in the back row. The ringtone's "Fuckin' Problems," because of course it is.

"You are responsible for ten hours of community service per year. If you forget to turn in your forms, you'll be prohibited from having lunch off campus."

"What about theater? I want to hear about *theater*," someone near the front says. The voice sounds familiar. I scoot out of my seat to try and catch a glimpse of the speaker, but I can only make out a head of curly blond hair and a giant bedazzled flower barrette.

"There will be an informational meeting, I'm sure, but you have to check the website calendar. I'm not an oracle," the teacher says.

"*Theeeeater,*" someone mimics from the back. The girl whips around, furious. And here's the kicker: I *know* her. Her name is Zoe Melton and we did community theater together in the sixth grade. We were friends. Both of us, theater dorks who were way too into *Glee* covers and the *Camp Rock* soundtrack. I sink into my seat.

"Shut up," she says to her heckler. And then she sees me. "Olivia?" she says. Far too loud. "Oh my God. Do you remember me? From theater?"

I look her up and down. She's wearing a blue fur vest and a pink tutu and neon yellow knee-high socks. She looks like she just waltzed out of the Justice catalogue. I have to make a split-second decision. For survival purposes.

"Actually no, sorry," I say. "I'm Via."

Kim Kardashian Stole My Salad

Here's the problem with LA.

It's not the traffic.

I mean, it *is* the traffic. And the lines: seventeen minutes for a food truck bagel, infinite hours for a DMV visit. And how everyone's too attractive (seriously, you hop off the plane at LAX with a dream and a cardigan and you drop three points before you reach baggage claim).

But all of this is fine. You can put up with it. You can arrange to leave forty minutes earlier than you usually would, or Grubhub all your meals, or invest in a vampire facial—a skincare treatment that involves the rubbing of one's own blood onto the face. These are the kinds of things a person can get used to, I suppose. But Los Angeles' most irredeemable fault can't be brushed away so easily. It sets in so slowly that you may not even notice anything's wrong until you've already subscribed to the whole Southern California shtick. Maybe it'll creep up on you as you finish up your trial workout at a boutique fitness studio, or it'll hit as you drive eight miles out of the way to buy pet-friendly CBD therapy oil for your epileptic Maltese-poodle mix. It'll stand dormant, a silent aggressor, until you finally realize—while examining the caloric value in a bottle of kombucha, no less—that there's something missing, and for whatever reason, you're hopelessly, eerily, unfathomably lonesome.

To live in LA is to experience a unique sort of isolation. The urban sprawl is too great, the goal of an advanced aqueduct system and the Californian preference for wide driveways and rambling backyards. We aren't friends with our neighbors. In fact, most communities have forfeited neighborhood watch groups in favor of motion-activated security cameras. Thanks to this, in all my years of teenage debauchery, I never once try to sneak out of the house. And because of the immense spread, the city doesn't have a singular thesis. Unlike New Yorkers or Chicagoans, with their shared metropolitan identities and staunch loyalties to pizza crusts, I don't feel any sort of default camaraderie with the 818 area code. It's rare when something worthy enough to rally behind materializes.

The first time I experience such LA cohesion, I'm growing up alongside the greatest lunch place in the whole entire world. It's located not in a Parisian square or Italian plaza, but in the dreary nook of a San Fernando Valley strip mall.

The front patio has overlooked a sun-bleached parking lot since the store's inception in 1971. It's a hop, skip, and a jump away from a McDonald's, flanked by a budget hair salon and a mom-and-pop pet store. It's accessible from the freeway. Thousands of cars bumble past every day, and it's in close enough proximity to Calabasas High School to milk a booming teenage lunch rush.

It's called Health Nut, and it's a vitamin store first, eatery second. The shelves are packed with tinted bottles of herbal remedies and sweet-smelling teas. A hodgepodge aisle of lotions and sprays provides a tricky barrier between customers and the lunch menu. Worse, there's hardly any seating. But this unintentional obstacle course doesn't sway its loyal customer base. In fact, students at CHS guarantee that Health Nut is the best-kept secret in the greater Los Angeles area.

The menu is small, offering only a few lunch options. Owned by a Korean family, the Chois, the place is run with the help of just a few employees. One works the register while another tosses salads and toasts sandwiches in the back. You can order a BLT or a tuna salad. But no one ever does. If you're going to Health Nut, there's really only one thing to order.

It's called the noodlerama. They serve the salad in a clear plastic bowl with a domed top. Order like this: extra ginger, avocado, fork in the bag, please. And to drink, an iced mango greentini.

I lose my Health Nut virginity halfway through my freshman year, when I'm smuggled off campus by some newfound upperclassman friends. Brooke and Melissa bring me with them during lunch period. They teach me the routine. Pour the dressing, close the lid, and shake. And with my first bite, I come to understand that there are about three things I am absolutely positive of. First, this salad is delicious. Second, there is a part of me—and I don't know how potent that part might be—that will hunger for this eleven-dollar salad on a daily basis, from now until the end of time. And third, I am unconditionally and irrevocably in love with it.

My palate is romanced by a near-perfect flavor profile. The dressing, a spicy concoction of sesame with notes of cayenne, engages in a perfect dialogue with the cool tanginess of the mango greentini. It clings to rice noodles, smooth and bouncy and piled on top of the lettuce in a glossy heap. The ratio of spice-to-sweet is sublime at a mathematical level, proportionally rounded so that I finish both the salad and the drink at the same time.

Health Nut has awakened a cultish following in the Calabasas High student body. It isn't mainstream, like Chipotle or Starbucks. And it fits neatly into the Los Angeles healthy-but-make-it-cute expectation. A salad from Health Nut is delicious, for sure. But it is, above all things, an accessory.

The salad says I'm locked in to a symbiosis with the rest of my school. It's the final stage in achieving a mid-tier Calabasas popularity (the first being a significant drop in grade-point average, the second being a re-wardrobing of Brandy Melville sunflower print). I guess I've done a decent enough job of conforming, because here I am, sitting across from two upperclassmen, a privileged Calabasas inductee with a fast pass to total blend-in-ability. And an eleven-dollar salad.

"It's not as easy as everyone thinks," Brooke says, manicured fingers picking a particularly girthy chunk of chicken out of her salad. "Like yeah, we live in a nice place. And it sounds great. But, like, it's hard! And sometimes . . ." She lowers her voice and takes a dramatic sip of iced tea. "I wish I was more . . . you know . . . *normal.*"

"No, I totally get that," says Melissa.

This isn't the first time I've heard these, shall we call them, confessions. Brooke, Melissa, and I are all involved in the theater program. Theater kids aren't ostracized like they are at other schools—instead, they're the ones considered closest to the entertainment industry. Rich kids with C-list parents give up hoity-toity private schools for our theater department. We've got an unreasonably high budget and brand-new, state-of-the-art performance space (so nice that it's actually called a performance space instead of a theater). I've received the supreme luxury of a background role in the fall play, *A Midsummer Night's Dream*. Brooke laid herself bare with aspirations of economic averageness a few weeks ago, at Pass the Candle. It's a bonding tradition among theater kids; we all sit in a circle at someone's house, monologuing our teenage ire through the early hours of the morning. One girl, Jennifer St. Claire, had broken into tears about her parents' broken marriage, the expensive consolation presents, the loneliness that arises when you live in a house so big it requires an intercom system.

"So fucked," Brooke says. "The only reason we're doing that stupid play is because it's in the public domain and Purcell blew too much money on last year's *West Side Story*."

West Side Story was a big deal. It sold out almost every night and was even nominated for a Jerry Herman Award (the SoCal high school equivalent of the Tony Awards). The cast performed "Jet Song" at the Hollywood Pantages Theatre, a vaudevillian relic that houses traveling troupes of ongoing Broadway shows. *West Side Story* set an impossibly high precedent for all subsequent plays at the school, and it's rumored that the musical's success was directly responsible for a huge uptick in enrollment this year. The school even had to put up temporary lockers to accommodate the surge.

Of the three or four other freshmen in the cast, there's Zoe Melton (my old community theater friend) and Elijah Fisher. Elijah's not from Calabasas either, hailing instead from the fringes of Woodland Hills. When we met, we'd both been waiting for our parents to pick us up. He offered me a Gusher.

"No, thanks," I said. "I have braces."

"Sike. I wasn't going to give it to you anyways."

I decided then and there that Elijah would be my number one enemy. He's the lead of the play, our director Mr. Purcell's favorite new prodigy. I'll admit he's a good actor. But regardless of his talent, I've made it my goal to supersede him in all other things. It's totally not because I'm jealous, though. Like, dude, I swear. Halfway through the Health Nut lunch I mention him casually, clueing in Melissa and Brooke to my distaste.

"He's so immature," I say. "I think he subsists off of Gushers alone."

"I dunno," Melissa says. "Not to be creepy or anything, but he's cute."

"Mm-hmm. He has good bone structure," Brooke adds.

"I heard he hooked up with a senior girl at the district relay last year," Melissa says.

"No way. My gaydar goes off on him." Brooke pauses, then shakes her head. "No, sorry, that's problematic of me."

"He's probably just another Valley douche. They all are. I thought this one guy in my chem class was cool for like two whole seconds before I heard he had"—here Melissa leans in and lowers her voice—"the *Drive*."

"What's a drive?"

"You sweet child," Melissa says. "It's not *a* drive, it's *the Drive*. It's totally controversial. Some people don't even think it really exists. It's this game a bunch of senior boys supposedly came up with years ago. Someone drops a flash drive into another guy's backpack or locker anonymously and it's filled with girls' nudes from this school. The new guy has to import all the nudes he has from his past hookups or whatever onto the Drive and then he passes it on the same way." She shudders.

"Pretty sure my boobs are somewhere on the Drive, if I'm being realistic," Brooke says. "And anyway, I doubt Eli has the Drive. He doesn't seem the type. Maybe I should go for it."

"He's not cute at all," I say. "I think he's annoying."

Brooke's fork clatters to the bottom of her plastic bowl. "Oh. My. God. Do you like him?"

"No, I'm just saying."

"Because I will totally back off. That's girl code. So let me know."

I'm haunted by visions of Gushers. "I promise."

The rest is history. Like when you learn a new word and then see it everywhere, the salad makes similar repeat appearances. In post-lunch classes, the dressing's scent wafts through the air like the first trace of spring wildflowers. It's impossible to walk through the quad without catching the twinkle of a plastic bowl from a campus recycle bin. Even my desk in Spanish class is sticky, and it only takes one whiff for me to identify the residue of a mango greentini. But it's wonderful. The most perfect salad in the known universe belongs to us and us alone.

The Chois prep extra noodleramas just in time for our lunch period. When fifty of us spill through the front doors, packing the vitamin store with knobby teenage elbows and Herschels, they accommodate us, making sure we're all fed in the forty minutes before the last bell rings.

Months flirt by; the fall play is a moderate success. The spring musical, *Young Frankenstein,* tempts wider audiences, only stirring up trouble when a handful of parents complain about one scene that calls for a seventeen-year-old cast member to mimic an orgasm onstage. But that's only a minor blip, and the show is otherwise well-received, at least according to the county newspaper.

In regard to my self-engineered rivalry with Eli, it's business as usual. We've degenerated into hallway shoulder-checks. It's something to occupy the time.

I'm glaring at him from across the room when Brooke grabs my hand and yanks me into the lobby of the theater, where a crowd of kids is hunched over someone's laptop. An episode of *Keeping Up with the Kardashians* is playing, full volume.

"What's happening?"

"Watch," she says.

A wide shot, and I see it. We all see it. I gasp.

It's *our* clear plastic bowl, filled with *our* noodlerama, situated next to *our* iced mango greentini. And a forkful of *our* lettuce is headed directly for Kim Kardashian's mouth. The on-screen conversation is something along the lines of:

"Mmm, I love salad," Kim says, poking at a piece of avocado.

"Salad is good," Kourtney adds.

"This mango iced tea is *literahhhhly* to die for," Kim says. "I just love supporting small businesses."

"Bible," Kourtney adds.

And then the scene ends and cuts to Kardashian baby daddy Scott Disick brandishing an electric razor while Kourtney giggles in a bathtub. "I can't believe Scott is gonna shave my hoo-ha for me," she says, before someone in our crowd yells to *please turn that shit off.*

We're quiet.

"Well, fuck," someone says, breaking the silence. "RIP."

But maybe it's fine. Perhaps the camera hadn't zoomed in enough on the logo for anyone to see where it was from. Maybe our secret is safe after all. And during the next lunch period, there don't seem to be any more customers than usual. Because it isn't until Kim hosts a Twitter Q&A that a curious fan asks for clarification and thrusts us into the mainstream.

"It's from Health Nut! And the drink is the mango greentini," she answers. And Calabasas High devolves into chaos.

"What are we? Second-rate citizens?" Lindsey Webster screeches, when we go to Health Nut next and can't get through the door. Whatever salads the Chois had prepped for us have already been sold to fans, and what was once a clubhouse for students has become diluted with unfamiliar faces.

"This is the worst thing I've ever heard," Melissa says, when the cashier tells her that they're out of ginger, that they've been out of ginger since even before Calabasas High let out for lunchtime.

I make eye contact with a woman carrying her baby—the kid's in a TEAM KOURTNEY onesie. I wait in line: Five minutes.

Ten minutes. Fifteen minutes. Twenty minutes go by, and I have to leave, or else I'll be late for my next class.

We're all seething. Why couldn't Kim like Arby's? Carl's Jr.? Christ, we'd even be willing to bargain with Stonefire Grill.

Student sleuths perform a frame-by-frame analysis of the episode. The worst part is that the family isn't even eating the noodlerama. They've ordered chef's salads. But without cheese. Easy on the avocado. And low-cal dressing. It's blasphemy. Like. Who *does* that?

As I grow up, so does Health Nut. Eventually, the shelves are cleared of vitamins. The skin-care aisle is removed in favor of chic white tables and chairs. The owners install a TV, which doesn't play cable, but instead a looping slideshow of celebrity tweets about the restaurant. The menu expands, too, now offering poke bowls and pho and different variations of the iced teas. The sons don't work the register anymore. They hire an entire team, all sporting black visors emblazoned with their new logo on the brim. And it isn't uncommon to spot a KarJenner assistant at Health Nut. We see the G-Wagon parked outside, a black-haired woman with a Bluetooth and a grimace at the wheel. I wonder if this is what the elusive American Dream looks like.

Summer comes and goes. The Valley slips further into drought. Kim Kardashian releases a video game to the App Store called Kim Kardashian: Hollywood. You can dress up your character in digital lookalike outfits: Balmain and Juan Carlos Obando, cartoon imitations of Kim's real life red-carpet-wear. The goal of the game is to social climb for Star Points until you reach the final level: A-list. Everyone plays it. It makes $1.6 million in the first five days through in-app purchases alone.

We come back to school from summer vacation and I make a visit to Health Nut. But it's not there. I'm met with a stripped facade, an empty storefront. The El Camino Shopping Center looks bleak. I'd been annoyed with Health Nut's sudden popularity, but I would never have wanted it to go out of business. It was the only thing I held in solidarity with my classmates. And the employees were always kind to everyone.

I begin to walk away—until I notice the tail end of a line. It's almost twenty people, single-file. I follow them to see what they're waiting for, and I'm introduced to Health Nut 2.0. The logo's been enlarged and hoisted to the top of a new storefront. There are posh chandeliers, a shabby-chic wooden deck. I step inside. Canvas, high-def prints of the noodlerama hang on the walls. Now four times its original size, the place resembles a Jonathan Adler catalogue. A backlit menu hands over the register station. There's a designated photo op area by the water cups. The store sells merch now, too: hats, tees, sweatshirts, and prepackaged dressing. I hear they're opening a second location in Sherman Oaks, and rumor has it they're looking to branch out to Venice Beach and Malibu, too.

But my salad doesn't look any different. I open the lid and sneak a bite of the chicken. Tastes the same, too. I carry the bowl at my side as I take a lap around the restaurant. There aren't any tables, so I go home. I'm not upset. The Chois are a success story, and I'm happy for them.

The next week, Brooke reignites the old group chat and proposes lunch. She's found a new place.

So we go to this new hole-in-the-wall spot in the middle of another bland Woodland Hills strip mall. It's tiny, tucked away behind a rug store and a Zumba studio. The woman behind the counter offers a free cup of frozen yogurt.

"The principal asked me if I wanted to press charges," Brooke says. "The *principal*."

As it turns out, we were mistaken about the Drive. It wasn't a flash drive that was passed around school. It was a Google Drive. There were dozens and dozens of photos, including nudes from girls as young as fourteen. There were even a couple of celebrity cameos in the mix; some horny freshman had tossed in a few of Jennifer Lawrence's leaks from the 2014 mass iCloud hack, dubbed "The Fappening" by Reddit's great thinkers. And as Brooke had predicted, she had indeed made an appearance in the Drive.

"Are you gonna do it?" I ask.

She sighs. "No, fuck it. All those boys will have to get lawyers and stuff. It'll be a hassle for everyone. And what about me? I don't have time to, like, go to court." She takes a forkful of salad. "I think the creepiest thing was that there were screenshots from girls' Instagrams. Like, innocent bikini pics they'd posted at the beach. And they were using them for a spank bank. Gross. Anyway." She unlocks her phone and refreshes Twitter. "It happens."

"It happens?"

"Yeah. Paris, Kim, you know. They all turned out fine. More than fine."

There is something seriously wrong with the world when a seventeen-year-old girl has to accept that her stolen nudes are just out there. "It's not your fault, though," I say. "You shouldn't have to take responsibility."

She shrugs and changes the subject. "What do you think of the new place?"

It's small and empty. There isn't much going on. Five or six tables, an open cooler stocked with Pellegrino, motel-caliber wall art.

The salad is good. Different, but good. The dressing isn't at Health Nut's level, of course, but there's something about this place that twists my heart in a funny kind of way. I watch Brooke pour a packet of Stevia into her iced tea and stir it with a spoon.

Then something catches my eye. From out the window. A glare.

It's the windshield of a matte black G-Wagon.

On Feeling Like a Plastic Bag

Like any other teenager, I hate my parents. More specifically, I submit to the inevitable adolescent feud of Girl v. Mother, a side quest in my journey of being a teenage shithead. I have to channel my unprecedented angst somewhere, so I suppose it's only natural that I should choose the person who's in charge of me. I feel grown up, but I'm restless; I'm at an in-between age, one that comes with a constant frustration at myself and the people around me. It's the specific burden of an undeveloped frontal lobe.

I find my mother's presence infuriating. I navigate my own house like a squatter, veering sharp turns into bathrooms or closets when I hear her coming my way. I don't speak to her more than absolutely necessary. I'm mean because it's fun. I don't yet have the self-awareness to see that I must seem ridiculous; I am, after all, an angry, pubescent blob of brace-faced hormones. From the outside, I probably resemble a rabid squirrel.

My mother's a writer. She isn't afraid of anything. She keeps a photo of a fat white worm on the refrigerator. It's called a witchetty grub, a local delicacy she'd eaten while on assignment in Australia. "Tasted like chicken," she told me when I was a little girl.

Before I was born, she was a travel journalist. Then she was a correspondent for *People* magazine and *Us Weekly*. She'd once arranged for an interview with the Olsen twins, and they wouldn't let her onto their yacht, so she stood outside on the loading dock in 95-degree weather to ask them about their success. They were ten.

Growing up, I had to accept that I will probably never know the full extent of my mother's adventures. In conversation, she tosses in references to stories she's never told like they're mundane comments about the weather. Watching the news one evening, Hillary Clinton's face flashes on screen. "I was once threatened by Secret Service for posing as a Stanford student to interview Chelsea," she says, then stands up and yawns. "I'm going upstairs to take out my contacts. Put away your dishes."

My mother introduced me to the legal pad, made sure I learned to walk by balancing a book in each hand. Toted me to book readings. I like to tell people that my first concert was a Joan Didion Q&A. Born in New York, she lived in a house with big beech trees out front and turned down modeling scouts that stopped her on the street.

On a Thursday night, I fold the napkins and allow—just this once—my mother to nag at me.

"Did you finish your homework?" she asks.

"Yeah." I fill the glasses with water.

"Because you know I will check online."

Forks. Knives.

"And after dinner you should study for your math test."

"Yeah." Plates. Butter dish. Serving spoons.

"Are you listening to me?"

"Yes." No.

"I was talking to your math teacher," she says. "She says you haven't been turning in homework."

"Oh," I say.

"I don't want you doing anything with friends until you get that grade up."

"Okay."

"Listen," my mother says, pausing from slicing a tomato. "I bug you because I love you, and I worry about you."

"I know. Love you too."

But inside, I'm furious. I give my father a look, praying for him to be on my side. *Give her a break, Irene,* I wish he'd say. But in reality, my dad's even more of a hardass. He's from Queens, New York. In college, he poured drinks at a Mafia bar; in adulthood, he worked in advertising at *Fortune* and ABC. He loves to call me a *snowflake.* His parenting style could be summed up in three words: cut the bullshit. "Do your fuckin' homework, Olivia," he says. "You're too smart for this shit."

My little sister, Jackie, observes quietly from her seat at the table. She's five years younger than me. She has a biting humor and a sense of sarcasm beyond her years. Jackie has mastered the art of the facial expression. Tonight, she's smug, her mouth hidden behind a cup of water.

Nobody understands, I think to myself, and wonder why adolescence has to be so infuriating, so absolutely unfair and enraging and uncomfortable.

But I think teen angst isn't necessarily a bad thing. While yes, my bursts of attitude are perhaps more *Diary of a Wimpy Kid* than they are *Rebel Without a Cause,* I maintain that it's still an important part of growing up. Some kids decide to use their angst for good. But some just use it to have a good time.

Valentino DeVito, for example, is the poster boy for Good Time Angst. He's two years ahead of me in school, a transfer as of a month ago. I don't know his real first name. Very few do. He only ever responds to his moniker, Valentino, both in and out of the classroom. Of unknown origins, he surges to the top of Calabasas High's small-time celebrity Rolodex overnight. One morning, he's all anyone can talk about. Because under the hazy cloak of a temperate autumn night, he snuck onto campus and put up posters of his official logo: a Valentino bucket purse, cut-and-pasted above the Wikipedia photo entry for Danny DeVito. And it is taped to every wall, column, and bulletin board at school.

Faculty remove them, but they're not fast enough for Valentino. When one's pulled down, three more pop up somewhere else. He must have secret associates. That's the only explanation. We don't know who's working for Valentino and who isn't. It's a schoolwide game of Mafia.

Valentino drives a 1970 Chevy Impala. There's a set of blue fuzzy dice hanging off the rearview mirror, and his vanity plate is, of course, VLNTNO. He wears vintage aviator shades like a crown above a head of long, shaggy hair. He's handsome. Stocky and well-dressed, he looks like he's just walked out of an '80s-era high school comedy. His voice is commanding, but soft; he's got a boyish mischief that both charms adults and frightens them. Youthful authority. It's the most powerful—and dangerous—combination a high schooler can possess.

We elect him as pep commissioner. He approaches this position with the utmost sincerity, reciting the Pledge of Allegiance over the intercom like he's performing voice work for the *Schindler's List* audiobook. He's got a taste for drama. He lets loose during pep rallies, usually to encourage some cockamamie plot by the student body: run shirtless through the quad, or pat Mr. Grisham on the back today, or bring water balloons to school.

His best friend and right-hand man, Norbert Cox, may be even more of an enigma than Valentino. Scrawny, quiet, and bizarre, he exudes dad energy, wearing ties to school and smoking cigars at parties where everyone else is drinking SKYY Vodka. Every two weeks he makes a mysterious trip to downtown Los Angeles to invest in platinum. "It's the only reliable currency," he claims, "if shit goes down." He once gained schoolwide infamy when, in order to win a scavenger hunt, he placed his manhood inside of a McFlurry; a few months later, CHS elected him as student body vice president. He and Valentino make for quite a team. Together, they make repeat trips to Nobu in Malibu, a celebrity hideaway where a salad costs seventy dollars. Norbert and Valentino sit in booths and order refill after refill of lemonade—and only lemonade—just to mingle with high society.

Monday mornings, Valentino wakes up early so he can drive

all the way to Santa Monica and pick up a trunkful of Krispy Kreme on his own dime. Armed with a bullhorn, he sets up a folding table in front of the main office and hands out free donuts to those on their way to academic dread. Where he acquires the funds to make such a generous purchase, no one can say; but then again, why look a gift horse in the mouth? "HAPPY MONDAY, CHS," he yells, the words glittering with his trademark smarm.

Principal Stack stands at the window of her office, gazing over Valentino's giveaway with a grim smile. Technically, Valentino isn't doing anything wrong. But all this hullabaloo doesn't sit quite right with her. She can sense his authority looming over the school. He's gaining control of the student body, and with every fried glob of sugar planted into an open palm, she's losing it. And there is absolutely nothing that she can do about it.

For now, at least.

Lily accepts a donut from Valentino and smiles. "Thank you so much," she says cheerily. She's wearing the same outfit she wears every day: navy polo, khaki shorts that come down to the knee. And tucked under her arm is her most prized possession. It's an outdated Acer laptop, the keyboard a charcuterie of Nature Valley granola bar crumbs.

Lily is a bit of an enigma. She doesn't talk much about her parents or her home life and she abstains from gossip. What we do know, however, is that she has big dreams. Lily wants to become a star. During lunch, she roams the quad. She holds her open laptop at an arm's distance from herself and films covers of Top 40 hits. Nicki, Ariana, Post. All full-volume, all a cappella.

Occasionally, she'll take a break from singing to vlog, skirting from table to table to introduce different cliques to her three or so subscribers. "Hey guys," she says, "today I'm at lunch with my friends. Everyone say hi!" Nobody dares make fun of her. She has an infectious confidence. Everybody loves Lily because she doesn't care what anyone thinks. She's similar to Valentino in that way. So it makes perfect sense that they should strike up a bit of a friendship.

He gives her shout-outs at pep rallies. High fives her in the hallway. If she had any form of social media outside YouTube, he'd probably hype her up on there too; it's a shame that she doesn't have a cell phone, or an Instagram, or a Twitter. Word spreads that he sometimes slips her an extra donut in the mornings.

In the meantime, Valentino, confident and backed by a throng of ardent supporters, escalates his antics. He locomotes from posters to chalk paint, scrawling his name in large block letters all across campus grounds. He discovers a doting lover in recreational drugs, upgrading his classes from drab to fab with the aid of a certain fungal psychedelic consort. One afternoon, he and Norbert drive his Chevy right onto the quad, bass-boosting Valentino's own mixtape over the speakers. It's a foolish mistake, a severe misjudgment of his own campus stature. Stack serves him a detention and trash pickup and delivers him Warning Number One.

At home, I'm also given Warning Number One. Though my case is a little different. I've been nursing a low D in geometry for three weeks.

My parents host an intervention when I come home far past my weeknight curfew of ten o'clock on a Wednesday night. I'd been at McDonald's with Melissa and Brooke. Most of my upperclassman friends at school don't have curfews, so it's easy to lose track of time. I can tell that I'm in trouble as soon as I twist the key in the lock. Kids have a sixth sense when it comes to parental rage. Danger is most certainly in the air.

I slow my steps and untie my Chucks. Maybe if I move quietly enough, I can escape to my bedroom unnoticed. But my father's throat clears. They're waiting in the living room.

"Come here, Olivia," my dad says. "Sit down."

I don't make eye contact. Instead, I fixate on a framed poster on the wall. It's my father at age eight, his little hand holding up a bag of Lay's potato chips. He was the original "Betcha Can't Eat Just One" kid back in the sixties. I concentrate on the chip in his hand. I bet the Lay's kid wouldn't yell at me. I bet the Lay's kid would think that I'm, like, really cool and stuff.

"Look at me," my mother says.

Enjoy it while it lasts, Lay's kid, I think.

"What's going on with your grades? Are you doing drugs?" my mom asks.

"Um, no," I say. Not yet.

"Then get your head out of your ass," my father says.

"So many people wish they had the opportunities you have. You should have straight As." That's my mom.

"I just don't understand the material," I say. It's a lie. I've been lazy.

"That's a lie. You've been lazy," my dad says.

"If you're really struggling, you should be going to your teachers during support periods," my mother says. "There's free tutoring at lunch and after school. You have the resources."

"She's always on that phone." My dad puts his head in his hands. "Steve Jobs," he mutters, to no one in particular. My father's biggest enemies (besides the government as a whole, because that goes without saying) are the recently deceased Steve Jobs, the Starbucks corporation, communists, and Rite Aid clerks who ask for ID when he goes to buy Modelo.

"Every time I see you 'doing homework,' you're playing on your phone. What are you even doing?"

"I dunno." I do know. I'm on Vine. Or Instagram.

"She's on Vine," my father says. "Or Instagram."

"Olivia, you're wasting your time," my mom says.

"That's not even true," I say. "I'm reading articles. Like ones in the *New Yorker* and stuff." This lie is so egregious that even I can't believe I'm saying it out loud. Since discovering Snapchat, my attention span fails to comprehend any reading material longer than a listicle. If it isn't interwoven with GIFs, it isn't getting read.

"Uh-huh," my mother says. "Suuure."

"That's even worse," my father says. "Get your grades up. Now." And then: the darkest threat, the ultimate punishment: "Or you're not auditioning for any more plays."

My life flashes before my eyes.

With the stakes heightened, I wake up early to go to support periods. I start asking for extra-credit assignments. Sometimes I hit the library after school—I develop a crush on my geometry tutor, so staying later isn't so bad after all. Of course, I'm not doing much learning. He has to explain triangle congruence postulates to me three whole times because I keep thinking about how cute it would be if we did the "Thriller" dance together at spring formal like in *13 Going on 30.*

Lily disappears from school for a week. Her absence does not go unnoticed. We're so used to seeing her traipsing through the hallways that it feels like a vital step of our everyday routine is missing. Valentino's morning donut giveaway seems a little bleaker than usual, too. Rumors spider about her whereabouts. "She got kidnapped," one conspiracy theorist says. Lily was known for hitchhiking from school to her home in Thousand Oaks, relying on the kindness of strange upperclassmen in the senior lot.

But in time, the real story gets out: her parents discovered her YouTube channel. When she does make her eventual return to school, she's without her beloved Acer. She deletes her profile. Her lunchtime patrol takes a turn for the somber. It's like her webcam was a social lubricant, and without the guise of a vlog it isn't so easy to slip from one table to the next. And anyway—why sing, if there's no chance of going viral?

I am at a rehearsal for the play when I hear the news, spread through the cast like a game of telephone. At first, I don't believe it's true. "That has to be a rumor," I whisper back. "There's no way."

But Mr. Purcell calls hold on the rehearsal and confirms it: a beloved faculty member, Mr. Donahue, has been harmed in an airport shooting nearby.

We aren't told the teacher's condition. We don't know anything. The adults in charge decide that we're too naive to keep updated. Rehearsal stops. It doesn't seem fair to expect us to remember lines when one of campus's most beloved teachers could die.

That evening, we learn Mr. Donahue is in stable condition. He was shot in the leg and is recovering in the hospital. He expects to make an eventual return to school.

The next day we are greeted by a slew of news cars at school, all backed up in the morning drop-off line like they are our moms' minivans. Reporters badger us as we make our way to classes. I take note of Principal Stack, giving a curbside interview.

Later, she announces a schoolwide walkout against gun violence. It's supposedly organized by student government, but somehow Stack is the one speaking, the one taking the interviews. There is so much media present. We are surrounded by cameras on all sides. I wonder who invited them. Some of the students seem to care less about our teacher than they do the opportunity to be on TV. They scan the crowd, searching for an unoccupied cameraman.

When the twenty-minute mark passes, Stack dismisses us all back to class. I watch the crowd disperse, leaving behind lunch trash and discarded posters. A reporter from the local NBC station points her finger in a circular motion. *That's a wrap.* Stack pats her on the back, smiles, and goes back to her office with tinted windows.

I take the slow route back to class, looping into the lower quad.

I refuse to enter a classroom until it's the absolute last minute—it's a small rebellion of mine.

And then I see Eli Fisher. He's listening to music on his phone, eating gummy worms.

"Go to class," I say, arms crossed.

"Cop," he says, then pats the space next to him.

"I have math."

"With who?"

"McKenzie."

He shrugs. "Whatever."

I shrug back. Then I sit next to him. "Did you do any interviews?" I ask.

"Nope."

"Yeah. It's kind of weird, right?"

"So weird."

"Like, someone got shot, you know?"

"Yeah. And everyone's like, 'Oh shit, my time to shine,'" he says. "Mostly theater kids."

"Theater kids suck."

"Takes one to know one, dummy."

"Yeah, I was making a joke, duh." I open my palm. "Gummy worm?"

"No. Get your own." He tips his head at the vending machine. The Calabasas High vending machines are a different breed. They're stocked with Voss and Perrier and Cheez-Its, but only the whole-grain kind. The gummy worms are organic, made from real fruit. You can't buy a snack or a water without setting yourself back at least eight packages of Top Ramen.

"What's with you and sharing?"

"Um? I don't like to do it?"

"You must be an only child."

"Actually, no, I have three sisters," he says. "I'd say you give off only child energy way more than me."

"I have a sister."

"Hmm," he says. "Surprising."

"Why?"

"I dunno. You're annoying, I guess."

"*You're* the annoying one."

"Yeah," he says, "but at least I'm self-aware."

"I bet you wanna be a famous actor, huh," I say.

"Yeah. What do you want to be?"

"A writer."

"Like, actually?" He looks surprised.

"Yeah."

"Oh. Shit. That's kind of cool. My dad writes for TV." He flicks the open bag of gummy worms in my direction. I accept the olive branch. "But you're too much of a goody-goody to be a writer."

"Why's that?"

"All writers smoke weed. I bet you've never smoked weed in your entire life."

"Have too." I reach for another gummy worm and he claps his hand over the bag.

"Have not." He narrows his eyes.

"Okay, so I haven't."

"Me neither," he says. "But I will, soon. Just waiting for the right time."

There's a crackle of a faculty walkie-talkie somewhere close by. "We should move," I say, so we relocate to a spot behind the science building.

"You're actually not *that* bad," I say. "You seem more annoying from afar, I guess."

"Well, you seem like a whiny princess baby," he says. "True from afar, and also close-up."

"Don't call me that."

"Whiny princess baby?"

I glare at him. "I hate that, seriously," I say.

"Yeah, alright," he concedes. "I guess a whiny princess baby wouldn't skip class."

"Most of all," I say, my voice haughty and matter-of-fact, "a baby wouldn't steal candy from Mr. Purcell's hiding spot."

His eyes widen. "No way," he says.

"Yup."

"Show me."

"Nope."

"Well, then you're lying," he says. "So you're a whiny princess baby who lies."

I cannot allow for this heresy.

We sneak into the theater. Normally, I hoard candy during rehearsals, when I know Mr. Purcell's not in his office. But now he could be anywhere. Eli assures me he's in the main office, but I'm not so sure. "You look first, then," I say, and he dips his head in the doorframe.

"All clear," he says.

His office is stuffed with old props from past shows. Up on the shelf, there's the beast's head from *Beauty and the Beast*. Eli points at it. "Purcell's a furry," he jokes. "You know what that is?"

"I'm not stupid," I say.

The desk is lined with trophies from local theater festivals. Calabasas High has quite the reputation at DTASC, the Drama Teachers' Association of Southern California. We place almost every year. The rules are as follows: no costumes, no instruments, and no backing tracks. The only props allowed are four chairs. You have to get creative, especially when working under a wicked time constraint—I'd once watched a group turn three chairs into a bicycle for an *E.T.* reenactment. A couple of months ago, Purcell rejected the scene I'd prepared. The category was Book Adaptations and I, along with some friends, had chosen a selection from Snooki's debut novel, *A Shore Thing*. It was deemed too raunchy, but I recognized a lapse in Purcell's appreciation for the avant-garde.

I crawl under Purcell's desk and produce the treasure: a wicker basket full of Laffy Taffy. There are fewer strawberry than any other flavor. (That's my doing.) Eli's eyes get big and he stuffs them into his pockets. "Chill, take less," I say. "You're gonna ruin it if he notices all this candy's missing."

We walk back to the main campus together, jaws sore from chewing. He asks me what music I like. "The Rolling Stones," I say.

"*The Rolling Stones,*" he mimics. "See? Annoying."

"What about you?"

"Vampire Weekend," he says. "They're my favorite band."

"See? Annoying," I say.

"No, listen, they're great," he says, and hands me an earbud. He plays a song called "Obvious Bicycle."

"Sounds like the end of a teen movie," I say.

"Yeah, that's why I like it."

I take out the earbud. "I thought I hated you."

"What the hell?" he says.

"Yeah, I think it was the sharing thing."

"I don't hate you," he says. "I think you're cool."

"You said I was a baby."

"A cool baby," he says. "A cool snobby baby."

"Ew."

"Yeah, gross, I take it back."

"But I've decided I don't hate you," I say. "So, congrats."

"Gee, thanks."

"You're welcome."

"So we're friends?" he asks.

"Yeah, I think we are," I say. "It was kinda fun skipping class today." I think about my grade in geometry for maybe half a second before shoving it out of my mind.

"Well, don't get used to it. I feel like you have strict parents."

"Not really. Well, maybe. They're normal, I guess. What are your parents like?"

"Divorced," he says. "I can do what I want, pretty much."

"Oh. Lucky."

He makes his mouth a straight line. "Lol," he says. "Well, see you later."

* * *

They run a segment about the student walkout on the news that night. I spot Eli and myself in the background of some B-roll. I pause it and stand close to the screen. Those are my arms, my jeans, my hair. TV is weird. It's disorienting to see the backs of my own legs.

I'm surprised by my own surprise, because I'm being filmed all the time. It's the nature of the twenty-first century. Even my recorded voice doesn't catch me off guard anymore. I've had it bored into my skull by Snapchat more times than I can count. But still, there's a disconnect. I wonder if my shoulders really look like that.

The only reason anybody ever uses Facebook anymore is because of school. There's a page for the theater program, a page for kids in AP US history. Tonight, the class of 2021 is spammed with screenshots from the broadcast. There's a kid who'd managed to speak to nearly every reporter, promulgating his love for Mr. Donahue, his mouth frozen in a permanent O.

I'm examining the comment section when my mother interrupts in a fury. "Olivia, what is this?"

"What's what?"

"This," she says, and shows me her phone: she's received an alert from the truancy officer about my absence today. "Are you skipping class now?"

"There was a walkout. Against gun violence."

"Yeah, I know. During lunch," she says.

"Well, we all stayed longer, 'cuz we were so fired up," I say. "Everyone got marked absent, but it's all a part of the movement, you know?"

"No, I don't know, and I think you're lying," my mother says.

"I'm not."

"Should I email your teacher?"

"She said she doesn't like getting emails."

"Do you realize how ridiculous you sound?" She presses her hand to her temple.

My father, sensing dramatics, emerges from his home office. "What's going on?"

"Your daughter skipped class today."

"Yeah, to make a change," I say. "They played that Bob Dylan song and I thought of you guys."

"Olivia. You're a knucklehead."

"Don't criticize what you can't understand," I say.

Jackie glances up from her times tables worksheet and snorts.

"One day you're going to look back and realize you were a dumbass," my father says. "Give me your phone."

"But I need it," I say. "What if there's an emergency?"

"Then borrow someone else's. You know, people used to survive without these things."

"Yeah, and they'd get kidnapped."

"You're too annoying to kidnap," Jackie says. "They would literally send you back."

"If you want to be a writer so badly you should look up from your phone and notice things," my mother says.

"I was on TV," I say. "You didn't notice *that*." I gesture to the screen. "Those are the backs of my legs."

"A man was shot, Olivia. Get some perspective."

My father leans into the screen. "Who's that next to you?"

"A kid at school."

"Oooo, she's got a *boyfriend,*" says Jackie.

"As if," I scoff. "He steals candy from Mr. Purcell."

"Oooo, she's in love with a *bad boy.*"

"Is this who you're skipping class with?" my father says.

"I wasn't skipping class."

"You're at school to learn, not to make goo-goo eyes at some dope," he says. "Right now, no phone. Don't play hooky again. You don't wanna know what comes next."

"I would never skip class," says Jackie. "FYI."

I make a face at her and surrender my phone.

It's Spirit Week, and there's a pep rally right around the corner. Which means Valentino DeVito is once again the star of the campus. It's his job to organize lunchtime events. He drives a golf cart around campus and hauls massive speakers to the lower quad. There's an outdoor stage, where local bands sometimes come and play for us. Today he DJs a playlist of clean radio hits. Microphone in hand, he volunteers compliments to all passersby. "Love the shoes," he shouts to a sophomore eating an Uncrustable. Valentino's friend Norbert, perched at his feet, nods in agreement.

Principal Stack watches from above. She's become stricter than usual. At the beginning of nearly every period, she takes to the loudspeaker to announce a tardy sweep, requesting teachers lock their doors. Faculty members inundate the campus, stopping any student left behind with a late slip and a trash pickup assignment. If you get trash pickup, you have to spend your lunch period collecting litter. Today, Lily's carrying a trash bag. We're disgusted. Giving Lily a tardy sweep is the stuff of revolutions.

She comes to our table. I give her my sandwich wrapper. "No vlog today?" I ask.

"Nope," she says. "Just trash. I don't have my laptop."

"You excited for Spirit Week?"

"Not really," she says. "Maybe I would be, if I didn't have to do this shit." She glances around us, then grabs an empty Health Nut bowl from the trash and puts it in her bag. "Shh," she says.

"Gaming the system?"

"Yup." She drifts to the next table.

"Lily," Valentino calls from the microphone. "Say it ain't so."

She waves her trash bag.

"She got tardy swept! I just can't believe it," he says.

Norbert stands, legs akimbo. He looks directly at Stack and shakes his head. "This is cause for warfare," he shouts. "Nobody messes with Lily!"

Stack crosses her arms in warning. Lunchtime chatter is suspended. Childish Gambino's "Sober" takes a turn for the ominous.

"Just kidding," Norbert says.

Stack raises an eyebrow. He sits back down.

Valentino pulls off his aviators and raises the microphone to his lips. "Lily! Come up here."

She points at herself.

"Yes, you."

"But I have trash pickup."

"Trash shmrash," he says. "Can I get some hype for Spirit Week?"

Nobody applauds. It's too dangerous.

"Alright, alright," he says, and pauses the music. "I'm bored. We need something fresh. And hell, we've got a world-class singer right here. Lily, come give us a song."

She takes a hesitant step forward. Stack cocks her head, daring Valentino to proceed.

"Let's hear it for Lily!"

Norbert stands again. "Lily. Lily."

A chant is every teenager's weakness. Once it starts, it can't be stopped. Some others join in, repeating her name in time. We crowd the foot of the stage. Valentino hands Lily the microphone. Campus quiets down, awaiting her first note. She clears her throat.

"This is the song 'Firework' by Katy Perry," she says. Someone offers an encouraging *woot*.

"Do you ever feel like a plastic bag?"

She holds up the trash bag. A prop. Her voice shakes on the word *plastic* and she flats a couple of notes. But as her voice strengthens, more kids approach the stage from their tables. They line the stairs, squat on the planters. We've transformed from a small group to a throng in a matter of seconds.

She starts belting. Her voice isn't particularly show-stopping, but it's enthusiastic, and she's hitting the notes. She has the kind of voice that makes you want to sing along.

The whole student body has gathered into an amorphous clump. Not even the promise of a free donut could incentivize this many teens to step out of their apathy. I glance to where Stack once stood. She's gone now. Norbert steps next to Lily. He sings along, too, a rich baritone supporting her falsetto:

"'Cause baby you're a firework, come on show 'em what you're worth . . ."

Valentino joins in.

"Make 'em go 'Oh, oh, oh!'"

More and more start singing along. It's like a movie. Calabasas High brings it home.

"As you shoot across the sky-y-y . . ."

I feel my own mouth following the lyrics. We're singing, all of us. Somewhere below our mishmash of musical keys, the bell for next period chimes. We don't pay attention, because we're too busy yelling for an encore.

Next is "Honeymoon Avenue." And when that's done, she launches into Lorde's "Royals." Halfway through that, Stack's voice erupts over the PA system; she's decreeing a tardy sweep. But we don't budge. They can't write us *all* up.

Nicki Minaj. Miley Cyrus. Christina Aguilera. If they've made a scene at the VMAs, Lily covers them; whenever it seems like it's time to pack up and go, Valentino points a finger and she starts again. It isn't until her voice falters on the bridge of Bruno Mars's "Grenade" that we decide we ought to give her some vocal rest. We disperse.

Eli finds me outside of my history room. "Holy shit," he says. "What just happened?"

"Where were you?"

He shrugs. "Theater. Candy."

"Lily just gave a private concert for, like, a half hour. It was crazy."

"Are you serious?"

"Yeah. Stack's furious."

"'Course she is," he says. "Send me a video."

I'm reaching for my back pocket when I remember. "I don't have my phone today," I say.

"Huh?"

"Yeah, I'm grounded for a week," I say. "I couldn't record anything."

"Your parents took your phone away?"

"Yeah."

"What if something happens?"

"That's what I said."

"Well, that sucks. It's like you weren't even there."

"You literally were not there."

"Yeah, we were not there together," he says, and smiles. "Good times."

If a tree falls in the woods and no one is there to hear it, did it make a sound?

If Lily sang an a cappella rendition of "E.T." and rapped the entire Kanye West part without messing up once and I didn't catch it on camera, was I really there? Philosophies aside, the answer is always yes, because my mother receives an automatic truancy notice about it.

I come home to my bedroom. It's small and lime green with glow-in-the-dark stars on the ceiling; wall hangings include a poster of the Cabazon dinosaurs, drawings my mother bought in Australia, and different hands I cut out of a manicure magazine I stole from a dentist's office. I lie on my bed and pick up a book. I decide I'm too dumb to read today and I put it back down. I change into sweatpants. I stretch. I sit at my desk. I fold my arms and purse my lips, because something is definitely off here.

I look around my room.

It's the door.

Or lack thereof.

The hinges are bare. I walk through the doorframe once. Twice. Three times. I run my hands along the side. No, it's gone. It is definitely gone. I am having a Lindsay Lohan experience. And just my luck, it doesn't involve cocaine and Aaron Carter.

Jackie's bedroom door is right across from mine. She comes upstairs, her math workbook tucked beneath her arm.

"Hey," I say. "Did you know about this?"

She stops, looks at me, and blinks. Then she backs into her room and, without breaking eye contact, closes her door.

The fall of Valentino DeVito occurs at his graduation. We knew it was coming. All good things must come to an end.

In the weeks before the ceremony, the senior class decorates their graduation caps with emblems from their schools of choice; they host get-togethers on the weekends, make group errands to Michaels for supplies. It's one of Calabasas' most wholesome traditions.

But on the day of the event, Stack interrupts the grad procession. "It's against dress code," she hisses, plucking at their heads.

At CHS, you don't have to be a valedictorian to give a speech. Stack works with a handful of English teachers to audition student speakers. It's fairly competitive, so nobody is surprised when Valentino's speech isn't picked. But of all the applicants, he was the only one with an active mythology backing him, and it seems absurd that he wouldn't be given the last word in all things high school.

The graduation cap confiscation is the final straw. He's disgruntled. So much so, in fact, that when Stack finishes up her words of goodbye to the senior class, he storms the graduation stage, mustering only a sentence or two into the microphone before he's restrained by two history teachers. Stack snatches the microphone back.

"Logan," she says, her voice booming. "Logan Ahmadi."

It is the dox heard 'round the world. Warning Number Three.

"Nobody's called me that in years," he shouts, his escorts herding him off the stage. "It's Valentino to you."

When graduation ends, Stack places a permanent campus ban on Valentino DeVito. The security guards are notified, the campus cop alerted. She has her slice of satisfaction pie. Valentino becomes Logan again, even going so far as to change his Twitter handle. He enters the workforce. Enrolls at a real college. And I never see him again, except for the odd Instagram post here and there.

But his influence remains. Lily sings again, sometimes with her Acer, mostly without. She auditions for choir and doesn't make it. It doesn't matter, though, because the next day she's skipping through the quad once again, singing just the same. I don't listen to the radio very often but I know the lyrics to all the hits because Lily keeps us very much in the loop.

Eventually, my parents put my door back up. They haven't received a truancy notification since Lily's concert. It's not that I've stopped skipping class. It's that I've gone online and set my own email address as the attendance system's default. Big brain stuff.

Eli and I become friends. First we stick to the theater, stealing candy or playing hide-and-seek in the woodshop. Then we walk to Gelson's for cookies, or Golden Spoon for frozen yogurt.

"I know a lot of you get scared giving presentations," my history teacher says. I'm in class for once, listening to the usual pep talk: Speak up. Don't read off the slide. Keep your hands out of your pockets. "But if I have any advice for you, it's to imagine your best friend is in the classroom. Pretend you're talking to your best friend."

I entertain her little thought experiment. But the first face that pops into my brain is Eli's.

It's a strange feeling, having a best friend.

Months after graduation, there is a district-wide meeting where parents and students are given a chance to air any thoughts and grievances. Present at the event, of course, are Logan Ahmadi and Norbert Cox. The meeting lasts for nearly four hours, and each presenter is granted three minutes of speaking time.

Logan approaches the podium and makes his statement. His hair has grown to his shoulders; he walks slowly and sedately. The last few months have drained him. But he still has a job to do. It's time to stand up for his fellow classmates. Faculty isn't being, quote unquote, "one hundred."

There are a few chuckles in the audience as he chews out faculty with his usual colloquialisms. "You're almost out of time, Mr. Ahmadi," the superintendent says.

"Alright, I'll take these last few seconds to say thank you," he says. "To everyone. Let's change the world!" He pumps his fist in the air. It's one last display of Valentino spirit. As he steps down, the room breaks into applause. For a split second in time, it seems that maybe, just maybe, Valentino won.

But come fall, a strict no-cap-decorating policy is put in place for that year's graduation, and Valentino is gone, replaced for good by a Mr. Logan Ahmadi.

Please Don't Eat the Oranges

In Calabasas, all anybody cares about is Kylie Jenner. On Monday, in history class, the boy next to me is babbling about driving past the youngest Kardashian sister's matte G-Wagon this past weekend in Hidden Hills.

"She's hotter in person," he says. "I feel I witnessed history, you know?"

"Totally," a girl in front of him says. "Do you still sell Adderall?"

I find myself hearing more and more about Kris Jenner's holy uterus and less about the outside world. Six girls from the dance team get lip injections one weekend. There's a hostage situation somewhere far away. Will Kylie and Tyga get back together?

The Kardashian-Jenners live in a gated residential area of Calabasas called Hidden Hills. If the Valley is a zircon, Hidden Hills is the Hope Diamond. It's Shangri-la, dropped just on the outskirts of the San Fernando Valley's collection of tract houses and Red Lobsters. In the third grade, rumors spread at school that the Hidden Hills' public drinking fountains spurted Evian. And to nine-year-olds with hyperactive imaginations, the steady stream of Teslas and Maseratis is proof enough that just beyond the Hidden Hills' gates lie the illuminati's meeting grounds.

Once past the gates, it's easy to forget where exactly you are. Is it even Southern California anymore? On the outside, each house has been designed to imitate and exaggerate the homes you could find anywhere in rural America—there are front porches and wicker rocking chairs, white picket fences, shutters and shingles. You've landed in Stepford, or perhaps you're an accidental cast member on *The Truman Show*. There's a feeling of artificiality in the air; the squirrels just might have wind-up keys in their backs. Be sure to drive good and slow—everyone knows that Hidden Hills contains quite a few stables, and it's not uncommon to pass by a family casually riding horseback down the street.

I first venture past the gates when I'm invited to Thomas Lopez's house. Thomas is a sophomore transfer from Viewpoint High, the private school up the street from Calabasas. We all know and hate Viewpoint because it's our school on steroids. They've got an omelet bar, plaid uniform neckties, and a forty-thousand-dollar price tag. Tiffany Trump is a Viewpoint alum. Tom Cruise's kids skipped through the hallowed halls. Charlie Sheen once called on his Twitter followers to send bags of shit to the school after his enrolled daughter was bullied. If Calabasas High is a B-list celebrity with a superiority complex and a deviated septum, then Viewpoint is its hotter, high fashion, A-list competitor.

"The performing arts program over there was literal shit," Thomas explains. I'm honored to be in his presence. Even though he's new on campus, he's already earned a crowd of adorers. It's not hard to see why. He looks like a *Tiger Beat* pullout poster and he's got the kind of movie-star charisma that pretty much guarantees free shit for life. In a few years he'll date a closeted pop star who'll release an EP about him (with the pronouns strategically ambiguous). His parents are eccentric TV producers—there's a giant catapult in his backyard; there are silicone breast implants framed on the living room wall.

Here, in his neighborhood, Thomas walks me down the street. Hidden Hills is filled with citrus. In the springtime, the air carries the smell of the eucalyptus trees, the swimming pool chlorine, the orange groves. California perfume, a spritz of eau de Suburbia. It's a major talking point of any real estate agent hocking a double-H mansion. Tempted, I reach toward the bough of a nearby orange tree.

"Don't," he says.

"What?"

"Don't pick that," he says.

I drop my arm. "I'll Venmo you, asshole."

"Very funny," Thomas says, "but you'll die if you eat that orange. No joke. It's radioactive."

Not quite a joke. Most of the West Valley—Hidden Hills included—sits uncomfortably close to the site of the 1959 Santa Susana Field Lab nuclear meltdown. For decades, the accident, one of the worst nuclear disasters in US history, remained undisclosed to the public. Today, rare pediatric cancers are found in an alarming number of children born and raised in the area. Perhaps it's no surprise that such coincidences never seem to make it into the news cycle, but among locals it's an open fear that every bite of a grapefruit or slice of a lemon grown there carries the risk of whatever effect radioactive fruit may have on the human body. For some, I assume, the citrus is strictly decorative.

The mansions are gimmicky and over the top. Think fewer infinity pools and Jacuzzis, and more along the lines of jellyfish tanks, bowling alleys, movie theaters, topiary trees, and waterslides. Behind the Cape Cod facades lie the sort of extravagance you may have thought only existed in movies or in Barbie Dreamhouses.

Britney Spears lived in Hidden Hills for a while. So did Drake and Miley Cyrus and Angelina Jolie. They're probably gone by now, though. The turnover rate is very high in these places. Rich people never know if they're satisfied or not.

The one Hidden Hills constant? The Kardashian-Jenners. They're the unofficial lords of the fiefdom. You may own a house in Hidden Hills, you may've raised your kids there, but who are we kidding? As far as Hidden Hills goes, it's a Kardashian world and you're just living in it. Kim and Khloé and Kourtney jammed their Kolumbus flag in Calabasas' dirt the first time that they shared a Snapchat story with Hidden Hills' trademark three-rail fencing in the background.

It's embarrassing to admit, but we envy the Kardashians, a family from our hometown that seemingly tripped upon immense success with minimal effort. They're a family driven by sex, by clothes, by makeup, by rap, by all the cool and amazing things that a high schooler wants to have.

It's easy for people to judge matriarch Kris Jenner with her overly Botoxed face and her Tory Burch accessories. *Yes, they're famous, but for what? A sex tape?* But there's a part of us, the

Valley kids, that wishes, when we see her at the local Gelson's, deciding between Tuscan kale or foraged chickweed, that she'd just accept us with open arms and bring us into her world, where we wouldn't have to worry about college or summer jobs or mediocrity. And if the cost is a sex tape, well . . . you know, it's worked out pretty well for others, historically speaking.

Calabasas High reveres Kylie most of all, because she's closest to our age. When she posts videos of her Italian greyhounds frolicking in her yard, we examine each frame like we're forensic scientists piecing together a criminal trail. She's breathing the same air as us, she's living through the same weather. When it rains in the Valley, a rarity in itself, we remember that Kylie's probably staying inside today. The same rain that we're looking at is gathering in her gutters, dusting her three-thousand-dollar lace-front wig when she pokes her head out the window to gauge the temperature. Maybe Kylie and I both rolled our eyes that morning, allowed a guttural *ugh* to escape our lips when we dodged puddles on the sidewalk.

At Calabasas High School, the Kardashian-Jenners hold an invisible power. When a photograph circulates of Kylie perched in the passenger seat of a Bentley, her little pink wrist stacked with six Cartier Love Bracelets—worth over $40,000 total— suddenly everyone at school except me, it seems, has a Love Bracelet or two of their own. When Kanye West launches the latest Yeezy season, this time an Adidas collaboration that's been themed "CALABASAS," the quad fills with students dressed in comically oversized sweatshirts marked with our high school's name. When Kendall Jenner praises ginger green juices, Calabasas High's trash cans transform into toxic waste bins, housing bottle after bottle of thick brown health sludge left to bake in the heat. We're all in this together. We're all Calabasas kids. Kylie, Kendall, Khloé, Kourtney, Kim: we *get* it. We're not so different. Right . . . ?

"I dare you . . . to go knock on Kylie's door."

Junior year. I'm at a sleepover in Hidden Hills with my all-girl a cappella group, Bare Rhythm. We're one of two a cappella groups on campus; the other one, Unstrumental, is co-ed, so everyone dates each other and it's all very histrionic. Unst regularly competes against college groups—and wins. Bare Rhythm has performed in Carnegie Hall and starred in a CoverGirl ad campaign. The head of the school vocal program, Mr. K, is a legend in the a cappella community.

But because Unstrumental competes and we don't, Mr. K typically spends most of rehearsals prepping them in a separate room. Since we're left to our own devices so often, Bare Rhythm is exceptionally close-knit, more so than Unst. We get regularly reprimanded for talking, for whispering, for using each other's abdomens as pillows. We know each other's business. Our periods are synced. We learn gibberish and double talk. Unstrumental is an a cappella group. But Bare Rhythm just might qualify as a girl cult.

This is our annual slumber party, traditionally held in the living room of the girl who has the most square footage to spare. This year, Lauren Campbell is hosting. There are sixteen of us sprawled out on the hardwood floor of Lauren's Hidden Hills mansion at one-thirty in the morning.

Normally, Bare Rhythm's time spent together is in the context of rehearsal, around a piano, where we're placed on a tight schedule to keep our bonding to a minimum. But these sleepovers are an exception. In Lauren's kitchen, there's a spread of junk food—brownies, pizza, tortilla chips, pails of ice cream. Her living room has been taken apart, armchairs and love seats dragged aside to make way for our sleeping bags, zipped open and laid out over an expensive Persian rug. We share stories (the tale du jour is a recent graduate's foray into soft-core porn) and engage in "bonding exercises" (typical slumber party games) until we eventually fall asleep, exhausted and bloated with cheese pizza and rainbow sherbet. Right now, the lights in the living room are off, except for a salt lamp in the corner. But none of us are tired yet.

"What?" I say, nearly choking on a mouthful of Sprite.

Ashley Maron repeats herself. "I *said,* I dare you to go knock on Kylie's door."

"Oh my god. She literally just moved into a new house on my street. She's, like, a really short walk away," Lauren says. "Hol-ee shit."

Ashley folds her arms, flashing a toothy smile. "Via. Do it. I bet you won't."

The entire room turns to look at me. Fifteen girls, absolutely quiet.

I guess it's time to divulge why it is that I'm the daredevil of the group. I've had a bit of a reputation since the Catwalk Incident, in which I accidentally established myself as an anti-cop figurehead at CHS.

It was my freshman year, and I'd forgotten that I had a sixth-period class after lunch. So instead of going to history, I walked to the theater for play rehearsal. When I was greeted with an empty stage, my eyes immediately met the forbidden fruit: the catwalk.

Suspended fourteen feet above the stage, the catwalk is a grid of invisible fishing line and it's strictly off-limits unless you've had proper stage crew training. And even still, anybody who walks across it must empty their pockets first. Even a quarter dropped from that height could seriously hurt someone.

Of course, finding myself alone in the theater for once, I decided it was my time to cross. When I made it up the stairs, prepared to take my first step, I heard voices from below and realized I'd had some atrocious timing. A few days earlier, someone had swiped hardware from the sound booth in the theater. Today, the stage manager was giving a police officer a tour of the premises. And the two were about to walk directly below me.

I don't know what came over me. Maybe it was demonic possession. Perhaps my childhood epilepsy was returning, only this time, I was being granted precise motor skills. It could've been any number of things. But before I knew it, I was sending a glob of spit through a gap in the wire, watching it land directly on the toe of the officer's shoe.

I scrambled back, squeezing myself into the wall and out of sight. "Who did that? Who's up there?" the cop yelled.

"It wasn't spit, I swear," I yelled back, weakly. And then I sped down the stairs and burst from the back exit and sprinted all the way across campus, where I hid in the bathroom for an hour and a half. I told a select few of my misadventure and within a couple of weeks I was both a no-fucks-haver and a baby Antifa. I decided to go with it, and here we are.

There are more things to be worried about, I've decided, than the possible repercussions of a ding-dong-ditch. I shrug. "I'm not a little bitch," I say. "I'll do it."

The room erupts in shrieks. "Shut up, shut up, you guys," Lauren whispers. "My parents are literally asleep upstairs. Shut the fuck up." She raises her eyebrows at me. "Are you serious?"

"Yeah," I say. "Like, what's the worst that could happen?"

"She calls the cops and you get arrested for trespassing," Amanda Franklin says.

"It would be funny as fuck," Ashley says, "if you got put in jail because of *Kylie Jenner*."

"It's dumb," Amanda says. "If you got arrested, that could fuck up college."

"Watch," I say, the support of fifteen girls giving me a sudden rush of invincibility. "I'll ask her for free lip kits." Kylie's cosmetics brand famously started with her lipstick/liner duo, called Lip Kits. When she began making public appearances with significantly larger lips, she'd first ascribed it to her liplining routine. When she finally confessed that the change was the result of a Juvéderm injection, she decided to use the press to kickstart her makeup career—customers didn't seem to care about the plastic surgery anyway. It was an instant success.

As I announce my plan, the room explodes into chatter again.

"Okay, literally you guys, if you start yelling again, I'm gonna get really mad," Lauren whisper-shouts. "My parents are right up the fucking stairs and they have craniosacral therapy in the morning."

"It's two a.m.," Zoe Melton speaks up. "You'll wake her up." Since the orientation debacle, Zoe joined Bare Rhythm at the same time I did, and we've been friends since.

"She's probably not asleep. She's clubbing. Or throwing a party. Oh my God, Via, what would you do if she invited you inside?" Courtney says.

"She's not going to invite her in," Amanda says. "She's gonna tell her to get the fuck off the property, and then she's gonna have her bodyguard kick her ass."

"Her bodyguard's hot," says Calista. "I would *not* be mad if he pushed me around a little bit."

"Pretend you live next door and that you're just welcoming her to the neighborhood," says Alice.

"Puh-lease," Lauren says. "This is Calabasas, not Kansas. Nobody does that here."

"I know it's stupid," Courtney says, "but I feel like me and Kylie would really click. Like, we'd definitely be friends."

"No, yeah. We like the same music and everything. She seems cool," Alice says.

I can understand why they feel this way. I think of the way she addresses her fans on social media, like she's a friend. *Was thinking of you guys today. What do you all think of my new lip kits? Thank you all so much for the support. Love you.* She seems to be playing along just the same way we all are. She's trying to convince us that we're all on the same team. We like her pictures on Instagram, promote her makeup line. When she graces the cover of a magazine, we feel a sense of pride. That's our girl Kylie. She's one of us. She's a Calabasas kid and she's kicking ass out there, and if she can do it, if she can date rappers and wear Valentino and tweet all day and make money, we can too.

"I just think it's a bad idea," Amanda says. "Do whatever you want, but it's dumb."

"Listen," I say. "I've never backed off of a dare in my life. I'm not scared of Kylie Jenner or her hot bodyguard."

"Wait," Serena says. "Alexis Neiers."

Silence. Calabasas is the former stomping ground of the Bling Ring, the notorious teen crime group that broke into the homes of Paris Hilton and Lindsay Lohan and other celebrities in 2009 to steal thousands of dollars' worth of clothes and jewelry. Alexis Neiers is the most infamous of the gang. Played by Emma Watson in the Sofia Coppola film, *The Bling Ring,* Neiers owns a special place in Calabasian lore because of the reality TV show, *Pretty Wild,* that followed her around in the aftermath of the crime. She is the ultimate niche pop-culture icon because she effectively balanced villainy with bubblegum stardom. We love to hate her. We hate to love her. She's our own personal antihero. A perverse Robin Hood in four-inch little brown Bebe shoes and a tweed skirt. Calabasas kids quote her like the Bible. I was once at Sephora with a group of girls when I witnessed one of my companions discreetly pocket a high-end highlighter compact that she'd seen on beauty mogul Jeffree Star's YouTube channel. "I wanna *rob,*" the girl giggled, quoting the catchphrase from the movie adaptation. But as much as Neiers is beloved by Valley dwellers, she also proved two important things: celebrities are not untouchable, and teenage girls are not harmless.

And even before the Bling Ring there was the Manson Family. Before things got bloody, the group held nighttime crusades in elite Los Angeles neighborhoods under Charles Manson's direction—they were instructed to "creepy-crawl," the Family's term for sneaking into rich people's houses late at night with no agenda other than to see what it was like.

So it would seem that LA girls have somewhat of a stereo-type to uphold. It's an infatuation with a certain lifestyle, an all-encompassing obsession with wealth, and cases range from checking a star's likes tab on Twitter to, well, theft and murder. Like I mentioned before, Bare Rhythm already veers dangerously close to girl cult territory. To creepy-crawl onto a Kardashian property late at night would be to follow in a long line of crazy California bitches.

"Well, it's not like she'll be trespassing," Courtney says. "Like, if she was sneaking in, that would be creepy, but if she's, like, ringing the doorbell, that's, like . . . pretty conspicuous. Like she's obviously not trying to be discreet."

"I guess," Serena mumbles.

"Who's coming?" Lauren says, standing up.

"Not me," Amanda says.

"Me neither," says Mia.

We divide into two groups: those that will journey to watch me step on Kylie's front lawn, and those that won't. Eight of us squeeze into Lauren's white Benz.

At night, Hidden Hills is especially dark. Streetlights are banned, likely a violation of one of the hundreds of Homeowners' Association rules to upkeep. As we continue down the street, the headlights of the car cut into front yards and horse stables and rosebushes. We catch the moony glow of a raccoon's eyes. The back seat buzzes with teenage prattle.

Then the car slows. "Here we are," Lauren says.

I take a look at Kylie's house. I can't believe someone only three years my senior is living in a place like this. It's a white cluster of peaked roofing and bleach-clean columns. Through the French windows I can just barely see the silhouettes of what appear to be a staircase and a Swarovski chandelier. It's dark, save for one single light in an upstairs room.

"Oh my God," someone says, hardly above a whisper. "She's totally home."

Lauren turns off the headlights and looks over at me. "You still going?"

"Um," I say, and swallow hard. We're at the curb, and the walk from the sidewalk to her front door is fifteen yards at least. Which isn't *that* long, I guess, but then again, it's 2 a.m. at the household of America's most famous teenager.

Before I can change my mind, I open the car door and step outside. It's cold. The one misconception about the Valley is that it's always hot. Nope. Like any desert, once the sun drops, so does the temperature. I pull the hood of my sweatshirt over my head, shove my hands in my pockets. No big deal.

"I'll come, too," Zoe Melton says. She hops out of the car and gives me a nod of solidarity.

My first step onto Kylie's property is accompanied by the hushed cheers of my friends. My foot is officially on Kardashian territory. I've crossed the line. There's no turning back now.

To stand on Kylie's front lawn is to tread upon blessed ground. She's at the top of a hierarchy for a school she doesn't even go to, a school she's maybe overheard in conversations a table over at Nobu or Villa Restaurant. Kylie never attended CHS—before switching online, she spent a couple of years at Sierra Canyon, a private school in Chatsworth. And yet, here we are. She, the young and beautiful and rich princess. Me, the lowly subject, chained into a never-ending cycle of tabloid perusal and Snapchat subscriptions.

As I walk forward, I run through a script of what I'll say when she answers the door. *Hey, Kylie, big fan.* No, that's wrong. I'm not a fan. We're supposed to be, like . . . equals, right? Both kids in the Valley. *Hey, was just passing by, and—* No, that's ridiculous. I can't pretend that I don't know her. It's two in the morning. Two in the morning! Okay, so maybe I should front with an apology. *I'm so, so sorry to disrupt you, but a dare is a dare—*

Hold on. Did the upstairs light flicker? Or was that just all in my head? Holy fuck. I'm totally bugging. I stare at the window, frozen halfway between the Benz and Kylie's front door. A warm, yellow light streams through the frosted pane.

I can picture her stirring from her desk, where she's sending an email to her manufacturers about restocking her cosmetics brand. Or perhaps she's in bed with a midnight snack, china dishes dressed with egg whites and plain oatmeal. Or maybe she's in her closet, thumbing through Balmain, Fiorucci, Versace. She could be frozen in her tracks, her hand paused over a wooden hanger, the dull sound of my footsteps bouncing through her marble hallways and sliding over her mahogany floors. Maybe her security is rushing down the stairs, prepared to grab me in a headlock and present me to Kylie like an eager-to-please housecat bestowing the corpse of a sad, mangled rat. She could even be peering through the blinds at this very moment, calling to her bodyguard as she watches the stupid kid loiter over her carefully manicured lawn: *There's a PEASANT out front, and she's dangerously close to the magnolias, and Christ! She's wearing leggings from Target!*

I consider that last possibility. Suddenly I'm not dressed well enough. I'm in a sweatshirt and Chucks. I look up at the second-story window, half expecting to see a sudden movement, maybe a shadowy profile or a strand of glossy black hair. But the house is still. When I stop moving, the sound of my steps dissolves into the air, and I'm left with nothing but a dog's bark at least three blocks away and the *ch-ch-ch* of an unabashed sprinkler system scurrying next door. (Magically, the California drought doesn't seem to exist behind the gates, and water conservation is the folly of plebeians with mere six-figure incomes.)

And then I'm there, on her front steps. She too has stood here, right where I'm standing. Zoe holds back, standing a couple yards behind me.

I glance back at the car and raise my finger to the doorbell. It's now or never. I'm already doomed to security camera footage scrutiny, I may as well complete the mission.

I do it. I press the button.

Her doorbell is a single flat tone.

A dog barks.

The sprinklers break into their chorus: *ch-ch-ch.*

I wrap my arms around myself, shivering.

Behind me, I hear turning gravel. Lauren's Benz is backing away. I remember that I am an unwanted guest in a community where security cameras are surely hidden in every hedge, light, and bronze decorative horse statue.

"Oh shit," I say, way too loud, and we sprint back down the driveway and away from Kylie's front door.

"Get in!" Lauren says. The girls in the back are onto something else, discussing some other drama. "We heard a neighbor come outside and got scared."

"Did you see anything?" someone in the back seat asks.

"No," I say. "I didn't see anything."

There is an episode of Kylie Jenner's TV show, *Life of Kylie,* where the nineteen-year-old spends a week trying to embrace the farm life.

"The farm, for me, is just, like, really how I want to, like, raise a family," she says. ". . . And I wouldn't like, trade my life for anything, but I do get lost. I'm like, what do I really want? What I *really* want is to live on a farm and have chickens and raise animals."

For the next twenty minutes Kylie confides in Caitlyn Jenner and tours a 106-acre, sixteen stable, guard-gated farm. Cue the adorable clips of Kylie holding chickens and collecting eggs. She's just *so* sweet. The producers edit in upbeat music while she *oohs* and *ahhs* over the cows and goats. "I just want to live the farm life," she says.

"Do you know how hard the farm life is?" Caitlyn says.

"I do, but that's cool!" Kylie says.

As she takes a step toward her assistant, her phone clatters to the ground. She gasps, prolonging the breath. Her assistant turns, sees the disaster, and clutches her throat. They stare at the iPhone, then at each other. The music cuts. This is it. Right here. The episode climax. Finally, Kylie sweeps an arm down and picks it up. "Phew," she says, examining the sleek, unbroken screen. "It's okay, it's okay."

I've often wondered where the Kardashians fit in in the pantheon of famous American families. Are they the Kennedys or Clintons without the politics? Are they the Barrymores without the talent? The Fords without the cars? The Vanderbilts without the railroads? But here, sitting in my bedroom the day after ding-dong-ditching her house, her spinoff show booted up on my computer, my eyes glued to a montage of Kylie petting ponies and goats while dodging dirt clods in her Yeezys, I have a sudden revelation: that the easiest comparison to make is one that connects the Kardashians to French nobility, and Kylie Jenner to Marie Antoinette.

Antoinette notoriously ordered a "little farm" to be built on the Versailles property ("little" being a mere eighty-six acres, complete with three separate mansions, twelve cottages, and orange groves) because she wanted to play dress-up and play pretend peasant every once in a while. She'd be escorted from the main Versailles palace to her hideaway, where she could pet her cows and chickens and make-believe poor. And strewn throughout the entire property were orange trees. Louis XIV fancied himself a collector, as a matter of fact.

Of course, the Kardashian-Jenners *have* accomplished something exceptional. They hold power—so much so that Kylie was able to drop Snapchat stock by one billion dollars with a single tweet. And to their credit, they have used this power for good in the past. Kim is vocal about her dedication to prison reform, even helping to free incarcerated people. Kendall has donated large amounts of money to clean-water funds. Kris's fundraising helped renovate the Watts Empowerment Center in downtown LA. Kylie, philanthropist extraordinaire, even went so far as to open up a GoFundMe to crowdsource money for her former stylist's hospital bills. :-)

But it can be argued that their dynasty was founded on tragedy, their earliest and most blatant tie to celebrity being the most high-profile murder case of the 1990s. Rob Kardashian defended O.J. Simpson; in this sense, it was Nicole Brown Simpson's blood that served as their celebrity baptismal water. Maybe they're cursed, and it's just an incredible PR team that keeps them riding the TMZ fluff wave. Because if you were to ask anyone for a summary of the Kardashian-Jenners' greatest hits, they'd probably mention Kylie's billion-dollar makeup brand, Caitlyn's Woman of the Year award. But if you were to subtract all the Instagram-mable news and Facebook-appropriate headlines, all the pseudo-journalism that plagues Twitter feeds worldwide, there'd be a lot more talk of Kim's murky, exploited beginnings when her sex tape was leaked. There'd definitely be more discussion of how the dozens of complex surgeries and injections administered to each Kardashian-Jenner woman are less about empowerment and more a symptom of toxic trend culture and perhaps even appropriation, of how their continued endorsement of appetite suppressants and stretch-mark creams and corsets only enforce the unrealistic body standards that impact millions worldwide. I have seen the consequences of this myself. It's twelve-year-old girls, Facetuning their undeveloped hips into perfect half-circles. Or posting ass photos, because they've been taught that hyper-sexualization is the last word in empowerment. Don't get me wrong—I think that celebrating your body is a wonderful thing, and (of-age) nakedness is beautiful. But I am wary of mistaking commodification for celebration.

I suspect that we will one day see Kylie Jenner's fall. Not as severe as Marie Antoinette's, of course, but the public eye does seem to behave in a pattern: First we love them. Then we hate them. The public has an insatiable appetite for schadenfreude. We've done it before and we'll do it again. But I think it's important to recognize that Kylie Jenner hasn't looked like Kylie Jenner since she was seventeen, and that alone hints at a profound insecurity. I have scrutinized my face in the mirror and wished I looked different, too. But to have the kind of wealth to make actual, drastic change? To pay paparazzi to doctor your images? That is a scary thing. That is a lonely thing.

When we watch Kylie talk "candidly" to the camera, we aren't seeing a real person. It's not actually her on the cover of *Paper* or *Forbes*. It's her brand. We're seeing a character that's been carefully choreographed. A persona. Her relationships, and her social media, and even the public parts of her family life are all fake. The citrus is strictly decorative.

So. If Kylie had opened the door on me last night, what would I have said?

What *can* you say to someone who has never known a normal day at school? Who's never had to accept her own flaws? What can you say to someone who, quite possibly, could be the loneliest girl in the world?

Who am I kidding? I know exactly what I'd say.

Selfie?

Stalling for Cub

Cub's in love. And this—oh, man—*this* is the kind of stuff they write songs about. Cub's on that decadent, highfalutin shit. I'm talking harps and cherubs and divine revelations all day long. He's up there with Paolo and Francesca. Rhett and Scarlett. Cub and (drumroll, please) *Vicki*.

He slips out of class to meet up with her in the senior parking lot, right behind the tennis courts. He takes long, libidinous hits of Sour Diesel, his preferred aphrodisiac. When he's sure they're alone, he unfurls his fingers from the shaft of his Brass Knuckles dab pen and, with all the erotic precision of an X-Acto knife wrapped in skin-safe silicone, strokes her. He runs his palm along her smooth, soft inside. Fondles her trunk. Her, um, glove box. He flicks at the air freshener he's installed in the air-conditioning vents, fingers the center console—ah, yes, Hawaiian breeze. She's so . . . *mmm* . . . fuel-efficient.

Cub's lover is a 2012 two-door Honda Civic Si Coupe in the factory paint Dyno Blue Pearl.

This car is his real home. Back at his address, he's at odds with his parents. They don't approve. But you have to understand— the red rim to his eyes is a metaphor. They're glasses of the rose-colored kind. And the smoky halo around his head isn't em- anating evidence of a habitual addiction—rather, it's a religious nimbus. Weed is, like, sacred, in, like, a lot of other countries, did you know *that*? And hence: Vicki's his place of worship. "She's tricked out," he announces to any potential carpooler, gesturing to the miniature disco ball that he once spent an entire Saturday afternoon installing. "Chicks dig it."

Meet Cub Birnwick. Teenage comedian-to-be. Deliciously awkward concoction of the three great Hormonal Boy Motiva- tors: unquenched sexual appetite, untempered pursuit of "class clown" designation, and the unchallenged belief that the high school social ladder is the most urgent and important matter in the whole world, even more than Haiti, or, like, *feminism,* dude. A newer addition to Los Angeles' ever-expanding cast, he hails from Philadelphia. What he doesn't know yet is that he will move away as effortlessly as he came, returning to the east at the di- minuendo of his high school career like a last-minute warbler to spring migration. For now, though, he lives in a lower-tier gated community with his parents, sister, and pair of brain-damaged poodle-Yorkie twins. (Lower-tier means there's a gate, but in- stead of a guard you have to punch in a code.) Clothed in mesh sports jerseys and acid-wash joggers, he's got all the makings of a grade-A certifiable fuckboy but without the "fuck."

My freshman year, we're enrolled in the same English class. A shared last initial designates us seating chart neighbors. Ms. Jäger-Vogt, an untenured campus newbie, stands near the smart board and asks us to share something interesting about our summers. Cub volunteers first.

"I went to Jew camp," he says.

"Vunderful," she says.

"Well, actually," he says, clearing his throat. "Not your kind."

The male faction of the class is thrilled. Frenzied, newly-pubescent laughter bounces off the walls, a decent imitation of the harpy chorus you probably hear upon entering Hell (or 4chan). And this is only the *first* step in Cub's four-year-long campaign for the class clown yearbook superlative. There is plenty more to come.

The next three years are a glorious ascension to the top: he's picked to play games at the pep rallies, he's named team captain of the school's improv team, a Facebook video of his standup set makes it to four hundred views. He's featured on the local Snapchat story when he makes a classroom game of stacking nickels on the neck of a sleeping Lil Shrimp, student DJ and SoundCloud rapper. He brings his knowledge from temple to the lunch tables, teaching everyone at school how to say *fuck off* in Hebrew. He memorizes a handful of Shakespearean quotes and doles them out to girls like Dum Dums, and sometimes, they work. The V-card that he carries in his wallet (cardboard laminate scribbled in Crayola) is eventually torn to shreds in a public show-and-tell during sixth-period economics. And Cub's virginity, much like his ability to read a room, is gone with the wind.

Like most whirlwind love affairs, Cub and Vicki are eventually confronted with passion's number-one adversary: time. Come senior year, Cub breaks Vicki's heart (engine?) when he meets a girl in his Second City Improv youth troupe. For weeks, it's all "girl from Second City this" and "girl from Second City that." And Cub's demonstration of the male attention span results in Vicki's neglect. Trash accumulates in her interior. The air freshener depletes. His seat fabric smells like mid-grade weed, the result of repeated late-night hotboxings. But Cub's got more important things on his mind than an auto detail.

We see it change him, this potential for romance. Regular old hookah-smoking, Civic-drifting Cub won't cut it when it comes to Mystery Girl. Suddenly, he isn't aching for the perfect wisecrack anymore; he simmers down, starts doing his homework. Takes a hiatus from his YouTube prank channel (he only ever made three videos, each with ten views). We know he's *really* metamorphosing when he trades in his trademark Samsung Galaxy S7 for the latest iPhone. He claims it was group chat mishaps that made him do it. But we all know better. This sudden makeover is too much for us. In the weeks before the dance, we convene into our lunchtime cliques, pontificating about everything from his suit to his girl. Maybe she's his cousin. Maybe he's paying for an escort service. Maybe she's a catfish.

"But a Cub Birnwick ten is, like, a real world six," Eli says, to Zoe and me. It's homecoming night. Lil Shrimp is spinning trap remixes of Chainsmokers songs in the DJ booth. It smells like fog machine and soggy corn dogs and Old Spice and general adolescent dread. The crowd is split into parts. Some offer a lukewarm sway from the safety of the punch bowl. Others assemble in line at the photo wall, and the final part—the horniest part—engages in a special kind of teenage grind that somehow clears both first and second base with heavy implication towards an eventual, more private shortstop.

The high school dance is a rite of passage. Sure. I've accepted this. If I'm being honest, I'm only here for Instagram fodder. Wearing a four-inch heel over sticky gym flooring, subjecting my olfactory senses to the acrid stench of mango JUUL vape . . . it's a gift. From me to my mother's Facebook feed, that is. The student body has decided that this year's theme is Circus. Maybe it's a stroke of brilliance on their part—after all, it's true that we do make for quite a menagerie, clumped in our loosely-coordinated friend groups. You're supposed to dress your niche: the dance team models the New Arrivals rack at Free People, film nerds are more apt to wear Urban Outfitters' renewal line, a cappella kids recycle their uniform performance suspenders. We're all here to further exacerbate the stereotypes we've been cramming ourselves into since freshman year. The phrase "stay true to yourself" is quietly incomplete; "stay true to your brand" is a bit more on-par with the mores of high school socialization.

The high school microcosm isn't as sequestered as you might think. In order to assimilate as soon as possible, you have to morph into an easily digestible category. Because we don't have enough experience to define our own social groups and expectations, these categories are extracted from what's presented culturally, in movies and television—products of the adult world. Basically, high school sucks because grown-ups make it so. And that's why the new-wave-scene crowd, still sore from the My Chemical Romance split, are coagulated over by the basketball nets. That's why the AP prodigies have assembled against the wall, why the codeine kids loiter near the exit. Because that's what every ass-backward adult in Hollywood has decided would happen.

But despite our predictable, boomer-sanctioned divisions, we're united by a common intrigue. We're waiting for Cub's big reveal. And finally: he and Mystery Girl materialize in the doorway, arm-in-arm, right as Bieber's "Sorry" ends and Mike Posner, in a fit of festival-induced Avicii ardor, decides to take a pill in Ibiza. And wow.

She IS pretty. Like, actually. Cub wasn't exaggerating. She's movie-star beautiful. As she steps into the dance, a party light bounces off her face. We're given a flash of cheekbone, a stripe of eyebrow. Wait. Hold on a minute.

"Holy shit," Eli breathes. "That's—"

"[XXXXX]," we all murmur in unison. Actor on an Emmy Award–winning drama, future star of her own successful TV show, [XXXXX] stands with perfect posture, hair curled, her designer dress swaying gently with each movement she makes. Cub places his arm around her waist. They make a clumsy duo. Imagine Kendall Jenner and Smokey Bear, or Tinker Bell and a gaming chair.

Our eyes lock with Cub's and he offers a nod in our direction. *Are you guys seeing this?* he communicates, with a glance toward [XXXXX].

Yes, YES, you absolute madman! we reply, with bulged eyes and raised eyebrows. *We're sorry! This whole time we thought you were the wise guy. We were wrong! You're the straight man protagonist! First billing on IMDb!*

There's an energy change as [XXXXX] establishes her presence. Collective awareness of proximal celebrity hovers in the air, thicker than the fog pumped in from rented machines. But because most Calabasas students earnestly believe they're already famous, it's an unspoken acknowledgement. Being "starstruck" implies the forfeit of your own perceived stardom. They amble around [XXXXX] without sparing so much as a single glance. It's almost a contest. Who can play it most coy?

"Guys, this is [XXXXX]," Cub yells over the music. "[XXXXX], this is Via, Eli, and Zoe."

We wave. She waves back.

"[XXXXX]'s never been to a dance before," he says. "She's looking for the *real* high school experience."

Between beat drops, Lil Shrimp flings bundles of glow sticks out to the crowd. One lands near [XXXXX], and she drags it around with the toe of her shoe, examining it like she's never seen one before. Perhaps I'm being unfair. After all, while I was picking at worms in my preschool playground, [XXXXX] was having catered fettuccine on the set of a $200 million TV show. Maybe they all just used flashlights.

"We're going to the big thing at Nora's later so she can see what a high school party's like," he says, while she stares blankly at the glow stick. "It's gonna be *lit,* you guys. *Major* turn-up."

"Yeah," [XXXXX] says, and shrugs. Wave of silence as we all try and think of what to say next.

"I like your shoes," I try, weakly.

"Thanks," she says.

"Yeah, those are some great shoes," Cub strains. "What is that, patent?"

"No, it's suede," she answers.

"Oh, cool," Cub says.

Eli clears his throat.

Zoe excuses herself to retrieve a Dixie-cup of warm soda.

Lil Shrimp directs a cross-fade into the next track, launches a couple more glow sticks into the audience.

"Did anything interesting happen before we got here?" Cub says.

"Not really," Eli says.

"Oh." He fiddles with the end of his tie.

I'm witnessing something new in Cub. He's faltering. For once, he doesn't have an endless backlog of one-liners. Panic arises in his eyes. He flounders. With each four-count in "Cheap Thrills" that remains unprovoked by conversation, a few things become more and more obvious: A) that Cub did not think he would get this far in the first place, and B) that [XXXXX] is having a terrible, horrible, no good, very bad date.

Cub's pupils dart around the room faster than you can say "*fortydollarsforagram.*" He sweats. Entertains a handful of canned conversation starters—first, a blah-blah about Lil Shrimp's DJ spot, then a ho-hum about the weather this month. It's brutal. I'm a terrible wingman, I will admit, but in my defense, there is no salvaging this (rapidly spiraling) situation. I excuse myself to go to the bathroom.

The bathroom is simultaneously the best and worst spot on campus. Saved only by its status as a safe-zone from faculty, it's haunted by a sensory mixture of sewage, menstruation, and Mario Badescu rosewater. There are never any toilet seat covers available, which of course prompts an avalanche of jokes about the school's skewed priorities. Calabasas High School, where multimillion-dollar theaters take precedence over *E. coli* prevention. Most of the sinks are in disrepair, and at least a few of the stalls have busted locks. But still, I take a weird kind of solace in our little shitstain of a bathroom. Therapy's a hall pass. As soon as you push open the restroom doors, you're untouchable. Plenty of time for tampon insertion, or a FaceTime call, or a full AV Club summation of *Glee*'s third-to-last season. What's a geometry teacher gonna do, ask for photo evidence of your scatological productivity?

A girl in a red shift dress hustles out of the big stall and I'm left on my own. I burrow myself inside the leftmost corner. A gnat beats against a fluorescent light strip. I scan the walls for any scribblings: phone numbers, or Instagram handles, or inspirational quotes. You can draw any number of conclusions about a school based on what's been etched on the walls. But Calabasas' bathroom stalls are scrubbed clean, a striking aesthetic, especially when compared to the grayish mold flowering in the tile grout. Eyes glued to the latch lock, I run through a mental slideshow of all the bathroom stall reflections I've had in my life. There's the eighth-grade dance, where I waited out "I Gotta Feeling" and instead took to a Genius analysis of Paramore's "Brick by Boring Brick" on my iPod Touch. Then my first day of freshman year, where I watched twelve minutes of *Pirates of the Caribbean* bloopers instead of attending the after-school barbecue mixer. And of course, I've escaped more than a spattering of family outings, all in the advent of my teenhood (Christmas 2014 comes to mind, when I left the table to play Temple Run in the bathroom because my dad called Harry Styles a soy boy). I've probably wasted entire days of my life just zoning out in bathroom stalls.

Having an intimate relationship with the stall is a symptom of the digital age, because a quick pee comes hand in hand with the social media catch-up. I don't think Twitter or Instagram or Snapchat are great for us, but there's no denying that there's something meditative about opening Twitter in a private setting. Outside, parents are checking online report cards or your best friend is ditching you at a party or you're somehow flunking Health 1—but hey, at least the Internet is still blissfully predictable. The world's going to shit but some "influencer" will always be getting exposed for saying a slur; recycled tweets are making the rounds again. The act brings a sense of normalcy: unlocking your phone with a glance, leaning against the porcelain back, watching corporate Twitter accounts latch onto memes like sea lice (I'm looking at you, Burger King): it's all easy and familiar. It's no wonder most younger people consider their phones a terrific ally and confidant. Those few moments of screen indulgence are a security blanket. And it's nothing new, either. My bathroom scroll is an evolution of the gather-round-the-radio experience, whittled to a solo venture with the birth of the iPhone. Even though the Internet is a cold, impersonal vacuum of AI and Captcha and phishing and password recommendations, I find myself strangely human in moments like these, ones where my boots are propped against a Hiny Hider, my bladder is empty, and my cell phone is loaning the stall a blueish-greenish wash.

So I take my pee and in the meantime I watch a couple of Snapchat stories. According to *Cosmo*, 20 percent of women have endometriosis. Someone from my history class is sucking a tequila shot from an innie belly button. *Elle* claims that everyone born between September 23 and October 22 will experience romantic dissonance in the next week, and *Vice* attests that everyone and their mother is microdosing their coffee. Bland, repetitive, average information settles into my brain while a radio-friendly version of "Bitch Better Have My Money" seeps from the gym into my stall, a nagging reminder that I'm still obligated to have forty dollars' worth of fun tonight. I stand up, prepared to wash my hands and reenter the dance when the bathroom door swings open and a set of high heels strut into the stall next to mine. There's the ruffling of toilet paper (a makeshift toilet seat cover, no doubt) and the trademark sigh of someone who has just escaped an awkward social situation. Curious, I lean over and peek at the shoes. And here's the kicker. I know them. They're suede. Wait. These are [XXXXX]'s feet. No doubt about it. I hold my breath. Famous people . . . also pee?

And then I hear it. It's an auditory punctuation mark, something as comforting as catered fettuccine, as familiar as the "Brick by Boring Brick" music video and as cathartic as Twitter's mute button. It's the universal signifier for alone time. The interlude of escapism, if you will.

It is the pluck of the iPhone unlock sound.

I hold my breath as one teenage girl's unfulfilled expectations of the "high school experience" collapses into its staccato *tick*.

At the end of the night, Cub appears at Nora's after-party alone. "She said she felt sick, so she went home," he says. "Probably the corn dogs they were serving at the dance."

For the remainder of our time at Calabasas High School, Cub doesn't mention [XXXXX] again. We don't prod. It's a pride thing. We get it. And Cub completes high school just as he started it—single and stoned. He buys Vicki a new air freshener. He sells the rest of his Adderall to freshmen. He hits on a born-again Christian with the line, "Wanna pray together sometime?"

"Via," he says to me at graduation, a cigar dangling from his lips, "one day we're going to write comedy together. Let me know if you're ever on the East Coast."

I'm sorry to say that this is the last time I ever see Cub face-to-face. He moves away shortly after, the first Valley defector of my graduating class. I don't know if he drove Vicki. I'd like to think he did.

As time passes and college begins, Cub is shoved to the bottom of my Instagram feed's algorithm, giving way to posts from new faces I recognize from campus. But he is far from forgotten. I give him an anecdotal legacy among my new friends.

Two years later, [XXXXX] snags the lead role of a hit teen drama. Her face is plastered all over stan Twitter. She's inescapable. Photos circulate of her brunching with A-listers and she shares scripted stories on the talk show circuit. She is a serious contender for the coveted role of Hollywood's newest it-girl.

On the evening of her TV show's premiere, I'm studying for midterms on the floor of my apartment. My housemates are scattered around me, bowls of Top Ramen and mugs of lukewarm coffee lined up on the kitchen table. We've been doing this all day. I haven't stood up in three hours.

I get up to pee. In the bathroom, I surrender to my instincts and I open the Facebook app for the first time in a hot minute. There he is, reigning at the top of my feed with a shared post from three years prior. It's a picture of Cub with [XXXXX] at the dance, a goofy smile on his face, his eyes wide like he's an eight-year-old at

Disneyland. I'm graced with the gift of retrospect. When I look at the photo I don't see the awkward silences or the glow sticks or the sterile inside of a bathroom stall door. I see Cub, the most excited kid in the world, and [XXXXX], one cool-ass girl making her distant friend's whole year.

Internet Safety

Zoe Melton will become a star.

It will happen a few years after graduation. I'll have lost touch with most of my high school classmates. I'll be fully acclimated to college life, having joined forces with cheap vodka, disposable vapes, and the library all-nighter. And news of her success will reach me while an ex and I are breaking up. "Pause," I'll say, wiping snot and tears from my face.

"What?" he'll say.

"I'm having an out-of-body experience," I'll answer. There it is again, the voice I know well. It's coming from a television set in the living room. I stand up and press my ear to the bedroom door. "That's Zoe."

But that is a long time away. As it stands now, the most famous members of the Calabasas student body are a relative of the Jacksons, a Mexican pop star on exchange, and an Instagram model who, according to unchecked sources, once went on a date with

Justin Bieber. Zoe is still relatively unknown. But that's not to say she doesn't have a résumé. She's a familiar face on commercials, network sitcoms, and children's TV shows.

She's talented. Always has been, even when I first met her at community theater back in sixth grade. Her vocal dexterity is unparalleled. She has a belt made for the stage. She's confident and poised and good with grown-ups. She has a distinct look, too, which is half the battle in Hollywood; her spray of freckles and curly brown hair allow her to respond to casting calls for ages as young as twelve. And she dresses like she's raided the wardrobe of a teen sitcom protagonist's zany best friend. Blue tutus. Cheetah print vests. Bubblegum-pink combat boots. I marvel at her confidence. Looking back, I'll realize she was ahead of her time; come 2020, thrift apps will be peppered with outfits not unlike hers, tagged as #y2k and #kidcore, marked up into the triple digits.

Today, tenth grade, she's toned it down, content in a Paul Frank T-shirt and purple tulle skirt. Butterfly clips and blue mascara. Zoe walked so e-girls could run. She enters our shared history class and plops into the seat next to me. We're in the back row. On the other side of Zoe sits Katerina DiCarlo, the daughter of one of the biggest rap producers in the game. She's one of nine siblings, all hip-hop royalty. She's beautiful, and her Instagram is a steady stream of bikini shots, designer sunglasses, and sports convertibles. In the future, she'll even star in her own episode of MTV's *My Super Sweet 16*—the climax will be, of course, her receiving two birthday cars: a Tesla from her brother, a Bentley from her father. I, uh. I won't be invited to the party. But it's cool. Not many people will be, I think. Very intimate scene. Yeah. Haha.

"I'm grounded this weekend," she says, and tells us about the rager she attended on Friday. A girl had stripped completely naked in the middle of the party and thrown Katerina's phone across the room. "Someone filmed me yelling at her, but that's it," she says.

"I'd have done way worse, honestly," Zoe says, adjusting her scrunchie. I raise an eyebrow. I'd consider Zoe to be one of the great communicators. She might still collect American Girl Dolls, she might be wearing Limited Too knee-high socks, but she somehow never manages to be out of place.

"I know, right?" Katerina says. "I just can't be getting into stuff like that anymore. TMZ always hears about it and then it's on their website like . . . '[XXXXX]'s Daughter Starts Drama in Malibu.' And then my dad looks bad." She sighs, doodles a flower on the corner of her study guide packet. "But I love my dad. I don't wanna be an asshole."

"Ladies, quiet down," Miss Branch says. "It's class time."

Miss Branch is only a little bit older than us. I'd estimate that she's under thirty, though everyone above twenty-one morphs into the same age group: old. She's pretty, with long blond hair and a perfect Malibu tan. She's coach of the Surf Club. It's her first year teaching, which means she hasn't yet lost the light in her eyes. Absent from her curriculum are the tried-and-true rhythms of the high school classroom. Instead, she introduces us to "alternative learning." Independent study. Makerspaces. Word webs. Group projects. Now, we're in the middle of our World War I unit, and for today's lesson, she has us rearrange the desks and divide into teams to reenact trench warfare, complete with crumpled paper instead of bullets. "STAY OUT OF NO MAN'S LAND," she calls as we hurl our supplies past a sea of desk fortresses. "YOU'RE FREEZING COLD. IT'S RAINING. YOU HAVE LICE AND TRENCH FOOT." It only begins to get out of hand when Owen Boyd hurls a clump of index cards straight at Zoe.

"Fuck you, Owen," she yells. "Asshole."

If Monster Energy had a face, it would be Owen. He lives in a permanent scowl. Big gamer energy. Assumed drywall-puncher. He wears mesh basketball shorts and extra-large sweatshirts with the hoodies yanked over his head and the strings tied in a bow. He and Zoe have a turbulent history. They've hated each other since middle school, when Owen spread a rumor about Zoe eating glue.

"You look like a Lalaloopsy, for fuck's sake," he responds. His *fuck* is jarring and pointed, the tell of a rookie curser. The particular cadence of a fifteen-year-old figuring out the ins and outs of the word *fuck* is as pivotal to the high school experience as fruit-flavored alcohol.

She smooths her tutu, tucks a curl behind her ear, and smiles. "Thanks." The doll line is actually one of her biggest style inspirations. She even dressed like one last Halloween.

"Whoa whoa whoa," says Miss Branch. "Stop. Wrap it up. We're done for the day." She flicks the lights back on. "Watch your language, everyone."

As we clean up the classroom, I mourn Miss Branch's spirit—it will surely be broken by high school entropy.

"Those soldiers had to survive in conditions you couldn't even imagine. What's the coldest you've been? On your family's ski trip to Aspen?" She sits on the end of her desk and folds her arms. "Kids not much older than you were dying of frostbite. Fever.

They had to kill or be killed. Can you begin to imagine what that's like?"

"All that and they weren't even getting laid," calls Owen. "A tragedy."

"Not funny," she warns and walks to the whiteboard and in big, bouncy letters, she writes *1918*. "Does anyone know why this year is significant?"

We give her nothing but blank stares.

"It's the year World War I ended. With a death count of forty million. It's an injustice, really." She turns around and writes another word on the board: *RESPECT*. "I'm a pacifist, which means I believe that no violence can ever be justified. Forty million deaths. There has to be a better way." She shakes her head. "And still, I believe in respecting the history and the lost soldiers. Many of them were drafted, or had nowhere else to turn but the military. You can laugh, but what happened in those trenches was a terrible, terrible thing. I want you to think about the word *respect*. Long and hard."

Owen Boyd guffaws.

"Shut up," Zoe calls across the room.

"I can defend myself, thank you," says Miss Branch. "But Owen. Be quiet."

When class ends, the halls are swarmed because pep commissioners are passing out T-shirts in the quad: black crewnecks with THE PACK written on them in thick white type. Anyone can wear the shirts, but only a select few are appointed to the Pack, a squad of male fans whose job it is to hype up the team (read: cheerleaders with masculinity complexes). Calabasas High football games draw crowds from all over the Valley, but it wasn't always this way. My freshman year, the team was so desperate for members that they didn't hold tryouts—anyone could just sign up. At orientation, they even tried to recruit me, which says a lot.

But at the time, the Calabasas Coyotes hadn't made state playoffs in a decade. They'd been on a two-year losing streak. Games were tragic; what audience they did draw seemed more invested in making repeat trips to concessions than cheering at the game. It's far easier to stomach a microwave corn dog than watch a vicious defeat unfolding on the turf.

Over the summer, however, Principal Stack decided it was high time to make some changes. She hired Coach Pete, a former quarterback at a major university, who'd been working at a rival private school in the Valley. He marched on campus with a whistle and a promise: that he alone could whip this team into shape—or, at the very least, provide some general, uh, *fluffing*.

Coach Pete brought with him his star quarterback, Andre Smith, the son of an NFL player. In a matter of days, Andre secured near-instant popularity on campus, driving the nicest whip and hooking up with the hottest girls. He was only the first in a new wave of student transfers. Soon afterward, more and more experienced football players materialized on campus, from Compton, Long Beach, and Torrance.

But however unsportsmanlike Stack's fluffing may be, at a surface level she did accomplish her goal. The Coyotes are underdogs no more. It's almost as if nobody can recall the litter of knobby limbs that used to traipse and hobble the turf like lost poodles. The *LA Times* has given us the nickname "Calabraska" because of the heavy recruiter interest that CHS draws from

the Cornhuskers. Like Andre. He's been granted early accep-
tance on the condition that he starts playing for their team in
October of his senior year. Meaning, he gets to cut corners on
high school.

An ASB—Associated Student Body, our student council—
commissioner tosses a T-shirt to Andre. I elbow myself out of the
crowd, where I'm yanked aside by a frenzied Eli. A film camera
swings around his neck. Photography is a quiet passion of his.
He doesn't talk about it much, but sometimes if he's feeling especially enamored with the light outside, he'll cruise campus with
a camera bag strap slung over his shoulder. "Andre asked to use
my GoPro," he says. "He's never talked to me before in his life but
he heard I have a camera and he wants to use it. Dude. Do I let
him or no?"

"Explain?" I say, my mouth full of a Rice Krispies Treat. Eli's
frazzled. I lean against a vending machine. One of my favorite
things about Eli is how he's so easily excitable. It's a good contrast
to my demeanor. My reactions tend to underwhelm.

"Nebraska wants him to come and visit for two weeks. Just
to see. Get to know the team and stuff. And Andre wants to film
practices, I guess. I didn't really question it."

"You never question anything," I say. "You don't even know
him."

"So?"

"I dunno."

"V," he says seriously, "imagine what it would be like if we
became friends with Andre and his group."

"Okay, so I just imagined it and it's lame," I say.

He props his backpack up on a lunch table and pulls out his GoPro. The lens catches the sun; it glitters like a holy object. "If he gets, like, super famous, it would suck if we never had any interactions in high school. I won't be able to tell everyone he used my fuckin' GoPro. Before he got big. You know what I mean?"

"Yeah, I do." He does have a point. In Calabasas, there's always the sneaking suspicion that some of us will ascend to real celebrity status. We make secret, unspoken bets with ourselves. *Well, Zoe's booked, like, three pilots. The next one will definitely get picked up. And Brandon's dad is a big music producer, and Brandon's met, like, Kendrick Lamar. And Adrianna's done some catwalk modeling in the past, and she's trying to go to New York Fashion Week.* You have to try and live your life according to the bar stories you'll get to tell once you're old and boring.

"I'm gonna do it," he says. "Fuck it. Should I text him?"

"You have his number?"

Eli blinks. "Um, well, not exactly. He messaged me on Facebook." He unlocks his phone. "I'll ask him."

I watch him draft a private message:

ELI

> Hey, dude! :) Can I have your number so I can tell you where to meet me?

"Don't send that," I say.

"Why not?"

I grab his phone, delete his message, and rewrite it.

ELI

hey can i have ur # so i can tell u
where to meet me?

"What'd you do that for?"

"You sounded like Ned Flanders."

He sends, and in a matter of seconds, Andre's responded.

ANDRE

nah fb messenger's fine

"Ouch," I say, and take another bite of my Rice Krispies.

"Don't make that face," he says. "You're doing your Via face."

"I'm always doing my Via face. By default."

We sit on the top of the lunch table while he goes back and forth with Andre. "Okay," he says finally, "he says he wants me to meet him at his table in the lower quad."

"Dun dun dun."

The *upper* quad, where my friends and I stay for lunch, is fairly low-key. Adjacent to the teachers' lounge, it's got a sprawling lawn and enough authoritarian presence to make sure lunchtime is strictly business as usual. The *lower* quad, on the other hand, is as far away from the administration offices as possible. There's an outdoor stage where Lil Shrimp sometimes plays sets during breaks. Take a second flight of stairs and there's a hideaway of lunch tables, with nothing but a rusty fence cordoning off the trail to the senior lot. In other words, it's a fantastic chunk of lunchtime real estate, private from the administration's watchful eyes, complete with the coldest water fountain. And this is where Andre and his friends have lunch.

Eli and I walk shoulder-to-shoulder, taking small, tentative steps. We dodge a set of lip-locked juniors called the Anal Couple (nicknamed for their incessant bragging about having engaged in back-door coitus), and step over a cheerleader and her Jergens Glow shins. Someone nearly whacks Eli in the head with a smoothie cup.

And then we spot Andre's table. A beam of sunlight pierces through eucalyptus leaves, laying a soft glaze over their heads in a heavenly display. A Beats Pill pumps out a Top 40 hit. Football parents take turns bringing hot lunches to the team, and today's menu includes In-N-Out Double-Doubles and fries. Eli steps forward, but Andre's mid-conversation with somebody else. I cringe as I watch Eli try to get his attention. He rotates around Andre twice, like a small planet, clearing his throat, crossing and uncrossing his arms.

"Should I message him?" he says to me, at the end of his third circle. "Or is that weird?"

I shrug. "It's weirder if we just stand here and wait for him to notice us," I say.

"One more try," he says, and circles the table yet again, until he's directly behind Andre.

"Hey," he starts, but Andre doesn't hear. Eli clears his throat and tries again. No avail. He swings around and gives me a helpless look.

"Hey, hey, hey, Andre. Kid's trying to talk to you," the fullback says, and points at us. Conversation pauses. Someone stops the music.

"Eli, what's up," Andre says. It's not a question, it's a statement. He doesn't know my name so he offers a nod in my general direction. And despite his passivity toward me, my face turns bright red. He's very handsome.

Eli rolls his eyes at me. "Nothing much," he says. "You?"

Andre takes a bite of his hamburger. "So. I can use your camera?"

Eli nods. "Yeah, I have it right here," he says, and produces the GoPro.

"Sweet," Andre says, and picks it up. He looks it over. "Okay, so. How does it work?"

Eli leans forward. "Um, so you press this button here, and then you press this to, um, zoom in. And it's out of battery when this light here flashes, so you'll, uh, want to charge it when that happens. Here's the charger. And um, you need a flash drive to back up your footage and stuff, and, like, download it or whatever. Um. So, yeah."

Andre shrugs. "Ok. Got it. Sounds easy."

"So I'll see you in ten days, right?"

"Mm-hmm," Andre says, already turning back around to his friends. Somebody presses play on the Pill. He cracks a joke and the table erupts into giggles. Eli and I have been dismissed.

"Where were you at lunch?" Zoe says, a few days later.

"In the library," I say. "Found the homework answers on Quizlet."

"There was a whole-ass fight," she says. "Two seniors. Clarity Martel and Jenna Phillips. Jenna was on *crutches*. She was, like, swinging them around and stuff."

"Are you serious?"

"Yeah. It was insane. They've been beefing for weeks online, 'cuz a video of Clarity sucking two dicks leaked, and then Jenna was like 'You slut!' or something like that. Then everyone commented that they should just fight already, so they did, but it only went on for, like, a couple minutes before a teacher broke it up. Super dramatic. Sad you missed it."

"If I had seen it on Twitter I would've come," I say.

"It wasn't on Twitter," Zoe says. "It was on this." She slides her phone across my desk.

"What am I looking at?" I ask. All I see is a blank green screen.

"It's loading, calm down." She sits down next to me and I watch as a cartoon yak appears before me. "There, see? It's called Yik Yak."

"Yik Yak," I repeat, scrolling. I catch on quickly. It's Twitter, only anonymous, and the content you receive is solely based on your location. Each *yak* is limited to two hundred characters, and the more upvotes it receives, the higher up your yak will be on the public feed. Right now, the number one yak, with sixty-five likes, is a sociocultural and anatomical critique of biology teacher Mr. Rhodes's technological habits.

mr. rhodes uses a loud ass keyboard from 1994 not just bc he hates us but to cover up his carrot farts

"Get it?" she says. "'Cuz, like, he's always eating those huge carrots dipped in peanut butter."

"I get it." I scroll further. I find a yak with four downvotes.

ms stack is a queen <3

"That's heinous," I say. "She probably wrote that."

"Dislike it," she says. "If it gets five it's automatically deleted."

I oblige, and Principal Stack's fan mail dissolves into the ether.

"We have so much power in our hands," she says. "Look, I'll write one."

Zoe Melton's outfit today >>>

"The whole school's gonna be checking out my outfit now," she says. "Watch." She refreshes the page, only this time, her yak has one dislike.

"Someone's finger probably slipped," I offer.

Katerina takes a seat next to us. "What's happening?" she says.

"This app. Yik Yak. Did you download it?"

She sits back and shakes her head. "I do *not* fuck with that." She points at Zoe's phone. "Twitter's bad enough. Whatever that is? It's cursed."

Katerina's got a Twitter chip on her shoulder. Last year, her father sent the Internet into a frenzy when he tweeted at LAPD, requesting help in tracking down his missing daughter. According to him, she'd been on the run with an eighteen-year-old. "He wasn't even eighteen," Katerina told us. "I was fourteen, he was fourteen. My dad just googled his name and found some older guy with the same name." Ever since, she's hated Twitter. "All these online journalists talk shit about me on their websites. Like. You're really gonna come after a fifteen-year-old? It's fucked up."

I continue scrolling through the app. The vast majority of posts are stolen tweets and harmless jokes aimed at no one in particular. And then I notice Miss Branch's name. Only this yak's not so innocent—in fact, it's so over-the-top vulgar that it could almost be a parody of itself.

Katerina looks over my shoulder. "See, that's what I mean. That's some pervy shit."

"Who would say that about her?" Zoe says.

"Like every guy at this school," Katerina and I say at the same time.

We refresh the app and there's already another yak about Miss Branch. This one involves various classroom accoutrements, namely a desk and a smart board marker. "My eyes," I say. "Jesus."

"Vote it down," Katerina says. I do, but it doesn't make much of a difference. Within thirty seconds it's been liked enough times to give it a spot high up on the feed. Even worse, a new yak has appeared, already six likes deep: another obscenity involving Miss Branch's appearance. We slowly look at her. She's grading at her desk, totally clueless.

"Damn," Zoe says. "Now I feel weird."

"I can't stop thinking about smart board markers," Katerina says.

Owen Boyd comes into class with a Red Bull and a Big Mac. He takes one look at Zoe and says: "Zoe, what the hell are you wearing?"

"Claire's," she says.

"The store for babies?"

"The store for *whimsy*," she corrects. "Where'd you get your outfit? Huf? I Heart Boobies?"

He narrows his eyes. "Nike," he says, and points at his feet. "They're called Elites, dumbass."

Miss Branch calls our attention to the board.

"I hate him," Zoe says. "His downfall will come."

That evening, I'm indulging in my nightly routine of screwing around on my phone for two to six hours before I sleep. I check Instagram first. Some girl who was in my English class last year got a nose job. Someone else's grandpa died. I throw them each a like and I comment a heart emoji for the kid with the dead grandpa. Then it's Snapchat. Someone's shared a story of Lil Shrimp's mixtape release party. I skip through most of what I see. When I get to Eli's story, a video of him doing skate tricks, I watch the whole thing twice in a row.

And last of all, I check Twitter. I scroll past memes and K-pop fancams and a photo set of Jeanette McCurdy's nudes. And then a name catches my eye. It's Andre, tweeting from Nebraska.

Rly lost the gopro ☺

Intrigued, I sit up in bed and click on his profile. He's verified, one of the chosen few at CHS to actually have received the blue check. His timeline is mostly high-def sport stills. His last tweet (prior to the GoPro) was:

just landed #calabraska

I compare the time stamps: six hours. Six hours. He lost it in six hours. I text Eli a screenshot. It's hilarious, a perfect I-told-you-so. And it's the kind of thing that would only ever happen to Eli.

Eli prioritizes being cool before all else. He pledges a silent loyalty to social hierarchy. I notice it in the little things; we'll be talking, and his eyes will drift behind me for a second and I'll know that someone's walking past my shoulder, maybe the best player on the lacrosse team, or someone whose parent used to be on MTV, or a member of the dance team with sixty thousand followers. Sometimes he'll ditch me in favor of upperclassmen. But they don't reciprocate the same loyalties. They forget his birthday, or leave him out of certain group chats. And so I strongly doubt that Eli will even confront Andre about the missing camera.

In the morning, I pour a bowl of Corn Pops and review Twitter again. Only this time, I don't even have to visit Andre's profile to catch whiff of the Calabraska action. Because it's trending. #FindAndresGoPro is actually, verifiably, ridiculously trending on Twitter.

I scroll through. First the official Nebraska U account, then NFL fans and Andre's friends at Calabasas. And of course, the man himself:

Can't believe I'm actually trending for the first time. Can't lie im lowk honored lol

I attend to Yik Yak, where Miss Branch is garnering a competitive level of attention. Every other yak is about her, and they're increasingly obscene. It's only a matter of time before campus intervenes, I'm sure. Principal Stack is a big fan of the assembly. I'd sat through one before, also about Internet usage. One of the campus cops, some guy named Deputy Danforth, had put together a series of PowerPoint slides and barked at us for an hour. Calabasas High has mixed feelings about Danforth. We'd hated him for years, until someone sifted through his tagged photos on Facebook and discovered a series of images, all of him taking shots from a stripper's cleavage. Now, he's earned our respect, both as a party bro and as a supporter of sex work. But even that couldn't protect him from our jeers at his Internet safety assembly.

First, he presented a grainy JPEG of a handgun and warned: "Do not send this image to your peers. It could be misinterpreted as a threat, and I know where you live. It's on school record."

Then, a stock photo of a noose: "It has come to my attention that it is considered trendy on the Web to say 'Kill Myself.' If you text 'KMS,' someone could very well have grounds to call a wellness check on you. Do not send pictures of ropes and do not say KMS."

"This makes me want to kms," Zoe whispered.

And last, a photo of a random child, his eyes closed and his tongue sticking out. "Do not send selfies like these to your friends, ones where you're pretending to be dead. Someone could think it's real. Take the Internet seriously."

"What about pictures of my ass," called Cub, from the back of the auditorium. "What if I wanna send pictures of my big ass?"

Of course, the assembly only inspired us. For weeks, every

student group chat was inundated with stock photos of various weapons. I imagine that any adult intervention in the Yik Yak ordeal will only exacerbate the situation. Grown-ups should know better: the online landscape is a no-man's land.

In the coming week, I start to dread history class. I feel guilty for the things I've read about Miss Branch. She teaches her class with a painful sort of ignorance, her tone enthusiastic. Zoe and Katerina and I wonder if we should tell her, but I'm not sure how that conversation would unfold. Maybe it's cowardly of me to choose silence.

Meanwhile, Eli considers the GoPro situation. "He didn't text me about it, so he probably found it," he says. He's walked me to class, and we stand in the hallway in front of Miss Branch's door. "Maybe he lost it for only, like, two seconds, and then just went along with Twitter for the attention."

"He didn't tell you he'd lost it? You found out on Twitter?"

"Well, yeah, which is why it's probably fine."

"Uh-huh."

"Like I know him, you know?"

"Right," I say dryly, "you guys are, like, best friends forever."

He winces. "You know what I mean," he says.

"The entire state of Nebraska's looking, so it's bound to turn up somewhere."

"Exactly." He doesn't catch my sarcasm, apparently.

The bell rings, and class is about to start. Eli peers into the doorway. "That's your teacher?" he asks.

"Yeah."

"She's, um." He watches Miss Branch calibrate the smart board. "Really pretty."

"Yeah, I know."

"What's her name?"

"Miss Branch."

"Oh, shit. Is she the—"

"Watch it," I say. "Yes."

As class begins, it's clear that there's something off about our teacher. She doesn't make banter with us like she usually does. Wordless, she plays a short YouTube documentary about POW camps and turns her attention toward a stack of study guides.

Zoe gives me a look and passes me her phone under the desk. I scroll through her Yik Yak feed, hoping to find at least a single thread uninterrupted by some salacious comment about her, but it's hopeless. "This is, like, obsessive," I whisper to Zoe.

"I know," Zoe says. "I didn't know we had this many creeps at our school."

"Phones away," Miss Branch says. She's looking straight at Zoe and me. She pauses the documentary. "Actually, I think we need to have a class discussion."

We know what's coming.

"I had some students in another class period show me some things that are being said about me on this app. Yik Yak. Hurtful, disgusting things about me. Every day I'm so excited for the opportunity to be in the classroom. I expect for you to give me the same respect I give you."

She picks up her phone. "These are horrible, horrible things to say. About any woman. I am hurt. And I'm disappointed in all of you. Not just the ones that typed out these things and advertised them publicly, but those who liked them and allowed the posts to do well."

Katerina leans in to Zoe and me. "Told you this app was *fucked up*."

"In this class, I try to keep politics out of the classroom. I provide information and I allow you to make your own judgments. But there are some basic values I hope to teach you. Like peace, tolerance, respect, and accountability. I would hope that whoever said such things would feel ashamed and guilty. I would appreciate an apology. I don't expect it—I know how teenagers are, and I assume that the kind of person to write these things would be too cowardly to speak up. But I hope for it just the same.

"I guess that's all I have to say about it. I feel a little uncomfortable lecturing today," she adds, "so we're just going to finish this documentary, and I'll collect notes at the end." She takes a seat at her desk.

And then: a voice, so small and meek it might've belonged to a mouse. "Miss Branch?"

It comes from the corner of the room. We turn around to face the source: Owen Boyd, his hand raised and trembling slightly.

"Yes, Owen?"

He straightens and pulls the hood from his head. He has an odd, crumpled look. "Miss Branch, there's something I have to say."

He closes his eyes. We hold our breaths.

"It was me who said all those things about banging you on the desks and stuff," he says, in one uninterrupted stream. "I'm sorry. I'm so, so sorry."

Katerina gasps. Zoe stifles a laugh.

"It was all you?" The look of horror on Miss Branch's face is unmistakable.

"Yeah, pretty much. I said the stuff about the markers and the desks." He gulps. "Also the stapler. I said that, too."

I cup my hand over my mouth.

"I just wanted to come clean," he says, and his voice cracks. "Can I please be excused?"

Miss Branch doesn't reply because she's still processing this information. We all are.

"I'm just gonna go, if that's okay," he says, and flees the room—a flash of purple basketball shorts out the door in a zip. In near perfect synchronicity, we turn to face Miss Branch.

"Well," she says, and adjusts her ponytail, "I guess that answers that."

Like all fad apps, Yik Yak dies out as quickly as it came. In a few weeks it's as if it never even existed. Neither Owen nor Miss Branch ever mention the incident again.

Andre returns from Nebraska, his mind made up. He's signing to the Cornhuskers. Eli greets him on campus, offers his congratulations.

"Thanks," Andre says. And that's it. Nothing else.

Eli procrastinates. After school, he sits with Zoe and me on the floor of the hall outside Miss Branch's room. "I don't know what to say," he says. "Or how to text."

Zoe presses her fingers to her forehead. "Eli," she says. "I will go up to him and yell at him if you want. I will do it."

I believe her, too. Ever since watching Owen's moment of humiliation, she's found a new sort of empowerment. It seems she's taken special pleasure in Owen's downfall, taunting him to his face. "And you called me a *glue eater*," she'll whisper. Nothing scares her.

She stands up and places her hands on her hips. "You're being ridiculous. Let me message him for you."

"No, no, I'm good," he says. "I just don't want to sound like a dick."

"He lost *your* camera," I say.

"Okay, fine," he says. "I'll do it, okay?"

ELI

> hey andre, can i get my camera back

I glance at the text. "Lowercase," I say. "You've learned."

The $18 Million Sandbox

Do not look the dog in the eyes.

I lean back in my chair. I'm in the black box theater at Calabasas High School, fifteen minutes into rehearsal for the spring musical. Our director, Mr. Purcell, is taking an important phone call outside, so the cast stands aimlessly around the room, reviewing lines and blocking directions and passing JUULs through closed fists. I remain seated in the bleachers. I'm entranced by the creature before me.

From my periphery, I track the animal's movements. What exactly are the specifics of this no-eye-contact agreement? If the dog initiates a glance, am I allowed to reciprocate? Or do I shield my eyes? What about sunglasses? If I'm wearing reflective lenses, then am I permitted to look? Or will the dog . . . somehow . . . *know*?

The dog's handler, a thin blond woman in designer wedge heels, scrolls through her Instagram feed. She's definitely got, like, ten thousand followers on Instagram. I can just tell. "Social Media Influencer" radiates off of her like electricity.

I can't handle the suspense anymore. I sneak a glance at the dog.

His little head is turned in the other direction, thank God, so I take time to give him a complete once-over. He's wearing a miniature pink vest with the word DIVA inscribed on it in gold sequins. He's shaking, as Chihuahuas tend to do, his Bedazzled leash vibrating around his throat. A pair of silver whiskers protrude from above his mouth and patches of his fur are totally gray. He's ancient. This is a dog who has seen a lot of theater.

I notice that it's begun to smell like cheeseburgers. The dog notices too, his tiny rat nose searching the air. I hurriedly look down at my shoes.

"I've been thinking," a voice from above says. I look up. It's Cory Tucker, his hand clutching the top of a paper In-N-Out bag. Cory's playing Elle's dad, and he's new to theater. His endeavor into the program is a casual one, a choice doubtlessly made post-A24 bender. (I have a theory that no one just "joins" theater halfway through senior year without the aid of a Certified Fresh coming-of-age movie.) Cory comes from the film program on campus. He smokes cigarettes and quotes the @dril candle budget tweet. He plops down into the chair beside mine. "Fry?"

"Thanks."

"So anyway," he says, "Have you ever thought about how this dog-rat-thing—"

"Has had a better career in theater than anyone in this room will ever have? Yes."

He smiles and takes a sip of his Sprite. "*Shhh.* Don't want

Madison to hear that." He tilts his head in her direction, where Madison Whitney sits alone across the room. She studies the script, her fingers tracing the words before her. Her focus is practically tangible. Maybe it's because she's realized that she has to work twice as hard now that there's a canine vying for her spotlight.

The dog in question isn't your average run-of-the-mill house pet. He's a star. His name is Frankie, and he is God in the theater dog industry. He's got extensive credits, having logged more performances of *Legally Blonde* than any other cast member in the history of the musical. Though he's never graced the Broadway stage, he toured nationally, barking and sniffing his own ass in professional productions all across America. And Calabasas High School has hired him to play Elle Woods's beloved pup Bruiser in our upcoming production of *Legally Blonde*.

Welcome to the Calabasas High School theater program. It is definitely unlike anything you've ever seen. Its home base is the brand-new, $18 million, 33,000 square foot Performing Arts and Education Center. Imagine the greatest high school performance space you can. Now stop. Whatever you're picturing, you're dead wrong. It is so much bigger. So much better.

The main stage seats nearly seven hundred. The theater is built with hardwood acoustic walls, red velvet seats, and a state-of-the-art sound system. There's a fly gallery where props (as well as people) can be flown down on wires from above. An orchestra pit on a hydraulic lift. Two stories. Exit the theater, and you'll find the lobby, its walls decorated with giant canvas stills from previous productions. There's a plaque with the names of the biggest donors—more than half are ANONYMOUS. Snack bar. Ticket office. Take the door that reads CAST ONLY and you'll find an entire woodshop where sets are built and designed by industry professionals, three sprawling dressing rooms, instrument storage, and a costume room with a conveyor belt and hundreds, if not thousands, of expensive, handmade garments flown in from all over the world. There's a green room and offices and bathrooms with polished granite countertops. And there's a black box experimental space that seats one hundred. It's used for rehearsals, and it's where I'm sitting now.

For this production, the director and head of the theater department, Mr. Purcell, has decided to take an especially extravagant route. The theater has been fitted with a rotating platform—basically, the stage spins. We take a week just learning how to move on and off of it without smashing our faces. A Broadway stage designer is brought in to transform the opening scene into a UCLA sorority pool party, complete with a columned sorority house facade, poolside bar, and rear screen projection.

And, of course, there's Frankie the dog, Frankie the scene-stealer, Frankie the diva who's been flown out first-class from the East Coast, Frankie the star who's being put up at the nicest hotel in Calabasas, Frankie the furry Mariah who we've all been instructed *not to look in the eyes.*

Our lead, Elle Woods, is played by Madison Whitney. She was born for this role. Her hair's been bleached and dyed a thousand times into the same butter-yellow shade Reese Witherspoon tosses over her shoulder in the movie. She's eaten like a Victoria's Secret model every day for a year to make sure she can properly wear a hot pink Juicy Couture velour tracksuit onstage. She's trained her voice to hit the G5 that Laura Bell Bundy belts in the Broadway official musical soundtrack. This show is for her, and we all know it.

Madison eats, sleeps, and breathes theater. She's a scrapped *Glee* character. And her mother is *the* stage mom. Within months, Mrs. Whitney climbed to the top of the Theater Parent Coalition, convinced Mr. Purcell to choose *Legally Blonde,* and brought in a famous dog, all while helping Madison to become the star she was born to be.

But. The amateurs in this theater program just don't understand. Madison *has* to be focused. She has people to please. Her mother, for example. She wants her mother to be proud. So she drinks her singer's tea, drills her dance steps, lives her life in a revolving door of local theater auditions. There's no time for silliness. She doesn't get the appeal of alcohol or weed or video games or TV shows or any of the stuff that everyone else her age wastes so much time on.

On the day of *Legally Blonde* auditions, we asked her if she was nervous. "No, of course not," she'd said, and placed her cup of Throat Coat down so that nobody would see it shaking in her hand. When she'd finished her sixteen-bar audition song, we'd asked if she felt good about her audition. "Yeah, it was great," she'd said. But then she'd disappeared. The day that the cast list was uploaded, we didn't see her around campus, nor did we hear from her at all, until we saw her name: MADISON WHITNEY, bolded and underlined just below the words: ELLE WOODS, noted in a pretty serif font.

We sent her congratulatory texts, added her to group chats, sent her pictures of Reese Witherspoon. She didn't respond—not immediately. I doubt she was surprised by the casting. She's been collecting professional credits ever since she was a little girl. Being "normal" was never an option. Boys love to make fun of her, circulating YouTube videos of her performances, memorizing lines from her one-woman show to chant at her during passing periods. Perhaps she makes for an easy target because she seems unfazed by it all. No matter what anyone says, she always laughs back.

The day of the cast announcement, Kate Gardener claimed to have spotted Madison parked outside the nearby McDonald's, eating fries in her car. "She looked kind of lonely," she said. "But I don't know."

"Well, that's stupid," Mark Lumes said. "Not like she's the star of the spring musical or anything. Literally everyone was congratulating her."

Back in the black box theater, the scent of Cory's french fries is overwhelming. Madison glances up from her script and is overcome with annoyance. Boys. They can just *eat that stuff.* She shakes her head and runs through her big monologue again.

"Did she hear me?" Cory says, suddenly concerned, half a fry in his mouth.

"No," I say. "She smells you."

"Hey, Maddy," Cory calls. "Do you want some fries? I can't eat them all."

Madison tears her attention from her script once more. She hesitates, then stands up and meets us at the chairs. "No thanks," she says. "Smells good though." She stretches her neck and sits down on the other side of me. "I need a break."

"You're doing really great," I say. Which is true. I'm playing one of Elle's best friends and sorority sisters. I perform in a lot of scenes with her, and I'm well aware that I pale in comparison. She's talented and energetic and I've never seen someone with so much drive in my life.

"Thank you," she says. "I'm trying really hard."

"Doesn't look like it," Cory says, his mouth full of burger. "I mean it looks effortless. Not like, bad. You know what I mean." He closes his eyes. "Fuck."

"No, I get what you mean." She shrugs, smiles. "Thanks."

"Come on, Maddy, you have your fitting right now," an insistent voice calls. It's Mrs. Whitney. She's a staple here at the Calabasas theater program, around nearly every day and night, usually lurking just behind Mr. Purcell. Madison would never speak ill of her mother, not in a million years, but we've all seen the way she sometimes flinches when her mother calls her name.

"See you guys later," Maddy says, and trails her mother to the costume room, where the designers are awaiting her entry with a hot-pink corset.

"Bathroom," I say to Cory, and he nods. As I navigate the hallway, I pass Maddy's dressing room, where her mother is helping to tie her into the Playboy bunny outfit that Elle Woods wears to the Harvard party in the play's first act.

I watch Mrs. Whitney clasp the costume at the top. The crew has spent hours on this playsuit, each stitch an exact replica of Madison's measurements. The effort shows; the silky pink material catches the light just so. Madison steps back and admires her reflection with a faint smile.

Mrs. Whitney places her hands on her daughter's shoulders, meeting her eyes in the mirror. Maddy is quiet.

Next year, once she's graduated, her mother will drive her to the plastic surgeon for a nose job.

But Madison—and I, and Cory, and everyone else—is simply signed on to a four-year contract. An elaborate gimmick. This theater program is a multimillion-dollar simulation of what it feels like to be a real Broadway star. You pay the donation (suggested minimum of $300, but sponsorships can range anywhere from $2,000 to $15,000), your parents volunteer, you compliment Mr. Purcell's genius—and in return you're given the make-believe session of a lifetime. You get the chance to listen to your own voice rise above a full orchestra pit. You wear beautiful costumes that have been hand-tailored to your exact size, contoured to transform your teenage body into that of a magazine model. You're given standing ovations by gigantic, shadowy audiences. You're given cheers and blinding show lights and props that move and fly across the stage like they're living things. Friends of Mr. Purcell who work at the local papers come and write glowing reviews. News stations that only broadcast to the local gym's treadmill TVs interview you, hanging on your every last word. And it's intoxicating. You get caught up in this little fantasy so much that it consumes every thought that goes through your brain. It's an addiction, the high that comes with performing onstage, the trip that comes with your accolades. You're at the top. You're Elle Woods. Or you're Elle's dad. Or you're Elle's sorority sister. Doesn't matter. You're *it*. And then . . .

You graduate. And you're met with the realization that this whole time you weren't really at the *Fame* school—you were at the *Fortune* school. And everything you were thinking, and everything that you were feeling, was manipulated. The Performing Arts and Education Center wasn't a theater at all—it was an $18 million sandbox. In real life, when you audition, you might not get cast. Maybe you won't even get called back. You can get that rhinoplasty, you can dye your roots, you can sweet-talk directors and laugh at their audition-room jokes. And maybe it'll work. Maybe you'll be a star, and the whole world will recognize your name and your face and the sound of your voice.

But maybe not.

Maybe it's Mr. Purcell's responsibility to tell us that we're living in a bubble. Maybe he should gather everyone into a room and let us know that we're being hoodwinked, that we're lucky for this opportunity but for the love of everything that is good and holy don't let ourselves fall for it. But he doesn't. And I don't really blame him.

Mr. Purcell is a Calabasas High School alum himself. He's an award-winning teacher in the district. A true CHS loyalist. He too once navigated the Calabasas High theater program as a student, back when the plays were held in the (now defunct) school auditorium. Clean-cut, mild-mannered, and tailored, Mr. Purcell is the kind of milquetoast authority figure that the Southern California stage mom can only dream of. When he announces the play at the beginning of the year, dozens of parents bring him gifts and pay him compliments and hand him checks with amounts so high that what can you do *besides* go out and hire a Broadway dog? He's an incredible director. The best, maybe. Well, that's what everyone says, anyway. And he's so swept up in the narrative that this theater program is self-made that he begins a fundraising campaign on GoFundMe and sets the goal at $100,000. Mrs. Whitney comes into rehearsals with her DSLR camera and takes students one by one into the dressing room where she feeds them lines: *Talk about how theater has changed your life. Tell them how it feels to perform. Talk about how it helped you deal with bullying and public speaking. Talk about how theater has saved you, about how it's the best thing that's ever happened to you.* And then she edits the interviews together and posts them on Facebook. Look, we need your money! Do it for the children. Little Jenny Sue will absolutely just *cry herself to death* if we don't get a levitating operating table complete with electric balls transferring bolts of lightning for this year's *Young Frankenstein.* (All donations are tax-deductible.) And even when the proposed dollar amount isn't quite met, a mysterious benefactor might sweep in at the last moment, an anonymous four-digit donation. If this happens, rehearsals become less about play production and more about sussing out who brought in the big bucks.

Some kids know it's all fake. Cory, for example, who saunters into rehearsal fifteen minutes late with a bag of burgers slung over his shoulder. He only memorizes his lines in his free time, when he's not occupied with something else. During dance rehearsal, when someone cracks a joke about Frankie the dog's salary, and the choreographer overhears and walks out because she's just found out that a dog is getting paid more than her, Cory laughs, bent over, clutching his stomach. "Don't laugh," Madison snaps, "it's not funny." When the leading man's girlfriend breaks down in dramatic sobs because she has to watch Madison kiss her boy-friend onstage, Cory doesn't rush to comfort her and fuss in her ear like the rest of the cast. Instead, he rolls his eyes and props his legs up on the seat in front of him until Mr. Purcell comes by and tells him that he's disrespecting the theater and *please put your feet down.* When Cub Birnwick gets the role of the UPS hunk and his rival, Brad Stanton, throws a fit because he's just lost the token hot-guy role, Cory sits back and doesn't take a side like everyone else in the theater program. Mrs. Whitney doesn't even bother to ask Cory for a filmed testimonial. Part of me wishes that I had the same level of nonchalance, that I'd taken the same route and waited until the last minute to waltz in to the program. But, no. I assimilate. I beg my parents to donate. "Oliva. Are you on drugs?" my mother says back. So I grovel in other ways: wearing CHS theater merchandise, publicizing heavily on my social me-dia, choosing extracurricular commitments over academics over and over again until my grades sink. Skewed priorities, sure—but I go to Calabasas High School, where pretending to be famous is practically in the curriculum. I'm fallible, I'm gullible, and most importantly, I'm sixteen.

I return from the bathroom and reclaim my seat next to Cory. Madison sashays back into the black box, this time in the Playboy outfit. Her mother totters behind her, adjusting her hair and fluff-ing her bunny tail. Cory and I watch her pick up Frankie and pose for her mother's pictures. Her eyes are glued to the DSLR lens.

"You look really beautiful," I tell Madison. She opens her mouth to respond, but before she can speak, her mother inter-rupts:

"Well, it's fine."

They leave the black box to run one of Madison's solos with a vocal coach. And then it's back to me and Cory and Frankie and the dog handler, who's now on the phone with someone, rattling about the show dog business, or maybe Instagram paid advertising.

The dog sits down and scratches its ear.

"Hey, Frankie," I whisper.

The dog pauses and his head jerks around to face me. His damp little nose twitches. I make sure no one's watching, except Cory, who's chugging down his Sprite. Then I lean forward.

I look this dog straight in the eyes.

The One Direction Essay

It was 2010, and the Doomsday Clock had granted us five roomy minutes until mass destruction. The world was still coming down from the cultural high that was "David After Dentist," *Piranha 3D* shocked and awed us all, and an eighteen-year-old Miley Cyrus, God love her, had just taken a massive hit of salvia in the presence of a surreptitious cameraman. Our Bieber had a bowl cut, and all our It girls wore UGGS. Placated by a recovering job market and the deceptive calm of an early Obama presidency, suburban America was relatively comfortable, but the arrival of the sleek, trendy iPhone aligned the Internet with social prosperity, introducing both a new mainstream and a strange undercurrent of teenage restlessness. Every ten years or so, news media slips into crisis mode and asks: what could be responsible for tempting America's honor students away from soccer practice and toward hormonal deviancy? Who will be elected scapegoat? But it wasn't 1969 anymore. Blameless was the sex cult, innocent were the Satanists. The culprit was a bit more abstract—and it was coming from inside the house. Call it an online era, one equal parts degenerate and wonderful. But we'd been coaxed into cultural stagnation by "Peanut Butter Jelly Time" and auto-tuned newscasts. We needed a catalyst, and it had to slip past a mother's radar. It had to be lowbrow, yet soft-core. Charming. Adorable, even. In other words, it was high time for a boy band.

It was primal. We required step-touch choreography like we required air, or another installation in the Taken movie franchise. Cable TV made an honest attempt at satiating us, delivering wholesome sweethearts who sang infectious, squeaky-clean pop songs about unnamed girls with indistinct features and quotidian personalities. The Jonas Brothers gave us purity rings and familial camaraderie. Big Time Rush provided twenty-two minutes of boyish antics and perhaps the most unexpected Snoop Dogg collaboration of the late aughts. But One Direction picked us up from Limited Too in the family car, slipped us copies of *The Care and Keeping of You*, and delivered us unto a definitively Internet teenhood.

You know the story. In suspenders and skinny jeans, five UK boys burst onto the scene under the guidance of *X-Factor* judge Simon Cowell. Harry, Niall, Louis, Liam, and Zayn charmed the world with their breakout single, "What Makes You Beautiful," a song whose topic sentence had something to do with low self-esteem being kind of hot. Whether they were singing to me, or to you, or my cousin, or your lab partner, it didn't matter; we were all now fashionably insecure. Quirky little sixth grade me, in her side ponytail and MUSTACHES R COOL T-shirt, was ugly and proud.

With One Direction came a new kind of fanbase. Directioners didn't faint, and they sure as hell didn't *pine*. They had goals. Aims. Agendas. Hacking airport security cameras? They did that. Desecrating Bibles? Yup. Creating gay relationship rumors so widely believed that One Direction's management had to intervene? Absolutely. (I hate to report that not even Hilary Duff's "That's So Gay" campaign could eradicate casual homophobia). One Direction grew to such a massive scale that the band's stardom wasn't even exclusive to the boys themselves. Directioners slung fifteen minutes of fame around like it was a game of hot potato, concocting a quasi-celebrity prototype that lived on the Internet first and planet Earth second. The key was to be palatably salacious. Such as seventeen-year-old Boopsie, known for her knack at tracking members of One Direction faster than the paparazzi. Or Anna Todd, whose BDSM fanfiction about a Christian Grey–type Harry Styles landed her a movie deal with Netflix. Or Acacia Brinley, the primordial Tumblr Girl, loathed by the fan community for her perfunctory dedication to 1D and overdocumentation of a clumsy adolescence. All scandalous in their own way, of course, but they were kept safe from any real criticism by a sacred reputation: the All-American Crazy White Bitch.

Directioners made a home of Twitter, sharing content like short-form fanfics, or Imagines, on "sass accounts"—a network of celeb enthusiasts that predates today's "stan Twitter." But the app had its limits. One hundred and forty characters, for example. And besides usernames and profile pictures, there wasn't nearly enough personalization—after all, this was a generation raised on Floam and glitter glue. So they relocated to Tumblr, which in 2012 operated as the Internet's subculture index. Directioners across the world befriended one another, as did furries and scene kids and shoplifters (oh, my). Stranger danger was a laughing matter, shipped to the old wives' archives along with masturbation causing hairy palms and LSD storing in the spinal column. Thirteen-year-olds navigated blogs dedicated to thinspo, serial killer worship, gore, and porn without blinking twice, and then they went downstairs for family dinner. They say generations fluctuate—that if one age group is particularly conservative, the next will counter it. It's hard to imagine conservatism in Gen Z's future, but I do think we're far too Internet-savvy to let our kids live online double lives in the same way we did. (That is, if a copious intake of yellow Gatorade hasn't rendered our generation's male population completely infertile.)

At the time, I was still in Catholic school. It's safe to say I occupied the brightly lit corners of the Internet. iFunny may as well have been the dark web. I liked One Direction, but I only consumed the parts of the band that had been preapproved by test groups and research departments. Still, I wasn't totally clueless. I'd stumbled across my fair share of online degeneracy, and I did know there were darker parts to the fandom. Kids in my grade occupied lunch hours by summarizing fanfictions they'd read the night before. "It was rated lemon," Kelly Parker said.

"What's lemon?"

"It means it's super graphic," she informed me. "Like with blow jobs and stuff."

"Oh, yeah. Blow jobs," I said, and nodded, even though I was confused as shit trying to figure out what body part was supposed to get blown on. "Who writes them?"

She shrugged. "I dunno. Fans? They're like, our age, pretty sure. This girl in eighth grade at Our Lady of Grace had one of her fics go viral." Apparently, you didn't need sexual experience in order to write smut. "You read other fics or watch porn so you know what you're talking about," Kelly told me. "Like I'm not *doing it,* you know, so if I wanted to write a lemon fic I'd probably just research on Tumblr or something. You can find out how stuff works on there."

One Direction wasn't just a middle school fixture. The group has followed me ever since. At Calabasas High, I undergo the expected phases with the usual suspects: Mac DeMarco, Lorde, Brockhampton. But thanks to Gen Z's sentimental nature, One Direction maintains a stronghold with the fifteen-and-up crowd. Or maybe it's thanks to the universal obsession with the suburban-nobody-turned-superstar trope. Either way, One Direction is a constant presence. Pep commissioners blast the early hits at rallies for old time's sake, and deeper cuts sneak their way onto party playlists by way of covert Directioners disguised in Arctic Monkeys merchandise. Because as every kickback host knows, the easiest way to social congruence is a trip down memory lane. With One Direction on the conversation card, carrots, spoons, and staircases suddenly possess meanings outside the domestic sphere, all coded in trendy nonchalance. Memes lie on a plane of post-irony. Ask any nicotine addict under twenty-five and they'll probably admit that they started JUULing as a joke. It's cool to like things that are unpopular, but it's even cooler to like things that are massively loved, but, like, in a caustic way. Then you're twenty-one and you're timing your morning dome to coincide with the guitar solo in Harry Styles' "She" and it's like, Oh fuck, maybe irony is a myth.

Ask a Directioner: *Where were you when you heard?* and they'll supply a detailed account of their whereabouts on March 25, 2015—the day Zayn Malik announced he'd be leaving the band. I was in the girls' locker room. I remember it in vivid, sensory detail. The smell of the place (sweat, piss, Victoria's Secret signature scent, Bombshell), the weather outside (suspiciously warm), the clothes I was wearing (flea market Docs, of course, I'd seen *Empire Records* at an impressionable age). I watched kids skip class to cry in their cars. Zayn's departure from One Direction might've been Gen Z's first collective memory of a major tragedy. We took it personally.

My junior year, One Direction announces their final record. Consolation prize. The band claims they're only going on a short hiatus, but the track list begs to differ. It's an obvious swan song. When I listen to it for the first time, I'm surprised by how different they sound. Their early work may've been a bit new wave for postpubescent tastes. But *Made in the A.M.* has a clear, crisp sound and a new sheen of late-adolescent nostalgia that really gives the songs a big boost.

It's the topic of discussion on a Sunday afternoon at the Peninsula Beverly Hills. Eleven-thirty a.m., a balmy seventy-five degrees. Rodeo Drive is humming. It's Rachel Lerner's sixteenth birthday, and her parents have booked a room at the five-star hotel for the affair. Her mother's in real estate and her father produces game shows. The room is organized by a seating chart. It's a physical ranking of Rachel's friends. I'm somewhere in the middle, slightly closer to Rachel. There are twenty-five of us present, even though there were technically only eighteen RSVPs on the Evite. In Los Angeles, no one ever RSVPs for anything. You're supposed to mark MAYBE no matter what. Flakiness is sexy. You want everyone to think you always have something better to do.

Noon sunlight streams through large glass windowpanes, filtered through Italian cypresses. The door to the lobby is propped open, so I watch as hotel customers check into their penthouse suites. Their veneers flash like Cheshire Cat half-moons, their T-zones Glossier-clear. They glide through the Peninsula like Nancy Kerrigan at the Sportovní, flirting fingertips up against the china vases, the pink upholstered wingback chairs. Offer a wink at the harpist. She's doing *great*. I'm only shaken from my meditation when an older man in a tuxedo hunches to my height with a platter of caviar spread on top of little gray crackers. I take one.

So. Anyway. We're eating caviar and talking about One Direction. As you do. Kendra Shin's favorite song on the new album is "What a Feeling." Corrine Emrich likes "End of the Day." Someone asks me to pass the Devonshire cream while Bryanna Hill argues on behalf of "Temporary Fix." Then the table looks at me. It's my turn to share. But this format feels like a classroom icebreaker, and a fancy little scone has dried the inside of my mouth. I take a sip of my tea.

"It's hard to choose a favorite," I say, "among so many great tracks." The glittery hum of the harp right outside has rendered my mind useless.

"Boo," Rachel says. "Just one."

I've entered panic mode. I can't remember a single song title off the album. Rationally, I'm well aware that this is a low-stakes situation. But there's something called an Elderflower Cordial Bonbon on the dish in front of me, and the hired photographer's camera is hoisted in my direction. "Stockholm Syndrome," I say, and it's completely wrong, because everyone knows that "Stockholm Syndrome" was a standout track off of *Four,* and honestly, this is one of the most egregious mix-ups a so-called fan could possibly make, even one admittedly past her Directioner prime. I dive back into my tea.

"Wrong," Bryanna says flatly. She's only kidding, of course. But the damage has been done, and I'm positive that this minor fuckup will play on loop in my head before I fall asleep for the next couple of weeks.

"I would pick 'Olivia' if I were you," says Rachel.

"I bet Harry was always your favorite," says Bryanna, and rolls her eyes.

This is a diss, but she's not wrong. Back in the sixth grade, your boy of choice said a lot about where you stood in the fandom. It was easy, albeit mainstream, to prefer Harry, with his dimples and cheeky Worcestershire accent. If you really wanted to prove your merit as a fan, you'd claim Liam or Louis as your own. As I've gotten older, I've grown impressed by Harry's staying power. He's a modern anomaly. In the advent of social media, teen idolatry has become democratized; instead of one Elvis Presley or Leonardo DiCaprio, there's hundreds of Insta-famous heartthrobs with their own miniature (yet equally dedicated) fan bases. But they don't last nearly as long. They're unvetted by record labels and management companies, so they're easy to cancel. They don't have first-rate publicists at their disposal, so their career moves are careless and unmonitored. The zeitgeist churns them out by the dozen, then exiles them to the graveyard of internet irrelevancy: Here Lies Magcon, or The Musical.ly Stars of Yore, or Twitter Experiment 39201. Yet Harry Styles somehow rises above the others, evoking from us a mass craze comparable to that of the Beatles. It's impossible not to dote on him and his rock-star charisma. He hasn't even gone solo yet. In the coming years, he will only skyrocket. For now, when we speak about him, it's purely in the context of One Direction. And still, he doesn't need an introduction. Call him by his first name only, because we'll know who you're talking about. He conquers the lunch table, the sleepover, the sixteenth birthday tea party.

The room has moved past my party foul; they're talking about something else now. I lean back in my seat and I take another sip of the tea in front of me. It's English Breakfast. The harpist outside the door launches into a new song. It's nice, but I wish it was "Stockholm Syndrome."

Several months after One Direction's *Made in the A.M.* release, my father takes me to the Thai restaurant down the street. I'm skipping class again. My grades are dropping.

"You're applying to colleges in fall," my dad says. "What's the backup plan?"

I don't know what the backup plan is. I'm busy eating pad see ew. I hear the same You're Not A Kid Anymore speeches so often, from so many different people, that all the lectures blur together. Of course, they never work. You can't just talk someone into growing up. But I take special note of this instance, because of the Thai place's choice in dining room music: the entirety of *Made in the A.M.,* subdued through second-rate speakers to match the ambiance of a late-night noodle run.

"Meth," I say flatly.

"You're failing chemistry," my father says. "Good luck with that."

I unwrap my straw and fiddle with the wrapper. "The future doesn't exist," I say. "There is only today."

"Do you want to be someone's receptionist? Is that what you want with your life?" He taps on the table like he's typing at a keyboard. *"What time is your appointment, sir?"*

"First of all," I say, "it's not nice to make fun of someone's job like that."

"Nice isn't important. Truth is."

"Okay, then," I say. "Truth. School sucks. I'd rather model chips, like you did." A guitar solo from power anthem "End of the Day" plays. "It's not even my fault. My teachers hate me."

"Why's that?"

"How would I know?"

"They probably hate you because you don't study," he says.

I feel a surge of defensiveness. "Um, no, actually," I correct. "It's because I talk in class."

He looks at me with incredulity right as Harry modulates to a rock scream on "Temporary Fix," securing a forever link between parental disappointment and stadium pop.

It feels almost karmic for One Direction, the first huge Internet boy band, to provide the backdrop for a Grow Up lecture. Each generation thinks that they've been cursed to grow up in a place that's uniquely unfit for them. But the truth is, young people will always feel a sense of personal injustice, because they're entering a world that's been designed for the generation prior. Thinking you're special and different is the entire point of being young. I know this. So it's with a degree of self-awareness that I introduce the bizarre conditions of Gen Z's coming-of-age. The online world and the IRL world introduced us to conflicting rules at a tender age, so our freedoms seemed kind of arbitrary; what was the point of a permission slip anyway, when part of the induction to the tween years is a Google Images search for "blue waffle"? We could see whatever we wanted, whenever we wanted, and we could do it all under our parents' noses. We didn't need to sneak out of the house. We had incognito mode. And because the honor system is the Internet's Constitution, we developed an intergenerational fellowship, one whose translation to the IRL resulted in a natural distrust of adults everywhere. A grown-up can only be one of two things: mal-intentioned, or so clueless it's cute. Your son isn't allowed to watch Adult Swim? Okay, but last weekend he and three other sixth graders saw *2 Girls 1 Cup* and washed it down with an ample serving of middle-aged Omegle dicks. They minimized the tab when you came in with chicken nuggets.

The Internet is seductive. It offers immortality. You don't have to worry about the future when you're online. There are no plans. And for hard-core Directioners, whose small-town idols were plucked from irrelevance and ushered onto the scene in a matter of months, reality offers some harsh truths of mediocrity: that we probably won't hold hands with Harry Styles, and what's more, we'll probably live our normal lives in normal places doing normal things with other normal people. It's easier to look away.

The album ends and my father and I leave the Thai restaurant. I've made the customary promises: I'll use my phone less, I won't miss class, I'll take practice ACTs. I can tell that my father isn't convinced. Which is fair, because I'm probably lying anyway.

And we go home. I hang upside down on my bed and declutter my camera roll, the task I've deemed most likely to domino-effect my life into homeostasis. I comb through stale screenshots until I reach a photo dump from Rachel's tea party. We look unenthused. Most of the pictures are faux candids, which are always easy to spot if you learn the idiosyncrasies: a distracted gaze, but a vigilant, angled jawline. In the photos, I'm doing it too, though I don't remember it being on purpose. It must've happened like a reflex. I want to fit in.

If you go to The Little Cafe on Ventura, ask for the Maya Rudolph veggie sandwich. If you go to Mon Sushi, ask for the Fabio Roll. In the Valley, we take "you are what you eat" to the extreme. It's a study in manifestation, like if we eat a turkey wrap named after someone we've seen on TV, we'll absorb their energy into our bloodstreams.

And if we can't order a celebrity, we'll make an effort to brush elbows. We'll go where they go: Banzai for Kanye West, King's Fish House for Howie Mandel. Celebrity saturation christens the LA small business, places little red dots on our maps. We're indexed by the passing starlet. Their tracks are invisible yet traceable, like strokes of synesthesia only visible to the London Entertainment Group and teenagers with Google Alerts. Even our roadsides work the fame hustle. In 2014, a stretch of the 101 Freeway in Calabasas was consecrated by Directioners when Harry Styles pulled off of the shoulder to upchuck a wild evening's worth of ethanolic gut stew. "Harry Styles Threw Up Here," the poster read. So flee youthful passions and pursue righteousness.

But those serious about seeing Harry Styles IRL know that the chances of spotting him at such a random location is nil. Because if we are to calculate a person's favorite place in terms of paparazzi sightings alone, then Harry Styles' favorite Los Angeles spot has got to be Café Habana, a Cuban/Mexican restaurant in Malibu owned by Cindy Crawford's second husband. It's known for the elote. For what it is, Café Habana is expensive, but I suppose it isn't the food that the clientele is paying for. Real Harry Styles fanatics will request his favorite table—the one underneath the succulent wall.

But when I go, the table in question's been claimed by a party of proactive Malibu locals. My group settles for a spot in the corner. We order taco salads and make routine glances toward the entrance. Today's celebrity activity at Café is limited to a pride of Real Housewives, all sharing a goat cheese quesadilla. I am only slightly disappointed. Harry is nowhere to be found.

I think One Direction remains important because it's a cultural gradient. The fanbase sits at the intersection of the wholesome IRL and the absolute anarchy of the online world. It takes the family-friendly teenybopper format and attaches to it a vitreous formula of hypersexed, hard-core digital lubricant. Growing up on such a strange combination of sensitivities makes for an uneasy generation. Our futures have always seemed malleable and hard to fathom because we are grown in some ways and stunted in others. And there's no suspension of disbelief in real life. It's not like Twitter, where photo evidence of a disheveled young lady leaving Harry's residence in the early morning might mean she was couch surfing, or perhaps that Harry had hosted a breakfast party and the other guests all took the fire escape. In real life, when things happen, they just happen and that's it. There isn't space for conjecture.

One Direction's breakup brings us back to the IRL. The band doesn't tour their final album, and they sign off with a final live performance at *Dick Clark's New Year's Rockin' Eve.* They sing the double entendre "History," a song whose true meaning—thank you to the fans—is hidden underneath an ex's pleas for reconciliation. The boys wear all black, as if to signify the death of an epoch. Perhaps it is. At the very least, it's a farewell. It's inevitable that the fans will scatter; maybe to K-pop, a genre partly kept safe from the IRL because the idols are contractually banned from dating, or to indie bands, ones whose audiences don't have to shroud themselves in a mushy layer of irony to have a good time.

But still, One Direction will always find a home at the bottom of our Spotify Liked. After all, they encapsulated the Gen Z fantasy: a forever kind of youth, mixed with the hellish candor of the online world. Being a Directioner meant you could dodge reality. You could be young without being innocent. When I see old pictures of the boys, I remember what going online used to feel like: strange and scary, but in a good way. We were shaking dollar bills from the cardboard seams of a Pandora's box. It was a preteen's fuck you to The Man. Sure, the act of going online may not have been as outwardly rebellious as dropping acid or setting banks on fire. But it was the best we could do in the era of the helicopter mom.

Gen Z is not a lost generation. In fact, it's abnormally found.

Our ability to organize ourselves is one of the best side effects of Internet literacy. I am optimistic about the kinds of things we can accomplish when we redirect our power from Harry Styles' airport gate to more pressing matters. Sometimes the Internet rules. When I'm online, I sense a collective consciousness: I'm part of something bigger. I'm part of a billion likes. I'm in on the joke.

But then my phone dies, and I am lonely. The comedown sucks. I'm outside of something so much bigger than myself. I am only one out of a billion. I cling to Internet memes because it makes me feel validated knowing I'm aware enough to understand. I question my own motives. Am I doing this because I want to, or because it will make for a good photograph? Social media creeps into my life like a warped step in my routine. I brush my teeth, wash my face, stalk myself so I can try and imagine how I must seem to a stranger. When you're online, there's a million people who are just like you. You can be in a room by yourself and feel like you're in a crowd. But off-line, when you're alone, you're alone.

I would like to revise my tea-party foul and announce that my favorite track off of *Made in the A.M.* is "Infinity." At face value, it's about pining after someone who's just out of reach. But there's something distinctly "Internet-y" about the lyrics. *"It's like I'm frozen but the world still turns,"* Niall croons. I find a sobering honesty in the words. The boys understand the isolation of the Internet, the subverted intimacy of it all. When Liam sings, *"I'm one step closer to being two steps far from you. When everybody wants you, everybody wants you,"* he suggests a social paralysis, an intangible distance not unlike the one between us and our curated Internet identities. Every conceivable personality fits neatly into any one of millions of online subcultures. But this niche comfort—and Internet literacy in general—doesn't quite translate when you're grown. It only complicates things. This guy you're "talking to" is several years older than you, and you feel lonely with him, you know it's not going anywhere serious, because a several-year gap is a whole lifetime in Internet years. You have a falling-out with your roommate and she moves away, but you don't cry until you notice that she's unfollowed you—not just on Instagram, but Snapchat, which you hardly even use anyway, so like, what's up with that? You become so recklessly infatuated with someone that you tolerate three whole seasons of *Riverdale* for him, but then it falls apart; weeks later, Twitter tells you that costars Lili Reinhart and Cole Sprouse have split up, and for reasons that you can't quite explain, the news makes you vomit. Then you think about how humiliating it is that a *Daily Mail* tweet about the *Riverdale* cast could make you physically ill, so you vomit again. Clearly, you are not in touch with your emotions. But you're sure as hell in touch with over three billion social media accounts worldwide. Niall gets it. The song's an undisputed masterpiece.

This is a hilarious reach. I am so lonely—shut up, we all are—and transmogrifying the mundane, the mass-produced, and the consumable is the easiest and most available form of generational catharsis. We are constantly overstimulated. My head hurts. I'm laid up with a bad case of I Saw His Twitter Likes. I'm seeing this targeted ad or that promoted story. I'm getting high and listening to a viral song, watching whatever's trending on Netflix this month, wearing the clothes I see on Pinterest that will likely fall out of fashion in three weeks. I don't know what there is to gain from all of this. Maybe our pop culture penance is overanalysis.

We have to pin meanings in the mainstream. We have to look for signs. I order a Happy Meal and I eat it slowly, carefully, like a caviar cracker at a rich girl's birthday party. What's it taste like? No, be more specific. How does it *feel*? Because I'd argue that the texture of a Happy Meal is more profound than that of caviar, if only because that's what everyone's eating.

Anyway, my *actual* favorite track off of *Made in the A.M.* is "Olivia," for obvious reasons.

At the end of my junior year, fires ravage the Calabasas hillsides. Faculty decides that finals are optional. Before my sixth period physiology exam, I'm invited to a celebratory end-of-the-year lunch. I decline.

And while I sit in my science class, like I'd promised my parents I would, a group of my peers takes the Pacific Coast Highway to Malibu. They sit at Café Habana's patio and place their orders. While I stare out the window at charred sagebrush, wracking my brain for key terms, they shift eyes across the seating area to the corner table. As I turn in a completed test, securing a score so average that it will ultimately make no difference whatsoever to my overall grade in the class, they notice that they're sharing a dining space with a very special someone indeed. While I mope my way out of junior year, my classmates meet a person worth skipping class for: our adolescent mainstay; Tumblr's participation trophy; the face of all things wholesome yet perverse and totally, definitively, how-many-retweets-for-you-to-go-to-prom-with-me, fuck-the-larries-they're-invasive, masturbate-to-a-Y/N, let's-sell-out-a-Chelsea-boot, *Internet*.

Harry Styles.

And *fuck,* I think, as I review the photo evidence. It's circulating on Twitter. Paparazzi are hounding the restaurant. No way I'll be able to get a foot in the door anytime in the next three months. *Fuck,* I say to myself, *try getting a reservation at Café Habana now, you stupid bastard.*

Depth of Field

Somewhere in the Valley, an anonymous pickup truck spins out of control on Mulholland Highway, veering off the road at an alarming speed and ramming straight into a power pole. A transformer explodes, showering sparks over a hillside of summer-fried brush. Flames travel up and down the fallen power lines. At 4 p.m. in Calabasas, the Old Fire ignites. In the time it takes for me to finish two incomplete assignments, it will have spread to over two hundred acres.

Here in the Valley, we're always waiting for our next fire. It's a natural culmination of a dry season: the Santa Ana winds come sweeping down over crisp, dehydrated bramble and Smokey Bear's eyes turn glassy and desperate. When I was a little girl, my father nicknamed the gusts "Johnny Wind," because it feels like they have a personality. They seem to listen, punctuating sentences with a long, moping whine that sounds far away and too close at the same time.

It may be twisted to say, but there is nothing like a fire sky.

It could be the eighth natural wonder of the world. My family drives out to a vantage point—perhaps Stunt Road, or the top of Winnetka—to get a good look at the whole thing. Windows look like pennies. My favorite view is the Honda dealership lot. Under a fire sky, the sedans look like dozens of ruddy beetles bowing to an inflatable eagle.

I sit in my backyard with my father. He plays the guitar, I sing along—"Georgia on My Mind," "Dream a Little Dream of Me," and "Tennessee Waltz." I've had a soft spot in my heart for classic country and blues since I was little, when my dad introduced me to Willie Nelson, Elvis, Ray Charles. We sing together for a little while, until the ash in the air makes me cough.

Our house is on a hill. From where we sit now, I can see across our little corner of the Valley. All the little windows look gold, reflecting the sunset and the smoke. I think of my dad's favorite story: "The Golden Windows." As I remember my father telling me, it's about a son who leaves home to find the palace across the valley whose windows shine gold at sunset. He travels for days, trekking over harsh terrains, only eating when the kindness of strangers allows. And then he finally arrives. Only it's not a palace. It's a house not unlike his own, with windows of plain clear glass. Confused, he asks the family who lives there where the palace with golden windows must be. "You're mistaken," they say. "We know where it is, but you can only see it at sunset." So they wait. And at sunset, they look across the valley. And the house with the golden windows? Of course, it's his own.

My sister stress-bakes. My parents keep the television on until bedtime. I hardly ever watch the news but they've got a live feed of the fires, so I pace back and forth in the living room, watching it spread to over five hundred acres. Calabasas High has been converted to fire department headquarters; they're drawing game plans on my Spanish classroom's whiteboard. But the flames grow and grow. I don't know what to think or how to feel. My school—and the Santa Monica Mountains—could quickly become nothing but ash.

There is something about the threat of a fire that feels impossible. I'm watching the flames on TV. I recognize the hills, the fence posts, the sagebrush. But somehow, it still doesn't click. There's a disconnect. I feel like I'm watching edited footage, or an outtake from a disaster movie. Fire? That's crazy. Too apocalyptic. That couldn't happen here, not really, no way.

And right now, I'm guarded from reality by a television screen and an aristocratic comedown from teapots and caviar. Maybe my high school will burn down. Good. Then I won't have to take my chem final. After all, I'm in Woodland Hills, and the Santa Susana winds push the sparks in the opposite direction. Our house is fine. I can't say the same for Calabasas.

Though it's the week before finals, I can't convince myself to put in the work. It's hard to focus when my phone is within reach, vibrating with updates every other minute. I submit to the temptation and check a headline. Attached is a photo. The fire is only feet from the edges of the baseball field. I put away my study guides. One switch of the wind, one rise in temperature, one wrong step could thrust CHS into an inferno. And then what? They have us take exams? Doubtful. But once in bed, I find that memories play in my head like a montage reel. I'm nostalgic for a time that hasn't passed yet, and I feel like a sap for it. But there I am, falling asleep in biology, or skipping a math class, or kicking the side of the vending machine to shake an extra pack of gum loose. I wonder if the last time I hopped the senior trail fence was just that—the last time.

The county sends out evacuation notices, text alarms with the buzzing urgency of a midnight Amber Alert. Like Oscar nominees coagulated in the coke bathroom of the Peninsula Beverly Hills, the Calabasas elite hounds the empty gym of A. C. Stelle Middle School. It's safe there. And temporary. They're promised that they'll only be held for a couple of hours.

I wonder what their last items to take were. I picture Cub, wrapping his glassware in a beach towel, stuffing it into a JanSport before his parents can see. Or Lauren, dumping Fenty into an overnight bag. Or even Valentino, who's rumored to haunt the Valley often. But he'd probably wing it. He'd probably go full-on *Easy Rider*. Nothing but him and the fuzzy dice and Mulholland.

But of course, not everyone stays in the gym. Some take to hotel rooms. The Kardashians hire a team of personal firefighters to protect their property.

Extreme wealth is flexed on the general public so often that we become numb to it. It's on TV, in magazines, on our Instagram feeds. So sure, richness can be fun and fluffy, like infinity pools and birthday caviar, but it's not so frivolous when over 16 percent of San Fernando Valley residents live below the poverty line and there are nearly sixty thousand homeless people in Los Angeles County. When wildfires nudge the air index quality to red, where can they go? Homeless shelters aren't always the answer, especially for marginalized groups, people battling addictions, or families who don't want to be split up by the system. I have a sneaking suspicion that the gated community is less about safety than it is about effective ignorance. It's the selfish way out. The gated community sends a simple message: Not my problem.

Come morning, the fire has been contained. School isn't going to burn down after all. My visions of a toasted Calabasas were only thought experiments.

Campus isn't the same, though. The surrounding hillsides, usually plush with wild rye and lavenders, are charred black. The eucalyptus looks like skeleton limbs. Usually, you can detect little hints that the ocean is nearby—seagulls pecking at schoolyard litter, for example, or wildflowers springing up from behind the baseball field. No more. Barbecue smells choke the air. Passing periods move slow and lethargic. At lunch, we stay indoors—the smoke is still thick, and soot lingers in the air. I tuck into a history classroom and nibble at a peanut butter sandwich. I've brought a tattered copy of *Rebecca* by Daphne du Maurier along with me. It's an old favorite, and it usually makes me feel better, like a cup of hot chocolate. But reading just isn't on my mind today.

Certain students enlist their parents to mass-email Principal Stack and request that finals be canceled. Screenshots of the messages leak throughout campus; they're ripe with phrases like "collective emotional trauma." Many of the families claiming to have been evacuated are lying, I notice. Stack emails us to say that she's heard our grievances and she's thinking about it. In the meantime, she advises, study anyway.

I am notoriously bad at taking advice.

* * *

By nightfall, Stack sends another email, this time to let us know that finals are optional. I'm at school again, ushering for a theater event. The parking lot's a desert and the seats in the main stage are mostly empty. I hand out maybe twenty programs. Eli ushers as well, distributing pamphlets on the other wing of the theater. "No one wants to be here," he says, "'cuz it smells like ass."

When the show ends, we leave the theater behind to explore the empty campus. After nine or so, Calabasas High becomes a liminal space. Eerie, yellowed fluorescents buzz jaundice above rusted lockers; moths beat against windows and awnings and light fixtures. You could get lonely fast. I flick a locker open and thumb through someone's neglected copy of *The Catcher in the Rye*. I've always liked to scan margins for other people's annotations. It's a miniature diary entry. Sometimes a stranger's handwriting can feel so close and intimate it seems wrong that they should even qualify as a stranger anymore. You really know a person once you know whether or not they loop their *y*'s.

I'm nosing through Holden's private school days when I hear the click of a shutter from the left of me. Eli lowers his film camera quickly and shrugs. "Good lighting," he says. "Here, let me show you something." He kneels down and shoulders against the bottom lockers, twisting the lens on his camera back and forth. "Alright," he says, "come look."

I sit next to him on the concrete and he holds the viewfinder out for me. "Come closer, I can't move it around too much," he says. I sidle in until our arms are pressed together. Through the camera lens, the string lights on the outdoor stage are unfocused, like little orbs of electricity. "It's called bokeh," he says. "You want a shallow depth of field, or else it won't turn out right." He snaps another photo. "Okay, last one, I'm almost out of film. Since I wasted one on you."

"Shut up, it's art," I say.

We walk up to the football field. It's dark, save for a flickering light above the men's restroom. And it's warm out tonight. In the first days of June, daytime heat spills into the evening. "Glad Stack caved," he says. "Now I can fail my classes without stressing about failing a final too."

"My parents are making me take my tests anyway," I say.

"That sucks," he says.

"Yeah, I know." We stand on the fifty-yard line, over a coyote paw print. "School's hard."

"Tell me about it."

"If I don't get into college I'm hitchhiking to Old Saybrook," I say. "Like Kerouac, or something."

Old Saybrook is a dot-on-the-map town on the Connecticut coast. The houses aren't anything like those in the Valley. It's quiet. There are some dogs, some mosquitos. On one side of Old Saybrook there's the Long Island Sound, with its ribbons of seaweed and thousands of small gray pebbles. And on the other, there's a salt marsh, acres and acres of cowlicked grass only tampered by the boots of crabbers who visit with pails of bait. My grandmother's house lies on the beach side, across the street from a small playground. It's a small yellow colonial with shingles and hydrangea bushes. It's my favorite place in the world. It's where I feel like I did most of my growing up.

"I would tell your mom," he says.

"No, you wouldn't."

"Yeah, I would."

"I'll murder you and then drive over the edge of the Grand Canyon."

"I won't snitch if I come to supervise," he says.

"You don't wanna get mixed up with a girl like me. I'm a loner. A rebel."

"Funny," he says, dryly.

"I live for danger."

"You walk into poles," he corrects.

"See? Danger."

"No. Dumbass."

"Natasha Regis gave Jace Mateo sloppy top right where we're standing," I say. "Isn't that historic?"

"This paw print is the most cursed spot on campus."

"Absolutely."

"Except for the football team. For them it's blessed."

"True."

"I bet you think Andre's hot," he says.

"Yeah, he's a dime. I cannot tell a lie."

He backs up a little bit. Then he runs across the field. "Go long!"

I run backward. He sends an invisible football my way. I sprint to the other end of the field. The air is tight and smoky and wonderful. We whoop and scream like little kids, making invisible passes to one another. Neither of us knows the rules to football but it doesn't matter much at all. We make it up as we go along.

It feels like we're caught in a time warp. We take stinging gasps, lungs filled with the smell of crumb rubber and polyethylene. The moon and the stars poke through smoggy air like beads of milk, all catching on the dips and rivets of the Santa Monica Mountains. Somewhere nearby, the frogs grumble from their lily pads in the Calabasas Creek. The air is thick and pulpy, and if I squint, the pieces of ash look like fireflies.

Out of breath, we collapse in the middle of the field. I lie down and press my palms into the Astroturf. "I hate the Valley but I love it," I say. I mean it. There's something about the parking lots and Olive Gardens and strip malls and talent shows, about all the marks of suburbia mingling with LA overspill. Most people who move to the Valley find it impossible to claim the Valley as their own. Maybe it's too transitional, too bizarre. But somehow, I know that I have the Valley for the time being. No place ever belongs to you as much as a hometown does when you're growing up.

And yes, I conform to the platitudes of adolescent boredoms. I talk about running away. I want to see New York. Et cetera. But I can't shake the feeling that a home can never really be left behind. At least not completely.

But there are different kinds of sad. There's the awful kind, the kind that hits when your dog dies, or you lose someone, or you remember that everything is only temporary. Then there's the good sad, like when you think about growing up, or when a sad movie ends. I'm the good sad.

Eli turns his head toward me and lightly clears his throat. "I love you," he says, quickly.

"Huh?"

"I love you," he says again. "You're my best friend."

"I love you too," I say. The words slip out by themselves. I've never said that to someone not related to me before.

I cross my arms over my chest. Suddenly, everything has changed. Growing up can be unbearably lonely sometimes. But I have a best friend.

We lie there for a hundred years. Two hundred, maybe.

"Should we go home?" he says after a while.

Instant Gratification

We're having a wine night. They're a tradition. Usually some-one's older brother goes out and buys us these big, clumsy jugs of cheap wine with little handles on the side. The varietal of choice is always rosé. We pretend like it's because we're particular, but really, it's just that rosé is the only thing sweet enough to stom-ach. Plus, it's pink. If it resembles a Starburst, it probably satisfies the teenage palate.

Tonight, we've gathered at Cory's house. He lives right by school. He has a good house for parties and a chill dad. We're drunk as lords. Whoever has the aux is playing the Smiths.

Michael Brophy shows us his stick-and-poke thigh tattoo. Zoe keeps swirling the wine in her glass around like she's some sort of aficionado. Eli takes bong rips. It's all normal kid stuff, I guess. Nothing out of the ordinary. Then someone suggests a game of Never Have I Ever. I say I don't want to play. I mumble something about the fetishization of women's sexuality, about how I find it regressive to accessorize with sexual benchmarks. Eli gives me a look like *oh, please, lol,* because we both know that the truth is I just don't want everyone in the room to know I'm a virgin. He's the only one that knows the truth: that the story I've been telling since freshman year about my first kiss, with a boy named Lucas at summer camp, is a lie. I've never even been to summer camp.

So I sit there on the couch, switching back and forth between Instagram and Twitter. My eyes feel huge in my face. I look at the same picture of Michelle Franchise eating a snow cone about a hundred times just from closing and reopening the app every two seconds. Adults are always on our backs for having short attention spans, but the big zoomer secret is that half the time we're just looking at the same things over and over again.

"Never have I ever . . ." Cub starts. "Shit. There isn't anything I haven't."

"Shut up," Zoe says. Zoe's into Cub big-time. You can tell because she's always going on and on about how annoying Cub is.

"Never have I ever fucked a relative," he says.

"You're disgusting," Zoe says.

"I *haven't* done it," Cub says, jamming a tortilla chip into his mouth. "That's the *point.*"

I wonder if Zoe and Cub have hooked up yet.

"I just hate how it has to go there," Zoe says.

"Did you fuck a cousin or something?" Cub says. "Jesus."

I determine that they have not yet hooked up.

It goes on like this for a while, this low-effort banter. I sink back into the couch and sulk at this miserable halfway-drunk state in which I've found myself. Zoe, frustrated with Cub's nonchalance toward her, leaves early. The conversation chugs along without me, until I hear Eli say my name. "Me and V are gonna go halfsies on a box vape one day," he says. "Vape Nation."

"Huh?" I sit up.

"We're gonna get flip sunglasses too. Commit to the bit."

I shoot him a look. I always feel uncomfortable when people are so flippant about nicotine in front of Cub. My freshman year, he confessed to me that his father had been in rehab for vaping for six months. He begged me not to tell anyone.

"Actually, we won't," I correct. "Vaping nic isn't a joke." I nod in Cub's direction.

"Why are you looking at me like that?" Cub says. "I *have* a vape."

I'm tipsy, so my inhibition is out the window. "But your dad," I say.

He narrows his eyes. "What about him?"

"Remember? What you told me," I say. "I don't wanna say it out loud."

"I'm an open book, dude," he says.

"Share with the class," says Cory.

"Didn't you say your dad was in rehab for vaping nic?" As soon as I say it, I wish I hadn't. Eli coughs. Zoe snorts.

"You believed that?" says Cub. "Oh man. I was fucking with you. You don't go to rehab for *vaping nicotine.*" He digs in his pocket and produces his dab pen. "Here, you need this," he says. "Sometimes you're Catholic as hell."

Ah, yes, my best friend: Cub's pen.

Months ago, I'd been introduced to cannabis not with a hollowed apple, nor a mutilated bottle of Dasani, but with Cub's

Stiiizy. I'm well aware that this is a crime against adolescence. I
should have respected the heirarchy of stoner paraphernalia. But
my first time smoking took place at a party, on a sofa, next to Cub
himself. "Do you feel it, dude?" he asked. "Cart's ninety percent
THC."

"Yeah, I feel it," I said. I felt slow and buzzy, if a little under-
whelmed. Nobody tells you that *yes,* weed is fun and everything,
but it's not, like, montage-of-sprouting-flowers-and-brain-cells-and-
large-gusts-of-wind good, and *yes,* everyone *is* exaggerating that
much. Turns out, nobody tells you a lot of things about high school.

Movies, TV, and grown-ups at dinner tables have always set
high schoolers up for disappointment. That's why every kid has
this irrational worry that they're missing out on a quintessential
experience. Nobody ever seems to mention how most of high
school is just a bunch of waiting around. And a lot of the action,
a lot of the gossip and the fun stuff, arrives in secondhand stories.
High school can be so boring that sometimes the only interesting
thing that will have happened for weeks was last Monday when
the third-most-relevant Ryan told everyone that he's "openly not
gay" and everyone was like, "lol." Or maybe it was when the
ASB vice president had to have a talk with the weird kid in my
Spanish period because he kept spamming the senior Facebook
page with shitty Republican memes and it was kind of awkward.
Maybe something really wild *will* go down, like Francesca Kate
jumping nude into the campus swimming pool during a drunken
scavenger hunt, but you won't see it or anything, because you
stayed at home or you didn't have a big enough group to form a
team or maybe you didn't even know the hunt was happening in
the first place, so you won't hear about it until lunch on Wednes-

day from someone who wasn't there either but talked to someone who was. Most depictions of high school are shit, because adult writers can't seem to understand that oftentimes the crazy stuff is happening somewhere else. If it happens at all.

And tonight, while I settle back into Cory's couch and muse about whether or not I'm a de-facto bourgeois asshole for having broken my gateway drug virginity with a piece of trendy, expensive hardware, something interesting does happen. But it's somewhere else. And we don't hear about it until the next morning, when we're in class, and Principal Stack is heralding over the loudspeaker at 8:05 in the morning.

"Last night, at eleven-thirty p.m., Zoe Melton was walking home from a friend's house when a distracted driver skidded off of the road and into the sidewalk. She was hit, suffered blunt force trauma, and passed away on impact. Grief counselors will be available in the library all week and there will be information about her upcoming memorial soon. Zoe was a beloved member of the community. She participated in the theater program and advanced dance groups and in her free time she volunteered at the animal shelter. She will be deeply, deeply missed."

The intercom clicks off.

The kid next to me raises his hand. "Do we have homework?"

As it turns out, the interesting stuff happening somewhere else isn't a fatal car accident, but the faculty's secret preparation for Every Fifteen Minutes. It's a biennial drunk driving program, designed to traumatize teenagers into navigating the roads very carefully for approximately one week before everyone forgets and re-enables Snapchat push notifications. It takes a dated statistic extremely literally: every fifteen minutes, the principal makes a somber announcement that another student has died as a result of drunk or distracted driving. And for the rest of the day, the chosen student mopes around campus in zombie makeup, not allowed to speak to anyone. When first period lets out, the quad is quieter than usual, a sudden melancholy dropped over an otherwise sunny day. It could be because campus socialite Parker Judge and her on-again, off-again boyfriend are splitsville once again. Or maybe, just maybe, it's because we've all been forced into a method acting experiment that involves the mourning of our fake-dead peers. Idk.

On the second day of the event we're led to the parking lot. There's a huge black curtain rigged in front of four or five bleachers, and a substantial portion of Mulholland Highway is cordoned off. Police cars line the street. When we settle down, the curtain drops and an audio recording of a major crash screeches through the speaker system. Laid out before us, like a sixth-grader's diorama, is a car wreck. A girl I recognize from my history class hangs limp like a rag doll through a windshield, her legs mangled and bloodied. We sit in a shocked silence, less so at the unfolding melodrama and special-effects makeup and more so in disbelief that this program is allowed to happen. I lock eyes with an open fracture. "BestGore," someone behind me murmurs. A girl stands and sprints to the bathroom; I'll later learn that she'd lost members of her family in a traffic collision.

An ambulance whirrs down the street, escorted by more cop cars. A paramedic pulls a boy from the wreckage with the Jaws of Life. Principal Stack makes her way to the front of the scene and collapses to her knees, wailing: "Oh God, oh God. My students. My poor, poor students." It's over the top. It's twisted. It's so deeply Calabasas.

Students selected to participate in the program are expected to keep it a secret, even though it's a tempting brag; it's considered a high honor to be chosen—everyone wants to play dead, to see how their friends would react if they died in an immediate and tragic way. Teachers nominate their students with the intention to create a valid sample size from all corners of the student body. They then meet in the early hours of the morning for educational workshops and rehearsals. I've been nagging Eli about this for months, trying to garner a confession out of him. But he's pled innocence every time. My suspicions are far from irrational, given his status not only as head theater kid but also as a bit of a heart-throb. He emerges from a crumpled Toyota Corolla, one of the few "survivors" of the episode. Discombobulated, he stumbles over a busted fender. "Knew it," I remark, to no one in particular.

He slumps on the curbside as the campus cop Breathalyzes the driver of his car. He's doing a good job. He has to. There is a decent chance that this might be one of the most attentive audiences of his career. Principal Stack kneels next to him and places her hands on his shoulders. If this were any other circumstance, he'd look at me and gag.

Two are pronounced dead on the scene and the rest are ush-ered to a hospital in an ambulance. They'll really go there, too—the "dead" will visit a mortuary, the "injured" an emergency room. The "drunk drivers" will visit a jail. At night, the "victims" convene at a local hotel and open letters from their parents and classmates. Each participant names three of their closest friends, who are subsequently taken out of class to answer the prompt:

"Every fifteen minutes, someone is killed or seriously injured in an alcohol-related traffic incident. Today you died, and I didn't get the chance to say goodbye. Here is what I would have said . . ."

I expect to be one of Eli's choices. After the presentation, I don't bother to focus on lecture, for two reasons: one, Stack interrupts every quarter-hour with another miniature eulogy, and two, because I know that at any minute I'll be summoned to the office to write my parting letter. Absentminded, I scroll through my phone from under the desk. My letter will begin casually. Maybe I'll bring up an old memory or two. Hide an inside joke somewhere. And then by the end I'll let myself get a little sappy. I'll figure it out in the moment, I guess.

The door opens and a representative from the office gives someone in the front row a pink slip. They're excused, gone to write a letter to a member of the robotics team who's been hit by a drag racer. I fidget in my seat, staring at the clock in the corner of the smart board, waiting for my turn.

When I'm eventually pulled from class, it's the end of the school day. There's hardly any time left for me to pen my letter. I'm too busy counting back minutes to notice that my slip isn't even pink, like the others—it's yellow, typically associated with misconduct hearings. And at the office, nobody hands me a prompt and a box of tissues. Instead, I'm ushered to my guidance counselor's office. Her computer monitor is angled in my direction, where she's logged into my grade portal. "Is everything alright at home?" she asks.

I stand in the doorway. "Yeah?"

"I'm only asking because I've noticed your grades have been on a steady decline," she says. I stare at my report card. "You have a fourteen percent in your math class. Are you planning on going to college?"

I take a seat. Her desk is covered in little trinkets: bobble-head dolls, succulents, holiday cards. I don't know her very well. Counselors come and go at such a quick rate that no student ever gets the opportunity to strike up a meaningful relationship. "Yeah, I think so," I say.

"Are you sure everything is okay?" she asks, her forehead crinkled.

I don't know what to tell her. I like to learn. There are things I'm especially interested in—writing, for example, and studying literature. Music, too, is something I really like. I even enjoy my science class sometimes. But the others aren't so easy for me. Calabasas High is a competitive school, and once I've already failed a couple math tests it's difficult to imagine myself joining the ranks of the AP students, ones who excel at everything and dedicate their whole lives to studying. So, I choose the short-term options. Skipping class, getting ice cream, making guesses on assigned worksheets. Besides, I already have a reputation here. I'm not tagged as a "smart kid." I've never told anyone about my stupid little pipe dream of studying English in college. But I'm not about to have a therapy session with a counselor, a woman whom I've only met once before.

"Yeah, I think," I say, except it takes much longer because I glance at my phone twice and fumble my words over and over again. "Just, like. I mean, well, it starts like how kind of when you go and stuff and it's just that . . . I guess I'm behind because of, you know, like, circumstances are . . . well. It's a lot of things, probably, and if I were to really think about it, you know, there's a lot happening there, I guess."

She watches me carefully. There's definitely a handbook she's flipping through in her head. "Well, Olivia," she starts, slowly, "I can transfer you into a remedial math class instead, if you're finding the material difficult."

I've heard of the class she's referencing. It's an extension of the Indian Hills program, a secondary school for troubled kids. It's where the Bling Ring met, so many years ago. Kids get bonus points on tests for drawing little pictures on the edges of the Scantrons. If my mother knew, she'd have a fit. "Will it look any different on my transcripts?" I ask. Translation: will my parents find out?

"It counts as a regular algebra II course."

"Okay," I say. "Whatever, I guess."

I don't know why I can't bring myself to care about anything. There's a contagion of apathy in Calabasas. It sets in slowly.

And now, as I get older, this attitude has set in long-term. It's almost a sadness, but it's a little too empty to be sad. I can't even remember the last time I felt emotional about anything. I don't like being alone, so I clog up my days making idle gossip with people from school. They talk about getting fucked. *Did they do anal? I heard he was really coked out. She got into all the UCs, but only because she paid somebody to take online AP classes for her. If you haven't lost your virginity by the time you leave high school you're basically screwed. They're dating now, but he cheats on her all the time. He's got chlamydia. Her dad works for the Kardashian PR. He's being held back a year.*

My parents say I'm drifting. "You're not yourself anymore," they say, and look at me like I've contracted affluenza. I don't believe it. I'm assuming that this must be what living in the moment means. That's how I justify it, anyway, when I skip my creative writing elective for the third time in a week to go window shopping at the mall. I stare at the display case inside Tiffany's, my skin soaking in all the halogen lights. I ask the man behind the counter if it would be alright if I tried on the silver necklace. He says okay. I would never—could never—buy something so expensive but maybe it's okay to pretend.

I wasn't on Eli's list, anyway. Aside from Alice, an upperclassman Eli's liked for years, he chose three acquaintances—popular ones. Of course. I don't know what I was expecting anyway. What would I have written? Probably something stupid.

When I get back to campus, Cub invites me to go drifting with him and some friends. Drifting is a typical Calabasas hobby. Some drifters are more dedicated than others. In 2014, a group of kids from different Valley high schools formed a gang, dubbed Taftco, whose main purpose was getting drunk and going fast. They'd been the number one Valley party clique until some of them crashed their parents' exotic sports cars in the middle of the night. After that, they became controversial, but not so controversial that they were removed from the pecking order completely. (In fact, Taftco served as a sort of pipeline to a KarJenner affiliation. Socialites Jordyn Woods and Anastasia Karanikolaou, both of whom have been featured on *Keeping Up With the Kardashians*, were known to be Taftco Mansion regulars back in the day.) We pay homage to Taftco's legacy in the school's after hours, coagulating in the senior lot to spin donuts. There's a certain rhythm to the whole thing. You've gotta go fast, finesse the perfect turn, and slam the brakes at the right second. A lot can go wrong. A few weeks ago, someone rammed into a lamppost and got suspended. Almost hit a squirrel. Cub and I figure we ought to hightail it out to Stunt Road this time instead.

Stunt Road is a windy switchback road laced with lookout points that the high schoolers like to use as sesh spots. If you keep driving, you'll end up all the way in Malibu. The road lends itself to various trailheads—a favorite vantage point is a chunk of graffitied concrete that juts out over a panoramic view of the entire city. There's a lonesome old sofa. An abandoned microwave tower sits just a few footsteps away. It's a view like no other—if you're brave enough, of course, to play footsie with a treacherous mountainside cliff.

We arrive at the top of Stunt at my favorite part of the afternoon. There are certain times of day when Los Angeles feels its best—I'm talking about, like, four-thirty to five-fifteen, when the sun hits the eucalyptus trees at just the right softness, and everything's hazy and warm and peanut-buttery. And we are sixteen, teetering between childhood and adulthood, lulled into a cushy invincibility. Cub's stoned, of course—out of his mind high, the kind of baked that belongs in a philosophy major's dorm room. We don't let it stop us, though. When you're sixteen, you're indestructible. He veers into the wrong lane, just to freak us out. "Okay, okay," he says. "Let's die." He hits the accelerator, and we're going incredibly fast, everyone's laughing, and I squeeze my eyes shut so I can remember everything just a little bit better. Because once you're out of high school, you'll start to forget the exactness of it all. Maybe it's some sort of biological tic, like how we're designed to forget the pains of childbirth. It doesn't matter. I want certain parts of my teenage years preserved like they've been on ice all this time.

"Hell yeah," I hear someone shout. And then an "Oh, shit." I open my eyes. Cub is panicking, struggling to regain control of the car. We haven't slowed down at all. And we are headed directly for the edge of the cliff.

But nothing happens. We stop just in time. We don't even acknowledge that we were ever in danger. High fives all around. A kantorei of "fuck yeah"s. Cub's the man. He's only giving us a cheap thrill. There never was any real danger. Nothing ever happens and it's all just pretend. The biggest dramas are fabricated by too-serious grown-ups like Stack and her minions. We're sixteen. We're covered in bubble wrap, and we're just getting started.

He drives me home. I don't speak to my parents. I haven't spoken to them in weeks. I head straight to my bedroom and I lie in bed. When I was younger, the lime-green paint on my walls was cool and cheerful. Now, it holds the light in an odd way and makes my skin look paper-white and sickly.

I feel like I'm looking at myself through a window. My words and actions crawl out of me on their own. Identity isn't an inherent thing. I know myself passively, like an acquaintance; I watch myself go about my day from a second perspective. I feel like a witness to my own life. Sometimes I'll access a memory out of nowhere, from a time where I didn't feel so detached. Diversion is an art, and the key is to push things out. I'll see something innocent online, like a photo of someone's little cousin drinking a milkshake, and I'll be transported back to elementary school. I'll remember how my parents used to take me to an old-fashioned diner for dessert after my school plays. We'd sit at the counter and order: a chocolate malt for my dad, ice cream sundaes for Jackie and me. My mom wouldn't get anything. She'd say she wasn't hungry, but my dad and I knew that was a lie, and she'd take spoonfuls of our dessert and we'd roll our eyes and give her a hard time but secretly we weren't bothered by it at all, and in fact we ordered large sizes just for that very reason. It's strange, the way things change. You don't notice how different everything is until it's too late.

The third day of Every Fifteen Minutes involves a faux funeral, hosted in the gym. The advanced women's choir sings "Amazing Grace" as an empty casket is carried down the aisle. Parents come and read eulogies. Principal Stack gives an impassioned address. She even cries. "This is what happens when you text and drive," she says. "Don't check your phone behind the wheel. Put it down."

That reminds me. I check my phone.

By the time I zone back into the funeral, an official Every Fifteen Minutes representative is already wrapping things up. According to the storyline, Eli isn't dead, only injured, so he sits front row with his arm in a cast. I stare at the back of his head.

I'm not empty-handed. Sure, he didn't give me the chance to write him a letter. But last night I took the liberty of printing out an old text conversation between us, one where he vehemently denied any association to the program. I sealed it in an envelope. He'll think it's hysterical.

When the funeral's over, the "dead" students are released

back to the student body. I don't give Eli a chance to find me in the gym's crowd. I go outside and buy lunch from the cafeteria and I carry it upstairs to the lawn. They've left the totaled car on display, complete with blood smudges on the window. I take a bite of my chicken tender and examine the fingerprints. It's pretty gruesome, but it's nothing compared to some of the stuff I saw online at age eleven.

"V," I hear. Eli's already found me. He's only sought me out because his letter-writers already said hi, I'm sure. "Aren't you gonna say you knew it?"

"I knew it," I say.

"That's my blood," he says, and places a palm over the hand mark on the window. "See? Perfect match."

"Incredible."

"How was my performance? I looked at you during the crash. Disappointed you weren't sobbing."

"Five stars. Your best work."

"I was thinking we could go grab some candy from Purcell's before lunch is over. Like old times," he says.

"I'm good." I lift up a chicken tender. "Eating."

He tilts his head. "Why are you being weird?"

"I don't know what you mean."

"I haven't actually lost my gaming arm. We should celebrate," he says.

"You didn't ask me to write a letter," I say shortly. "Not that I care, though."

He squints. "Oh," he says. "You're mad."

"Not mad, but my letter would've been, like, super dramatic

and emotional, so it's your loss." I shrug. "I'm just teasing. Really. I couldn't care less."

"I figured you'd think it's dumb," he says. "You're all cynical about this kind of thing."

"I'm not cynical."

"You're too cool, is what I'm saying."

"I'm not cool."

"You are."

"Tristan Laypalm is cool," I say. Tristan is one of the seniors Eli picked for his letter. He's popular and rich, always sporting Comme des Garçons and graphic tees that say shit like SOBER FREE. He's nice and all, but I didn't think Eli knew him that well.

"Tristan Laypalm . . ." He trails off. "Tristan didn't even show up to write it."

"Oh. Well, that sucks."

"Yeah, it does, kinda." He kicks at a dirt clod. "Hey, if it makes you feel any better, we submitted our picks six months ago. I was dumber then."

My feelings are hurt, I want to say. But it would be off-brand. Eli's right. I'm supposed to be cool. So instead, I say:

"You're dumb now, too. You finished a drunk driving campaign and all you can talk about is your gaming arm."

"But to be serious for a second. I'm sorry I didn't pick you. And um, you know this already, obviously, but you're my best friend."

"Same to you," I say.

Cub walks past, salutes Eli. "Glad you're not dead," he says, tipping his Snapback.

"Thanks," Eli says. Then he looks back at me. "What would you have said?"

"If I'd written a letter?"

"Yeah."

It always feels like there's a whole world of things at the tip of my tongue when I'm with Eli, but I can never figure out what they are. But something tells me my letter wouldn't have been cool or cynical at all. "I dunno," I say. And then I remember what I have stowed away in my back pocket. I pull out the envelope.

His eyes widen. "What's that?"

"I don't know if it's so appropriate now, all things considered."

He snatches it from me. "Guess Via Bleidner's not like everyone thought," he says, ripping it open. "There better be tearstains."

The screenshot flutters onto the ground. He picks it up, scans it, flips it over. The other side is blank, of course. "Oh," he says. "That's funny."

"Yeah, I saw DJ Khaled at the club last night," Michael is telling me. I'm at the Calabasas Commons, waiting for Eli to come out of the Fresh Brothers bathroom. In the meantime, Cub and I have run into a cackle of other CHS kids in front of the movie theater. I'm moderately stoned, and it's blatantly obvious that Michael is, too—he's been rambling for three minutes about his adventures at 1Oak, the eighteen-and-up nightclub on Sunset Boulevard. I've never been. I'm not eighteen, I don't have a fake ID, and the entire premise of "clubbing" is so foreign and terrifying to me that it's ranked up there with skydiving and bungee jumping.

"Dead meme," says Cub. "Don't care."

"Nah, he was cool," says Michael.

Eli exits the pizza place and spots Cub and me. "Show a picture then," I say.

Michael's caught off guard. "He wouldn't take one," he says.

"Hmm," I say. I can tell Michael's agitated. How dare I deny him his VIP romp. "Well, I once ding-dong-ditched Kylie Jenner's house in Hidden Hills."

"Oh, yeah?" he says. "Which one?"

I blink. "It was down the street from my friend Lauren's house."

"Lauren Campbell?" he says. Smirks. "On [XXXXX] Road?"

"Yeah?" I narrow my eyes.

"Kylie doesn't even live in that house," he says. "That's just where she receives packages."

I stare back at him blankly, but I can't think of anything else to say. "Cub, Via, we have to talk," Eli interjects.

"DJ Khaled, dude," calls Michael. "Scout's honor."

Eli pulls me away. "I don't actually have anything to say," he says to us. "Could just tell that conversation sucked."

"He's so pissed right now," I say. "I wouldn't believe his 1Oak story."

"Fuck 1Oak," says Cub.

"Keep hating from outside of the club," says Eli.

We walk toward Barnes & Noble. For whatever reason, Calabasas High has adopted the upper level of the bookstore. It's practically an extension of campus. The three of us regularly convene behind the romance novel section. I've made a game of choosing the tackiest cover and reading aloud the worst lines I can find: tonight, I've discovered a passage about a bagpiper seeking titillation from beneath the sensual folds of a kilt. When we get sick of that we sit on the floor and flit through our Snapchat stories. Someone's doing chops around a bonfire.

"FOMO," says Cub. "We feeling it?"

I am. Kind of. Our parents lived in simpler times. We've got the information superhighway delivering regular reminders of parties we aren't invited to, people who like us but not enough for us to make the kickback cut.

But when I picture myself at these events, I know I'd be too cold. Or tired. Or too drunk. Or not drunk enough. I admire the party-hopper, the social butterfly. But I can never seem to blend in quite right. I always find myself surrendering to my phone. I don't even notice I'm doing it until I'm already days deep into a peripheral somebody's Instagram profile.

Barnes & Noble is about to close, so we follow Cub to his car. He makes a grand show of dodging a puddle. "Can't scuff the Js," he says. "Car ride back, we'll play some beats. I wanna practice my freestyle." He opens the door. "Get in."

Eli jumps in passenger, I stay back. It's not that I'm averse to hearing Cub's flow (well, actually, yes I am). But we're all stoned. Last time I was in this car, I thought I was gonna die. For like two seconds, but still.

"I might stay," I say. I feel like a narc.

"Community curfew's in ten," he says. "Get the fuck in."

"I dunno."

Eli raises an eyebrow. "Are you being a cop right now," he says flatly.

"I just watched you fake almost-die," I say. "Literally yesterday."

"When have I ever let you down with my driving?" says Cub. "I'm insulted, not gonna lie."

"I'm gonna grab a coffee," I say. "From Starbucks." I back away.

"Suit yourself," Cub says.

"You're cool anyway," says Eli. "But fuck you."

"I don't care about the driving stuff," I say. "I wanna buy a book and a coffee."

"See ya, Via," Cub says, and they drive away.

I make good on my word—I buy a book, for the first time in a while. Truman Capote's *In Cold Blood*. I've read some short stories of his before. I especially liked the one about the old lady who kept dead cats in her freezer.

I take the book to another nearby Starbucks and I start reading. It's hard to stay focused. My brain has been fried by hundreds of hours of instant gratification. I take sips from a small coffee. WARM AND COZY LIKE A CRACKLING FIRE, the sign above the menu reads, and there's a picture of a caramel whatever right below. Cory's in line, headphones on. He doesn't see me. He gazes at the menu, conflicted; I narrate his thoughts. *Should I get a plain black coffee or a cappuccino? Or should I forego the operation entirely because there is no ethical consumption under capitalism?*

I finally catch his eye and he waves. We offer passing "heys" and he leaves, shaking off the slight chill that the Valley wears once it's dark. I lean back in my chair and open the book again, this time with my phone tucked under my butt. And I read until close, and after that I ask my mom to come pick me up, and she's annoyed that I didn't take a ride from a friend, and I could argue but I don't, because I'm too busy reading about the Kansas prairie in the passenger seat.

Jizzbag

God is real and She's supervising my morning school commute at seven-thirty a.m. on a Tuesday. She also has a toned physique, thanks to Dr. Fatoff's CoolSculpting technique. And she kind of looks like a Kardashian.

Each morning, it's the first thing I see upon leaving my neighborhood: a thirty-foot FREEZE YOUR FAT billboard. Kylie Jenner's lookalike smolders in a black bikini, bedroom eyes seducing a neighboring In-N-Out. And of course, the sign's not without a ringing endorsement (AS SEEN ON TMZ).

Only true Valley locals know the story behind the TMZ claim: that the Kardashians tried suing Dr. Fatoff for using Kylie's likeness, only to have their case thrown out when the CoolSculpting magnate revealed the billboard vixen was actually his own daughter. Now, the sign stands guard over Ventura Boulevard like a warped Dr. TJ Eckleburg on the brink of dystopia, monitoring our sins through the binoculars of a 1-800 number that passes over a (pretty much) nonexistent nose.

It's billboards like these that remind me that the romance of Los Angeles is largely fiction. The casual tourist is infatuated with a California ideal that's hard to find. And fair enough. We get good press. When you think of LA, what comes to mind? Is it that photo of Faye Dunaway, brooding over her Academy Award before a dreamy West Coast swimming pool? Is it the Hollywood sign, the entertainment industry's Christmas star, perched between sloping hillsides that play hostess to Lululemon hikers and Mansonite wayfarers? Is it sun-kissed Venice bodybuilders scooting down Sunset in a roll-top Mercedes? It's probably any one of these. But those bodybuilders are secretly fraught with the testicular consequences of steroid use, and I've seen far more sidewalk flashers than Academy Awards in my lifetime.

That's not to say that everything you hear about LA is a lie. It's fair to assume that at any given time, nobody's farther than six footsteps from someone in thrifted Rag & Bone jeans outlining a screenplay (*Titanic* meets something by Tarantino but with what's-her-face as the stripper with a heart of gold). Perhaps it's fair to accuse us of superficiality, drinking our sophisticated coffees from places whose interiors employ such architectural clichés as exposed piping and Edison lightbulbs. Maybe your vision of the LA dweller, dog-earing the middle page in a distressed copy of *Lolita*, retweeting GIFs of Lily-Rose Depp smoking cigarettes, and outsourcing Instagram bios to gothic font generators, is, from several steps back, pretty accurate.

The unfortunate truth is that most of LA is the stuff of Freeze Your Fat billboards. Lofted, cubic mansions are reserved for the richest of the rich—or they're unoccupied, or they're rent-per-hour video shoot settings for the likes of Team 10. The Walk of

Fame smells like pee. The people who dress like characters and hound tourists outside the Chinese Theatre aren't the Disney-lite; instead, they're aging actors in Party City capes trying to scrape a dollar or two in between cattle calls. During summertime, the city writhes as thousands of mechanical bodies roll through the Hollywood throat in LA traffic peristalsis. The air is sick, heavy with pollution and the cough-sweet smell of millions of backyard swimming pools gurgling chlorine just in time for barbecue parties and Marco Polo. You hold your breath.

But the most striking reality is the iron grip that the entertainment industry has on LA children. Every kid in the city either is, has been, or is trying to get signed to a talent agency. It's a tween rat race—a hustle dominated by unnaturally poised (and accordingly creepy) Valley children whose medicine cabinets are stocked with Ritalin and Crest Whitestrips. They've been trained. They introduce themselves like they're slating their names for a camera, perky voices dripping with faux acting-class charisma. *Do you have an agent?* is normal, after-school mall food court talk. It's almost a friendly opener. *Have I seen you in anything?* is a bit more violent. An LA tween actor only asks you this if they already know the answer is no. At this point, they're simply establishing a power dynamic in which you are certainly the beta and by the way, did you happen to see my Tooth Tunes commercial spot during last week's *Young Sheldon* season premiere?

It's a family affair. Hordes of out-of-towners migrate to LA from wherever to try and make it on the big screen. They become principals and real estate agents and pet photographers and dance instructors. Then they have kids. Their kids have kids. And now, all of Southern California is infested with these mutant nightmare children who've been steeped in Los Angeles' special brand of pseudo-ambition, kids whose birthright is a maniacal drive to play the shithead little brother on an ABC Family sitcom. You know them when you see them. They speak in catchphrases. They look like they're always about to dip a forefinger into a cheek dimple, and their first exposures to the word *book* were purely in the context of the casting room.

It's a dangerous formula. Where there's a surplus of telegenic children, there's a shortage of roles. Everyone's disposable. And by the time high school rolls around, the poison cocktail of puberty and Hollywood sleaze has jacked their potential. Their loss of innocence coincides with a loss of cuteness, and subsequently, a loss of marketability. They're caught vaping, they discover hentai, they fail their first test. Casting directors aren't so cloying anymore, shoving them aside for newer, cuter twelve-year-olds who can sing the alphabet backward and break-dance to radio-friendly rap. LA is the only place where the fifteen-year-olds are has-beens.

So. Meet Daniel Shepherd Summers. He enrolls at Calabasas High my junior year. Though he's about my age, he's two years below me in school—maybe it's an on-set tutoring confusion, because he's fresh off of the Nickelodeon roster. A recurring cast member on the original series, *[XXXXX]*, Daniel even had his name in the opening credits. He played the plot-B comic relief, the sidekick with the hijinks. But Nickelodeon has a tried-and-true rhythm when it comes to the longevity of their shows, and *[XXXXX]* didn't make it past one season. But given that he is the only freshman with a newfound entourage on the first day of school, it doesn't really seem to matter.

The second most valuable currency in the high school classroom (superseded by JUUL pods, followed by gum) is the aptly-delivered one-liner. And Daniel's been formally apprenticed in this art, having studied under dozens of soulless TV writers over at Nick. He's always at the ready, leaning his desk chair against the back wall of the classroom with a witty comment on reserve. He's got plenty of encouragement, too, since he's amassed plenty of admirers. But here's the thing. He's not necessarily *hot*. In fact, he's got . . . well, the sex appeal of a nerdy secondary character on a high school sitcom. He looks Nickelodeon. Thick-frame Clark Kent glasses. His hair is gelled and coiffed and he dresses in the audition room staple: black skinny jeans, white Chucks, primary-colored pullover. Daniel doesn't walk. He *struts*. His saunter communicates clearly: *I get stopped on the street by your little sister.* Daniel's newer to Calabasas High than me, sure, but years of schmoozing grown-ups have given him an uncanny slickness that I find slightly intimidating. He possesses a certain je ne sais quoi, a specific confidence that nearly places him in the same Hot Guy league as the basketball team.

The drama kids are distraught. How much disruption can one triple threat cause? A lot, apparently. What reads as campy and over the top on children's programming is just right for the stage. Daniel's a verified talent. We all know Mr. Purcell will eat that shit up. But when auditions for the fall play arrive, Daniel is nowhere to be seen. He's decided not to audition, a move that not only bruises the theater-kid ego but establishes Daniel Summers as a "real actor" and commodity.

Seven-thirty a.m., early October, junior year. Madison Whitney is dressed like she's expecting a talent scout to sweep her off her feet at any moment (this morning, it's three-inch heeled booties and a floral romper). I'm sitting at a picnic bench in the middle of the upper quad. It's overflowing with teenage bodies and portable breakfasts. We're all engaged in various cheating tactics—at one corner of the table, Michael Brophy programs the answer key to a history test into his graphing calculator. In another, a completed math assignment lends itself to five or six blank notebooks. If you're shocked, you must be old. School is less about learning than it is about scoring points. It's a game of percentages.

"Where's Daniel?" Maddy says.

"Wouldn't you like to know," Michael says.

Every sixteen-year-old is at least a little bit evil. They detect vulnerability like sharks smell blood. In this case, Maddy's weakness is that she is nursing an obvious puppy crush on Daniel. And the boys in particular have it out for her, shutting down anything she says with a half-baked classroom quip. Maddy brandishes her ambition with an unapologetic femininity, and boy, is she paying the price for it. She doesn't attempt to play the "cool girl," something that I cannot seem to wrap my head around. I'm still at an insecure stage where I find my own girlhood unwieldy, compensating for it with edgy jokes and "I'm not like other girls" attributes.

"I'm just wondering," she says. "I want to ask him if he's trying out for improv."

"Downgrade," Michael says. "Literally why would he do that."

"Because he's an actor, duh," she says, and squeezes herself onto the bench.

"He's an actor, duh," Michael imitates. "You're clout chasing."

"Please. He's not even that famous."

"More famous than you." He admires his calculator handi-work and slips it into his backpack as Eli, hands full with a half-eaten bag of Sour Patch Kids, approaches from behind and shoves a stack of books aside so he can sit. Every action he takes has to be obscene or outlandish in some way. He thrives off of attention, but we forgive him for it—it's part of his charm, like a little kid doing tricks on the monkey bars. He sits next to me and pulls out a textbook which, if I know Eli, will most definitely remain closed.

"If we're talking about Daniel," he says. "I'll make you all jealous."

"What," Madison says flatly.

"Nickelodeon party on Halloween. You have to sign an NDA and you can't bring your phone in. It's gonna be filled with fa-mous people. And I'm his plus one."

"Bullshit," Brick Weber says, his head finally bobbing up from his math homework. "Bull. Shit."

"I'm serious," he says. "We've known each other forever. Why wouldn't he take me?"

Eli and Daniel famously partook in the same production of *Bye Bye Birdie* in middle school, and Eli refuses to let anyone forget it. Perhaps it's because he believes that in a different life, it would've been him that got the audition for *[XXXXX]*, him that made it on TV, and it's only through a fluke error of the universe that he's now sitting at a picnic bench for school-enforced "extra study" because of an eternal placement on the academic proba-tion list. In a perfect world, he would be the one receiving a direct invite from the Nick clique.

"So he hasn't actually invited you and you're making as-sumptions," I say.

"Aw, is somebody jealous?" he taunts, shoving a Sour Patch Kid into his mouth. "Does Via wanna go to the big party and kiss a famous boy?"

Since his crush, Alice, left for college, I've found Eli to have grown obnoxious. He talks too much. I try to be sympathetic—it's an obvious diversion tactic, and he's only trying not to fixate on his heartbreak—but still, it takes every ounce of willpower I have not to offer a snide response to almost anything he does. Ascribe it to friendly competition, I guess, or maybe a general distaste for cockiness. Which is why, in this moment, I decide that there is no way Eli will attend this party before me.

"Yeah," I say. "I think I'll go."

"You don't even know him," he says.

"I will."

"Yeah. For sure. Go ahead and try to break this bond we've shared since sixth grade."

"Maybe I'll go," Maddy says.

The table falls silent, until Brick scoffs: "Hilarious."

"You're the funniest person at this school," Michael says.

"You guys are dicks," Maddy says, and the first period bell rings, and we disperse. Only now, I'm set on befriending Daniel. This challenge is harder than it seems. Tracking him down isn't so difficult, but getting a word in is a real bitch. He's not the most accessible person in the world. He's always surrounded by a clump of listeners. I see people like Maddy attempting to instigate the same friendship, though for a different agenda, of course. She hovers on the outskirts of his crowd, popping in at any gap in conversation. For the most part, however, it seems she's playing it cool. She's familiar with every One Direction fanfiction trope in the book, assuming the cold-blooded in-difference of a Y/N Betty Sue in a Forever 21 skater dress and inked-up Converse.

Eli, on the other hand, is an ass-kisser. It's obnoxious. He stoops. He goes out of his way. Rather than waiting for a break in conversation like Maddy, he dives headfirst, interjecting with an obvious bootlick.

I don't yet feel bad for him. I should. I should pick up on the smaller things—since Alice left, he's upped his Adderall pre-scription, smokes twice as much weed. We're both in the same first-period class, and he comes in late every day. At one time he regarded his theater involvement with a near piety; only now, he still hasn't memorized his lines for this year's role. And he doesn't ever seem to want to hang out anymore.

The biggest clue should be his second Instagram (or spam, or Finsta). It's an adult-free, unfiltered alternative to the (extremely consequential) main account. The username is usually something anonymous and tongue-in-cheek; with the barrier of a privacy setting, you don't have to be afraid to muddy up a grid with a crying selfie or a screenshot of a text conversation. Eli's account has, in recent events, taken a rather drastic turn. What was once a gallery of B-rate memes has veered into bummer territory. He posts black-and-white pictures of the pavement, screenshots of himself listening to sad songs. A better friend would reach out. At the very least, a better friend would see that for Eli, this party might be one of the only things he's had to look forward to in a long time. Unfortunately, I am not a better friend.

* * *

The first time I catch Daniel alone, he's in the black box theater. He's laughing to himself. I scope the room. Nobody's around. It's time. I move in.

"Whatcha looking at?" I say.

"I've been BCC'd on the greatest email chain known to man."

"What's that?"

"The Nickelodeon pedo chain."

"Nickelodeon has a pedo chain?" I don't even know why I'm asking, because *of course* they do.

"Duh."

"Well, what's going on?"

"Hmm," he says, then looks up from his phone. "[XXXXX] was mailed a bag of jizz."

"No way," I say. "My little sister watches her show."

"Imagine receiving a Ziploc bag filled with cum," he says, beholding a mugshot, "from this guy."

I can't believe what I'm seeing. "Is that a . . ."

"A throat tattoo of Abby Lee Miller? Yes."

Right there, on the bump of the suspect's Adam's apple, is a portrait of the *Dance Moms* reality matriarch. Except she's a zombie and her face is melting off.

"Good old Phoenix Sundown." He smiles.

"He's done this before?"

"Oh yeah, he's a classic. He served time with O. J. Simpson. He has a YouTube channel, where he, like, sets mice on fire and shit. He sends stuff to TV kids all the time. Finds their addresses online, I think. I will say, though, that this behavior's a little, uh, heightened. In most circles, a bag of cum makes a far more aggressive statement than a love letter."

"He's probably mad because they canceled [XXXXX]."

"Oh, yeah, for sure," he says dryly, "he's misunderstood. Just a simple stan."

"So when are you getting yours?"

"My bag of cum?"

"Yeah."

He laughs. "Via, right?"

"Yeah."

"I'll keep you updated. If I get a bag, you'll be the first person I tell."

That's how our friendship is sparked. It begins with little check-ins, here and there. "Still nothing," he says at first, passing me in the hallway.

Then we advance to more substantial interactions. He approaches me between classes, during the six-minute passing period, with a new email from the NPC. There's been another delivery from Phoenix Sundown. As the cum bags spread across Southern California, Daniel and I blossom from casual acquaintances to dedicated friends. We share a similar sense of humor. We click. He even starts sitting at my lunch table.

We're all squeezed shoulder-to-shoulder one afternoon when Maddy approaches, flailing her phone around. "You got a write-up," she says. "You got a write-up!"

Daniel's head nearly snaps off his neck. "Huh?"

"Look," she says. I peer over at her open Safari tab, where JUST JARED JR screams at me from a neon blue website banner.

Teen Hollywood Celebrity News and Gossip, it announces. It's MTV for the prepubescent crowd, reporting on tween heart-throbs from all over the map of cultural relevancy. Faces from *Stranger Things* as well as (less familiar) Musical.ly stars flank the article at hand.

And then: there he is. Daniel, last weekend, with his two former costars, [XXXXX] and [XXXXX]. They're in the parking lot of the Topanga mall. They're oblivious to the cameramen. It's a paparazzi photo.

His eyes widen. He scrolls through the page. "I mean, it's weird," he says humbly. "Like, it's a major violation of privacy."

"Totally," Maddy says. "You're an actor. You didn't ask for this kind of attention."

He furrows his brows and looks closer at the photo. "Yeah, that's the nature of the business, though."

"Crazy you're still getting press even after your show was canceled," Brick says.

"Uh-huh," he says slowly. Then a change of subject. "Did I ever tell you guys about the time I went to [XXXXX]'s eighteenth birthday and watched him get a lap dance?"

The lunch table erupts into ambient chatter; the teenybopper celeb in question's Instagram is pulled up and analyzed.

Daniel nudges me. "So here's where it gets really fucked," he says quietly, "and I'm only telling you this."

I take a bite of my sandwich.

"This is really sick, okay?" he says.

"Just say it."

"I kinda want him to send me a jizzbag. Is that so wrong?"

"Yes."

"You know what? Actually, the fact that he hasn't yet honestly hurts my feelings. I'm pissed, Via."

"I mean, it's only natural," I say, "to want to be hot enough to find cum in your mailbox."

"A desire for FedEx jizz is a part of the human condition."

"That could definitely be argued," I say. "A case could be made."

"I feel like I'll get it next, since I was paparazzi'd," he says. "I'm famous enough."

I pause, prepared to move this calculated friendship into phase two. "Maybe Phoenix Sundown will crash this Halloween party everyone's talking about," I say.

He looks at me, curious. "Maybe," he says.

Eli has this childhood tree house he goes to sometimes. It's hidden somewhere in his mother's neighborhood. It's gone through a few transformations over the years—first a playhouse, then a hideout, finally a ramshackle smoke spot. I've never been invited. He takes it very seriously. In fact, he's only brought one friend from his teenage life there, and that was Alice, just a few months ago, right before she stopped talking to him and went to college and fell in love with someone else.

She'd taken a Sharpie and scribbled a quote from a favorite Disney movie on the rafters. Something sentimental, about friendship or believing or growing up. I only know this because of a picture Eli's posted on his spam account, a grainy shot of her careful, prickly writing. It was strategically out-of-focus, and posted without a caption.

Maybe a year ago he would've told me about it in person. We

used to be like that. He'd tell me things about his sisters, or his mom, or school. We clicked because we had more in common with each other than we did with our other friends. Neither of us are from Calabasas, for one thing. When we started ninth grade, neither of us knew anyone or had a reason to be popular automatically. We were expendable. Sometimes I'd pace the upper quad at lunch because I had nowhere to sit. There were a few times I saw him do the same.

We enabled each other to fail in school. Both cursed with a fabulous disinterest in academics, we spent collective hours—days, probably—lying on the floor of the theater lobby not doing our homework. I used to try and press my favorite books on him but he would never read them. A few times he scanned the Shmoop summaries, and that was good enough. We reveled absently in the neutral space where a work ethic should be; we talked about the Internet or made prank calls; we examined old yearbooks and created code names for people we didn't like. We only ever drank together a handful of times, and it was always at parties, where we could separate ourselves from each other and dive into different social groups. We tried to keep our friendship away from anything unorthodox. It felt like everyone else was growing up, but Eli and I were perfectly comfortable playing children with each other.

I don't know where exactly our true-blue communication started waning. It could've been Alice. I guess that's the most obvious answer. The entire school found out they were having "everything but sex," and I, perhaps still in the grips of Catholic lunacy, realized my final link to childhood was about to snap. Maybe. But the truth is, I don't think the answer's that simple. It didn't happen all at once. In fact, the beginning of the end of our friendship happened so slowly I hardly even noticed it. Here and there, we'd miss each other during lunch periods, or we'd forget to walk each other back and forth from rehearsals. Pep rallies came and went, and we didn't text each other to meet outside the bathrooms instead. I found myself forgetting pivotal steps in our elaborate secret handshake. And then entire days would go by, and then weeks, and I never even noticed it because we were still Instagram mutuals and he sometimes liked my tweets. I saw his face all the time, but I didn't know anything about his day-to-day. The Internet has allowed for a kind of closeness without intimacy, a way of claiming a friendship without really knowing much about a person at all. Do you still know someone because you like each other's posts?

It's the Internet's magic word: *connect*. Any social media megalodon cites connection as the single best outcome of the digital age. And yeah, I love that I can talk to anyone at any time. I like that I know where my elementary school best friend is working these days, that I can see what my cousin wore to her junior prom. But social media lets you take for granted the people you see every day. It permits a newfound laziness in friendships. I saw your pic on Instagram, liked it. Task complete.

I hear little updates from others. The cast of the fall play is furious with him because he can't seem to memorize his lines. I catch glimpses of him in the hallway, poring over a ragged copy of the script with desperate fervor. I choose not to interrupt him.

In fact, weeks have passed with little to no interactions until he approaches me—again, in the hour before school starts—with his phone in hand. He wags it in my face. It's Daniel's Twitter, his handle decorated with the coveted blue checkmark. "Got him verified," he says, smug. "Filled out the questionnaire for him and stuff. It took, like, two hours."

"You did that all for him?"

"Yeah."

"Why?"

He jerks his head back. I'm being mean. But I like it. It's been settled—Daniel and I are friends, and Eli's an outsider. When I get older I'll understand that my new attachment to Daniel was perhaps a defense mechanism, a way to distance myself from Eli like how he had done with me while he was seeing Alice. "What do you mean, why?" he says. Offended.

"Just seems like a waste of time. He could've done it himself."

"Yeah, but I'm his friend," he says. "That's what friends do."

"Sure," I answer. "Aren't you failing English, though? Like, shouldn't you be studying?"

"I'm in the middle of a show," he says. "It's show week."

I shrug. I walk past him.

"Bleidner!"

I crane my neck and make eye contact with Cub, beckoning me from across the quad.

"Stunt after school?"

I flash him a thumbs-up.

I invite Daniel along. It's time to bring up the party, and by next weekend I'll have secured a solid TTI to present at all other Halloweens moving forward. We pile into Cub's Civic as soon as school ends and chug up the mountain.

We do it little by little, creepy-crawling only as fast as the

Civic will allow. Cub's on aux. He's playing Chance the Rapper. Cub only ever listens to Chance the Rapper. "*Acid Rap,* man," he says. "One day I'm gonna have sex to this whole entire album."

I watch the sky outside my window. It's almost Halloween but the Valley has not yet broken character. It could still be August. We engage in the usual mundane teenage chatter. Cub tells us about his life's dream. "I'm in college. Maybe, say, like junior year. Four years from now. And it's the big party. First weekend. I'm living in the frat house. I've got the best room. It's connected to the balcony. The party rages below. There's a pool. "Passionfruit" is playing. No. Not "Passionfruit." "Broccoli." And they're chanting my name. 'Cuz I'm, like, social chair. I come out on the balcony and they scream for me. Oh, yeah, we're also all in togas, did I say that?"

"I don't think so," I say.

"Well, we're in togas. That's important. When you picture this I want you to see me in a toga specifically. And I jump off the balcony and crowd-surf over my brothers. And it's, like, peak manhood, peak brotherhood."

We've made it to the top of Stunt. We climb out of the Civic. "Have some," Cub says, passing me his dab pen, "but I'm taking a break."

I've mentioned it before, this "I'm not like other girls" character guideline I've held myself to since starting high school. It's stupid, but high school is survival of the fittest—it's almost impossible to get taken seriously by boys my age unless I suppress the girly parts. I guess I've pulled it off pretty well, since I've noticed I'm not exempt from *guy talk* like some of my other girl friends are. I know everything from Cub's growing list of pursuable women to

Daniel's pornography habits. So I'm not excluded from the next conversation.

"So," Cub says. "Madison Whitney."

"What about her?" Daniel answers.

"Dude, she wants it." Cub flicks his head toward me. "Via, you're a girl. Confirm."

"How would I know?"

"You guys can sense it and stuff, right?" he says.

In my head, I see Maddy, clinging to any airtime she's granted in Daniel's company. I hate that Cub's kind of right. "Yeah, she likes you," I admit.

Daniel shrugs. "She's kind of a butterface."

I think about this word: *butterface*. As in, hot everywhere *but her face*. I've heard it before. Boys use it compulsively, without considering what it might be like for another girl to overhear. There's a twist in my stomach. I know what it feels like to be uncomfortable in my own skin. I wonder if there's a word used for me when I'm not around. I consider telling them that that word sucks ass, but *chillness* is a price you must pay to be a not-like-other-girls kind of girl.

I suck on the pen and fixate on a hawk floating above a rooftop somewhere in the hills below. I'm high. I'm a nice warm piece of butter. I'm having a great time. I'm having a true high school experience, just me and the mountains and the boys. I'm with Cub, I'm with Daniel, and I'm . . . I'm . . . hold on. Wait.

"I swear there's something I was supposed to do today," I say.

"Sucks," Cub says.

"No, I'm serious," I say. Technically, I *could* pull out my phone to check, but that would mean I'd have to reach into my back pocket and unlock it and poke around my calendar and that just sounds like a lot right now. I resort to leaning back on the side of the Civic. "Fuck, I'm high," I surrender.

"Riiiide it out, man," Cub says.

I'd wanted to mention the Halloween party to Daniel. But now, I don't feel like bringing it up. I don't even think I want to go, really. My only motivation was to keep Eli from going, which is murky, admittedly. What's the worst that could happen, anyway? He'd make new friends? Hook up with someone famous? Why do I care, anyway? It's just Eli. Eli. No, there was something besides the Halloween party that I'd forgotten. Something that had to do . . . with Eli. Shit. What was it? I rack my brain. I stare at my shoes and press my fingers to my temples.

"Uh-oh," Cub says. "Man down."

Across the mountains, the hawk dives into the canyon like a toga bro belly-flopping into a fraternity pool.

I forgot about Eli's play.

I don't say anything right away. He doesn't either. I test the waters and reply to something he says about it on Twitter. He doesn't answer. I send a text and I'm left on read.

For community service hours, I volunteer to help strike the fall play on Monday evening. I hear it was a moderate success. No sellouts or anything, but a much better turnout than the cast had expected. Mr. Purcell sends me off with a broom and instructs me to sweep the stage. I oblige.

It's pitch-black in the wings of the theater. My fingertips fumble along the wall, searching for a light.

"I got it," I hear. It's Eli, coming from the other side. I can barely make out his silhouette in the dark. He flips a switch and blue guide lights flicker on in the wings. He's holding a garbage bag of discarded tape. Face buried in his phone, he starts to walk away.

"Wait," I say. "Hey."

He drops his arm. "Hey."

I can't see his face, just his outline. I can't tell if he's looking back at me.

"Purcell's making me sweep," I say. The key to a successful strike is to figure out how to do the least amount of work possible without losing community service hours. "Forgot to walk with purpose."

"Oh, so you remember who I am now?" he says, curt.

"Funny."

"I'm serious."

I sweep up a dust bunny. He kneels on the floor and goes back to his job, pulling up old stage tape.

"Can I throw this in your trash bag?" I ask.

"I guess," he says.

For ten minutes we do our chores in silence. Mr. Purcell comes in to check on us. A couple of stray volunteers pass through. Someone in the building turns on the sound system and plays something vaguely familiar. I think it's an Anderson .Paak song. I don't know it very well but I focus my entire brain on it, like if I think hard enough about the lyrics or the beat, Eli will just go away and I won't have to feel guilty about anything ever again.

"Cassie's into me," he says, breaking the quiet.

"Oh, cool."

"Yeah," he says, "we've been hooking up, too." Cassie Forster's cool. Star of the a cappella program. She's crazy smart, too. I've never seen her cheat on her homework, yet she manages to keep a 4.0. She and Maddy are close friends.

"You're over Alice?" I say, casual.

He yanks up a strip of tape in one long piece. "I don't really think about her anymore."

"Oh, gotcha."

"Except Cassie wants to be serious," he says, "or something like that."

"Why not? She's nice."

"Yeah, she's really nice."

I walk over and dump a dustpan into his bag.

"I don't think I want to, though," he says. "We can't just, like, talk to each other."

"What do you mean?"

"It's a trust thing, I guess," he says. "Like I used to be able to tell you anything and it was fine, you know? But I always know that whatever I tell Cassie isn't really secret. Or special. Because she tells everything to Maddy."

"Used to?" I step back.

"But she came to see me, and that's important," he presses. "Because I was looking forward to her coming to my show, and she did. She doesn't flake on stuff and she means what she says. So I'm thinking that maybe all that other stuff doesn't matter as much anyway, because she cares."

When you're a self-determined outsider, it's hard to believe it's within your capacity to hurt someone. Eli's more popular than me, goes to more parties. He has the upper hand. Girls call him cute. I'd thought there was nothing I could say that would make him less cool, less personable, less likable.

"Yeah, that's good," I say.

He stands up and looks at me in disbelief, a tail of blue tape trailing off his finger. "It's fucked," he says. "Okay? You didn't even come to see me. I waited for you after the show and you didn't even come."

"I forgot, okay? I've seen everything else you've been in."

"Yeah, but."

"But what?"

"It doesn't matter," he says. "Forget it."

"What?"

"You took it too far. You and Daniel are, like, best friends now. And that's great. But we haven't talked in a while. Like—"

Approaching footsteps. He kneels back down to feign dedication to his task and I hold the broom like I'm mid-sweep. It's Mr. Purcell. "Pizza in the green room," he says. I respond with a thumbs-up and he leaves again.

"We're not best friends anymore. And it sucks." He jams the tape in the bag. "Do you like him or something?"

"Daniel? Absolutely not." The word *butterface* ripples through my brain.

"I know you better than anyone, Via. You do."

"Never in a million years."

"Well good, because he's a shitbag," he says. "It's, like, super obvious to everyone except you, apparently, that he's a huge dick."

"He's not that bad."

"We would've made jokes about him last year."

"That's mean."

"No, you know what's mean?" he says. "You. You're being an asshole. So if you aren't into him, then the only reason you're hanging out with him is so you can go to this stupid party. And the only reason you want to go to this party is so that I can't. Which is weird. Why can't we just be normal? For like five seconds."

I don't know what to say. This feud I've manufactured has been ongoing for over a month now, and fair enough—I'm beginning to forget my motivations.

"You're selfish," he says. "You're the most selfish person I know."

He waits for me to say something. A stage manager peeks his head into the theater. "Pizza in the—"

"Green room, we know," Eli interrupts, and looks back at me. "Well?"

"It's really not that big of a deal," I say. "It was just a joke."

"Is that it?"

I shrug. "Yeah."

"Fuck off, Via," he says, and walks past me.

For breakfast the next morning I have an apple at home. Usually I eat hash browns or toast in the car, but lately I've been feeling weird about it because of the way the Freeze Your Fat billboard girl's eyes follow me like a trick painting. Today, even though I've skipped the carbs, it still seems like she's watching me. She's even got an eyebrow raised. It would make sense that she's inquisitive. Because pressed between my legs is a little jar of turquoise paint and a wooden paintbrush.

The first thing I do when I get on campus is find Daniel. He sits on top of a lunch table, relaying a Nickelodeon anecdote to a group of avid listeners. I can't hear him but I assume it must be hilarious by the way everyone's laughing. He notices me and nods in my direction.

I don't have a problem interrupting anymore, now that we're friends. "Daniel," I say, "I wanted to talk to you about the Halloween party this weekend."

He hops off the table. "One sec," he tells his fans. Maddy looks at me curiously. I feel sort of queasy seeing her, now that I know what Daniel said. Like I'm in on a cruel joke that I want no part in.

We walk away from the table. He starts. "Okay, I was gonna bring it up too. It's complicated. Because it would be fun to bring you. Making fun of everyone, and stuff. But," he says, adjusting his glasses, "I, uh, promised Eli a while ago that I'd take him. Before you and I were friends. But I was thinking, you know, we could always talk to him, right?"

I imagine myself sharing posh giggles with the cast of [XXXXX]. It's nice to entertain. I could rack up blue check follows on Instagram. Maybe I could even blow up on Twitter. It's tempting. It really is.

But when you know you have to make things right with a friend you've slighted, well, good luck, Charlie.

"No, I think you should take him," I say. "I have plans anyway."

"Oh." He opens and closes his mouth. "Chill. That makes it a lot easier. Didn't wanna have to back out on Eli."

"Yeah, of course," I say. "Cool, then."

I feel better.

* * *

Eli is late to class again. While I wait for him to arrive, I tuck my knees under my chin and check my phone. One of my group chats is blowing up. Someone's sent a link to a *Just Jared Jr* article.

"*[XXXXX]* Spinoff Announced," it says. "Read All the Behind-the-Scenes Here!"

I skim the article. Daniel's name is nowhere to be found. In fact, every single one of his costars has been recast on the spinoff. Except him.

I read a little more; the show started preproduction early this year, and the cast was reunited this summer. Which means Daniel's known about all this since he started at CHS. All of the friends he's been name-dropping since his first day were rehired. And Daniel was left behind.

I realize that maybe all that stuff about wanting a jizzbag was less of a joke than I'd thought. A bag of semen in his mailbox would at least solidify his foothold in the Nickelodeon sphere. When that cum never came, it broke the last link he had to child stardom. Sick irony, but that's showbiz, baby.

Five minutes late, Eli walks into the classroom. He sits at his assigned desk across from me and promptly tends to his phone.

"Hey," I say softly. "Hey, I'm not going to Daniel's party. I asked but he wanted to take you."

He looks up for a second, then back down. "Okay."

"And also, I got you something." I reach in my backpack and pass him the jar of paint. "I, um, saw your post and I figured your tree house might need a paint job."

He inspects the color.

"I picked it out and everything," I say. "At Home Depot."

He doesn't say anything.

"I'm sorry, Eli," I say. "I've been a dick."

"Yeah, no shit."

"But I miss you."

Our teacher starts calling attendance.

"It's a nice color," he says. "Blue."

"Sea of Tranquility, actually," I say. "Very opaque. Should cover Sharpie."

He looks down. "I miss you too."

"Friends?" I hand him the paintbrush.

He takes it. "Friends," he says back.

On Halloween night, I take Jackie trick-or-treating. She's dressed as Raggedy Ann. She slings her candy around in a Hello Kitty pillowcase. I remember all the best houses from my trick-or-treating days, so we know where to get the king-size bars.

When we get home, Jackie empties her sack on the living room floor and I help her sort it. She likes to categorize things by size, color, and preference. I try to convince her to give me a Milky Way but she says absolutely not.

I pout. "Pretty please?"

She rolls her eyes. "Mooch," she says, and tosses me a Tootsie Roll from her bottom-tier pile. "That's all you get."

Then we watch TV and Jackie makes a big show of eating all the Milky Ways in front of me. Nickelodeon is playing [XXXXX] reruns. I've never actually seen an episode before. We turn it on for ten minutes.

"This show is trash," Jackie says.

I Can't Hang

"Let's go to the graveyard," Paige says, and so we start driving toward the cemetery, for no particular reason other than that Paige has named the graveyard as a potential destination and we have nowhere else to be on a Wednesday night in the summertime.

Cory drives a white Mitsubishi. A mom car. We've all joked about it because it's so unfitting. Something about Cory's demeanor says *I Brake for Bernie,* but the Mitsubishi screams *I'm a Maxxinista.* And so, the image is ridiculous, his six-foot-something frame tangled up in a 1999 working mother's dream car. Cuffed pant leg, propped against the center console. Sharpie'd Chucks, hovering over the brake pedal. You could take a picture and put it in textbooks in sixty years, presented as the perfect marriage of dueling cultures: soccer mom and teenage grunge, united, if only for once, in the name of reasonable gas mileage and easy-to-clean gray pleather interiors.

We're sitting like this: Cory in the driver's seat, me in shotgun, Paige in the center back seat. Paige works on stage crew. She hikes. Keeps essential peppermint oil on her person. Her religion is that of full moons and natal charts. She sits unbuckled, leaning forward, her hands clutching the backs of our headrests. It's long past midnight. Outside the car window is the splinter moon and a few miles of the Santa Monica Mountains. Cory's Apple Maps spits muffled recalculations from the cup holders.

At the graveyard, the Mitsubishi pins light to the wrought-iron gate, casting shadows on the headstones. It's small, the cemetery—just an old eucalyptus tree, a cluster of stone markers, some crawling ivy. Nobody gets out of the car. Paige yawns and collapses back into her seat. We came, we saw, we conquered. Cory puts the car in reverse, I make some dumb joke, and we're out of there, flying from the mountains into Van Nuys because we want to see if we can get into an eighteen-and-up strip club. This is how it goes in the Valley. The second that you sacrifice your stepdad's chicken parm in favor of Ventura Boulevard, you have to make your own fun or else you'll end up sitting on the kiddie swings for three hours like every other lazy weekend.

But first, Paige wants a Coke, so I ask Siri to take us to a drive-thru and we're delivered unto His Holiness, the Almighty Strip Mall. The storefronts are dark, hollow—save for one half-drained fluorescent light, tweaking above a mannequin in the window of a budget wedding salon. An old plastic bag scuttles like a crab across cracked pavement. On the edge of the parking lot, a dozen yards or so from the line of stores, sits a McDonald's, reeking of grease. OPEN 24 HOURS, a sign reads. BREAKFAST ALL DAY.

Paige gets a Coke and I get a Diet Coke and Cory gets a Sprite and then we drive to the strip club, which is nothing but pulsing pink lights, seriously, pink is emanating from every pore of the building and it's throwing a Pepto-Bismol wash over everything within a twenty-yard radius. I make a joke about how we all look like gingers now, which is funny because both Cory and Paige happen to be redheads, and Cory argues that Paige is strawberry blond and therefore is not accepted into the ginger community, and then Paige pleads honorary status and Cory is about to say no when suddenly we're at the front of the line and it's time to show the bouncer our identification.

Cory's first. The bouncer barely glances at his ID before he opens the velvet rope. "Have a good time," the guy says, and then Paige hands him her driver's license and the velvet rope opens again. I fish my high school ID out of my pocket. The velvet rope stays closed. "Yeah, right," the bouncer says, and we walk away, but not before Cory calls me a dumbass and I don't have to look over at him to know he's just messing.

We stay parked, Fun Dip pink, across the street from the strip club, trying to think of something to do next. I smoke Paige's weed and blow smoke out the passenger seat window. From the car in front of us, a stripper emerges, her hair pinned in rollers, a dark brown coat draped over her shoulders. She looks at her phone and crosses in front of our car. And then, shrugging her duffel bag to a more comfortable position on her arm, the dancer loses her balance, flailing her elbows all about, wiggling and wobbling toward the ground. She's going to fall. But in the nick of time, she skims her hand over the top of the Mitsubishi— thin, manicured fingers jittering over the hood of the car like a gnat trapped in a Mason jar—and she's saved, it's a miracle, her balance is regained and everything's well and good and fine. And it's in this moment, as she's righting herself, that she looks through our windshield for a single moment in time—a split, teensy-tiny, barely noticeable, universe-altering millisecond, the kind of look that you could miss if you weren't watching carefully. Cory's slurping his empty Sprite out of the straw when all of this happens. The dancer adjusts her duffel bag and crosses the street to the club, absorbing into all the pink froth, and I think that what might have happened is that Cory looked up at just the right second and made eye contact with the girl, that maybe when she looked up after she tripped it was Cory she was looking at, and now things have changed. Moment of silence in the car. I'm like, "Cory just had his sexual awakening," and Cory's like, "No, Via, I'm never having a sexual awakening, I want to be a virgin for life, just like you." And then: Denny's.

Because it was Paige's idea, I make her order first when the waiter comes to our table. She flips through the plastic menu and tells the waiter that she'll have an Oreo milkshake with peanut butter drizzle. I'll have the mashed potatoes. Cory gets fries and a root beer float.

The patrons at the Van Nuys Denny's don't talk. It's like in old Westerns, when the bright-eyed sheriff makes his entrance at the local saloon. We've been pinned as out-of-towners. I narrow my eyes, squinting over the vinyl seats and diner lamps, over the clinking coffee cups and angel food cake and sticky packets of Smucker's grape jelly. It smells like burnt toast in here. I take an inventory of all the night customers. Two people by the counter. Two at the tables. Three at the booths. Each of them all by themselves. A man in a Metallica shirt is husking over a turkey dinner, sloshing gravy over his vegetables.

I eat my mashed potatoes plain and Cory dips his french fries in honey mustard and Paige holds the end of her straw to trap the shake and bring it to her mouth. We talk about ayahuasca, the strongest hallucinogenic substance in the world. You can only get it from shamans in Peru, and before the trip starts, you gotta shit your pants and puke everywhere for two hours. Paige says she'd never do it, not even for, like, a thousand dollars and Cory asks: what's the harm in shitting your pants every once in a while?

We leave, and Cory says he wants to go to some kickback in the Valley. Paige says sure, if she can smoke free weed. *Good night, Van Nuys,* I think to myself, as the Mitsubishi climbs the freeway ramp. On the drive over, Paige tells us that she got ordained on the Internet last week and she's licensed to perform marriages. So, to pass the time, Cory and I exchange marriage vows on the 101 Freeway.

The party's in a gated community that I've never heard of before. I'm dubious. These are Cory's *other* friends, ones whose names I've only ever heard in tangents. They only exist in speech bubbles or sidebars. He comes from a *slightly* different social group, one with connections at our district rival, Agoura High School.

We roll into the driveway. This house is huge, a blurry mess of spiral staircases and sconces and tiered balconies and mismatched shutters. Cory leads us around the gate, and Paige and I make faces at each other because we can feel the bass vibrating against our ribs. This is a lot of volume for the proposed kickback.

A drunken fourteen-year-old boy shoves past us and hurls into a bush, his left hand clenching the neck of a bottle of Kirkland vodka. "Oh, fuck, what did we just walk into," Cory says, and we freeze as the kickback comes into full view: only it's a swarm of high school freshmen, drunk, making out and being stupid. I can smell the desperation (Axe Body Spray in the scent Anarchy) from here.

"Duuude," Paige groans.

Cory guides us through the backyard to his of-age friends, all sitting around the fire pit. I recognize some of them from Instagram. I'm introduced to the owner of the house, a girl named Lani. "Please excuse my little sister's stupid friends," she says, gesturing at the spectacle of freshmen trying to mosh on the trampoline.

Cory leaves to pee. I sit down next to some girl with her hair tied in a scrunchie. I try to say hello, but she's talking to someone else. So, I scroll through my feeds. Pretend to text. Read a Snapchat *Daily Mail* article about Ariel Winter's short-shorts. I get the same feeling as I did back in the Denny's. Like I'm the lone sheriff in a place where everyone knows everyone.

God must've heard my prayers because all of a sudden the bong's in my lap, and I'm inhaling, and someone goes, *Lani, your mom is literally the best.* And then Scrunchie Girl turns around and I'm coughing, not because of the rip but because that's definitely *not* an eighteen-year-old, or even a twenty-year-old, in fact, this is a forty-year-old mom, and everyone's just casually been hitting this bong and puking in bushes in front of her for the last hour.

"Don't worry," someone near me says. "She's cool."

I pass the bong to Paige. Immediately, I know something's off. I turn to warn her, but she's already exhaling. "What the hell," she whispers to me, after a minute. "This is not . . ."

My own heartbeat rings in my ears. "What did we just smoke," I say.

She yanks my arm and pulls me inside the mansion. I feel like I'm running underwater. We find an empty bathroom, a room of marble, and she locks the door behind us. "Where's Cory?" I ask.

"He's still in the other bathroom, probably shitting his dick off," she says. "Look down."

The sink is filled—I mean *really* filled—with vomit. I'm too high to react. "I think that stuff was laced," I say.

"I'm freaking out," Paige says. "I feel so weird."

I sit down on the lid of the toilet and stretch my legs out across the tile. Shit's weird.

"Dude," Paige says, "look at this stuff." The countertop is covered with prescription bottles. Three or four lonely pills sit on the soap dish. She examines the label on a bottle. "I seriously can't read this right now," she says. "I'm out of my mind."

I text Cory: *where tf r u.*

"Via," Paige says, "let's take something."

"What? I'm not stealing some rando's drugs," I say.

"She won't notice. She's so rich," she says. "Plus she deals." She shakes a couple pills from a bottle into her palm and tosses the rest to me.

"Jesus," I protest.

Someone knocks on the door.

"Hurry," Paige says.

"I can't, I—"

"I GOTTA PISS," someone says, and hammers twice as hard on the door.

"*Via,*" says Paige. I take a couple pills and jam them into my pocket. Paige opens the door, and whaddayaknow, we're face-to-face with Lani, the owner of the house. Paige and I look at each other, panicked, and dodge out of the way.

"Who the fuck yakked in my sink?" she says.

"Get Cory," I say. Before Lani can turn around and accuse us, we hightail it across the house, jiggling on random doorknobs until we locate Cory's bathroom.

"Occupied," Cory calls.

"We're leaving," calls Paige. "We gotta go."

"I'm literally mid-shit," says Cory.

"Hurry up," I say. "You've been in there for, like, a half hour."

Paige pauses her knocking and looks at me. "Cory has IBS but he refuses to admit it," she says seriously. "He's literally always shitting."

"I can hear you guys," Cory says. "Like every word." Then: a flush, and a running sink, and he opens the door. "What's wrong with you?"

"We have to go," Paige says. "I think that weed was laced with something."

"I'm ascending to another dimension," I say. "I know all the secrets of the universe. Ask me."

"I doubt that," Cory says. "Alright, let me say goodbye first."

"No," says Paige. "Please. Let's just dip."

The three of us split, Paige and I taking the lead with Cory dragging behind. The pills burn a hole in my butt pocket. We march down the huge driveway and get into the car. "Do you guys think there's a God?" I say.

Cory rolls his eyes. He turns the key in the ignition and maneuvers out of the gated community. Paige and I are too schlonked to go home yet, so we head to the beach.

The winds are high at Zuma tonight. When I step out of the car and into the sand, the chill bites through my shoes and socks and into my bones. The ocean rumbles, a thousand bowling balls. It's so dark that I can't tell how close or how far away the surf is. In the distance, Malibu mansions gloat, pinpoints of light scattered along the cliffs.

"This sucks," Paige says.

"Yeah, I forgot how dark it gets," I say. "When it's dark out, you know. Colors of the universe. All the stars. They join in song."

"Thanks for the TED talk," Cory says.

Our next destination is Universal Studios CityWalk. We park where it's free and take the rickety old trolley up the hill to the strip. The electricity is still running; the lights above Popcornopolis flicker, the Hard Rock Cafe halogens hiss. But CityWalk itself is a ghost town. Even the indoor skydiving tube is lonely, and I'm realizing that the three of us—Paige, Cory, and I— just might be the last three people in the world, just us and the neon BUBBA GUMP sign and the tinny schlock wavering in and out of the Universal Studios park-wide speaker system, faint and echoed. I'm finally beginning to feel normal again.

In the mood for some more mischief, we park outside a 7-Eleven and take to the age-old ritual: the prank call. Tonight's target is the guy who works at two different school libraries— one at CHS, another at a campus across the Valley. Mr. Warhol. He's short, squat, and balding. He claims to be related to the famous Warhol but refuses to answer any further questions pertaining to the matter. Through repeated stalkings of his Facebook page, we've deduced that he's a regular at the Renaissance Faire. He's strict and he's mean, and he hands out far too many dress code violations to the girls, so we don't feel bad ringing him at this hour.

We call him from Paige's phone, restricting the number. Cory takes the lead. He clears his throat, puts on an unidentifiable accent. "Is this Mr. David Warhol?" he asks.

"Who am I speaking to? It's late," the voice answers.

"I'm Carl Bacon and I'm here with my assistant, Amy, um, Adams."

Amy Adams? I mouth at him. Cory grins and puts a finger to his lips. He shoves the phone toward me. "Hi, um, we're representatives from Korky Plungers, and—"

"Take me off your call list." He hangs up.

"I literally hate this guy," Paige says. "He's the only person alive who can make prank calling lame." She sits back in her seat and pops her gum. "Bet he's a Virgo sun. Aries moon."

"Call again," I say. Cory does.

"Hello?"

"Hi, Mr. Warhol," Cory says. "We're calling to follow up on your recent bulk order of super-deluxe, heavy-duty plunging appliances."

"I'm not interested." Once again, a dial tone. I look out the window at 7-Eleven. A Slurpee machine chatters at me.

Paige scoffs. "Dick."

"One more time," I egg.

This time, he picks up before the phone even rings once. "What?"

"How are our plungers working with your massive dumps?" Cory says.

"Who is this? Give me your names. I'm tracing this call and I'm going to the police. This is harassment."

Cory fumbles with the phone.

"Hang *up*," Paige says.

"No shit, I'm *trying*," he answers. Then there's a beep. "Oh, fuck," he says, looking over at me. "Ohmanohmanohmanohman."

"Bluffing," I say. "He's bluffing. Nobody actually calls the cops over a prank call."

"My cousin's friend's mom did," says Paige. Paige always knows somebody who knows somebody who did something relevant. She's probably the most well-connected girl in the Valley. She's even three degrees of separation from Charles Manson.

"It's a waste of police time," I say.

"Fuck twelve," says Cory.

"Speaking of, I gotta get home." Paige takes her phone back. "If he does narc, there's nothing we can do about it now."

In a week from now, the news will circulate back to Calabasas High: that Mr. Warhol received a thread of prank phone calls and accused our rival school of making them. They'll have to attend an assembly on harassment and stalking, and certain students will have to pen letters of apology to the guy. The three of us will take a vow of silence never to speak of it again, and I will hide the stolen pills (high-dose extended release Adderall, as a Google search shall reveal) in my retainer case, where they will remain—that is, until college exams.

Cory drops Paige off at home first, then me. Next time we'll go bowling, or maybe we'll hit the arcade, or maybe we'll get burritos and dangle our legs over the 101 Freeway overpass. I squeeze some saline drops in my eyes and pop in a piece of gum. "Sorry I didn't have ID for the strip club," I say.

"Bring your passport next time," he says. "Valley's huge."

The Big Fuck You

"Christ," says George. It's a gloomy afternoon in the Valley. We're in cheap metal chairs, watching the cars go by on Ventura Boulevard from the side patio of the Woodland Hills Fatburger. We as in: George McCloskey, Eli Fisher, Cub Birnwick, and me. There's a twelve-year-old kid licking ketchup off his fingers a couple of tables away, but aside from that, we're alone. An unlit hand-rolled cigarette dangles between George's index and middle fingers. The whole scene smells like damp pavement and stale tobacco and grease.

"Christ *what*?" says Cub. There's unexplained animosity between the two. Maybe it's a clashing of the clowns. Who knows.

"It's damn beautiful today."

Cub frowns. It is most certainly *not* a beautiful day, at least in any conventional sense. "It's gonna rain."

"Come on, man," George says, "every day's beautiful when you're at Fatburger." He winks. Cub scowls. Someone across the way trips on a parking block trying to carry a bag of takeout from the deli next door.

My companions are eating cheeseburgers and Maui-banana milkshakes. I'm having a Diet Coke. It's 2 p.m. on a Wednesday. At George's request, we cut out of school early. "I'd hang right after school, but I have work at three-thirty," he said. George works at a local pizza dive. He sends us regular snaps of his creations: hunks of ungrated cheese, stacks of pepperoni, peculiar combinations of fruit and sauce slapped together on a thick crust of whole wheat. "Don't worry about it," he promises us, "I always use Purell after the bathroom."

He scooted us here in his vintage Chevrolet and almost killed us twice. The car drives like a tin can but it looks cool as hell. Forest green with white accents. He's been trying to sell it for as long as I've known him, but the Craigslist deals always seem to fall through. "Everyone's so flaky these days," he complained on the drive over, veering into the next lane and almost ramming into a US Foods truck.

It was Eli who found George. Two weeks ago, he'd approached me during a passing period and grabbed me by the shoulders. "McCloskey," he'd said. "Our fourth. George McCloskey."

So here's what we're doing. At the end of every year, the student body elects a new set of ASB representatives, most notably KYOTV: a group of four rising senior filmmakers whose job it is to release monthly episodes covering school news. They're the face of Calabasas High, and the lucky seniors earn an evergreen excuse to skip class and automatic priority with all school events. Also. Everyone knows who you are.

You're supposed to audition in groups of four. Since Cub makes us laugh, Eli and I decided to recruit him first. And then, Eli introduced us to George McCloskey, the stoner bizarro from his math class. George is an enigma. Every outfit he wears is some variant of the same uniform. Reflector sunglasses. Hawaiian dad shirt. Cuffed brown Dickies. He rolls his own cigarettes with tobacco he acquires from a plug somewhere in Van Nuys. Though he's an LA native, his voice is somehow devoid of any Valley inflection. And he's almost never on his phone. It's like he comes from a different time. To hear him suddenly swank a transatlantic accent wouldn't catch anyone by surprise.

Anyway, this is our first unofficial group meeting. We have one month before our audition tape is due. And lucky us, we're running unopposed. Last month, Eli made sure everyone knew of our candidacy, spreading the news by way of a couple of dance team girls. He exaggerated our progress, too. Scared off the competition.

"Now listen up," George says. "This is basically a courtesy thing. We've got it in the bag. No one else is going for it."

"Why are you taking the lead here? You were the last one to join," says Cub.

Eli kicks me under the table. The two of us have become the rational ones of the enterprise. We communicate through a secret code of side-eyes and elbow nudges.

"'Cuz I have a natural-born leadership," says George. "As I was saying, we—"

"We have thirty-three days to make the greatest KYOTV audition tape of all time," says Cub. "We can't slack off on this."

George whips off his sunglasses. "Birnwick, I can't *stand* that attitude."

"I kind of agree with Cub here," Eli says. "We don't wanna half-ass it."

"Look, we've already got everything we need. All the moving parts. We've got the brains. That's me. We've got the pretty boy. That's Eli. And we've got the boobs."

"I resent that," I say.

"Wasn't talking about you," George says.

Cub grunts. "Fuck off."

George puts his cigarette down and picks up a french fry instead. "Step one. Put a tape together, whatever. Step two. Win. Step three. Buy a van."

"What's the—"

"Step four, Cub my darling, is that we take this van to tail-gates. Grill hot dogs, pass out T-shirts, the whole shebang. And then we take a trip to the mountains in it and do every single drug we can find."

I consider my evening at Lani's house and squish a ketchup packet onto a napkin. "This is your brain on drugs."

"Alright, Via, we'll all do horse tranquilizers and you can read a book or something." He holds the fry up where the cigarette once was and slowly burrows a hole through its length. "Just kidding. Maybe. But that's the plan. Make good tape, drugs in van." We observe, careful students in the School of George, as he holds a lighter up to the french fry and inhales at the other end. He wretches and coughs, spattering little bits of potato all over the table.

"The brains," Cub says, and folds his arms.

* * *

It's no surprise that Cub's time with us is limited.

Because when the rest of us goof off, Cub gives us the stick. "Stop, you guys," he says, over and over and over again. He's the disciplinarian. Every group's gotta have one. Trouble is, being the boss is mutually inclusive with being the butt of the joke. It starts during lunch one day when he launches into a story and prefaces it with, "you know keg stands" and we're all like "yes" and he's like "you know, when people do handstands on top of beer kegs and chug?" and we're like "Jesus, Cub, we all just said we know what a keg stand is." And so it becomes a thing, overexplaining stuff just to piss him off. I say, "Cub, pass me a pencil. You know, the thing that is yellow and writes and you can also erase?" Or Eli says, "Hey Cub, where's the bathroom? You know, that place where you pee," and George chimes in with "that bodily process where you dispel of waste through your pee pee," and Cub starts yelling at all of us and storms out of the room.

It's the prelude for Cub's great tantrum. Late afternoon. We're about to start filming a sketch at my house. Eli's bringing his camera equipment and George is late because he's having lunch with his mom. So we enlist Cub to run to the dollar store and grab the only prop we need for the scene: the children's game of jacks. It's fifteen minutes before shooting time when he hits the group chat with a wall of text.

CUB

> no. im not getting the jacks. you're all taking this as a joke.
>
> you should have the jacks already. i'm everyone's bitch. it's
>
> always 'cub, do this' and 'cub, do that.' you all wanna ride

in my civic. how come we never go anywhere in george's prius? Or his chevy? he has two fuckin cars. you guys are always smoking my weed, trying to hang out in my car. and then you bitch me around. well guess what. not anymore. fuck you guys. i'm leaving this group.

GEORGE

did u workshop this in ur notes app

ELI

what the hell george you have two cars?

GEORGE

¯_(ツ)_/¯

ELI

seriously cub. you can't drop. the tape is due in two weeks.

CUB

beg me. tell me you'll quit with the "classic birnwick" jokes. no more with the overexplaining stuff. i have opinions and i'm more experienced in comedy than any of you. i demand respect. so. beg me.

Of course, no group chat stands alone. There's always whittled-down spinoffs. If you don't know what I'm talking about, and all

your group chats seem to exist in a vacuum, well, then I hate to
be the bearer of bad news.

I refer to our second group chat, the one sans Cub. George
is furious.

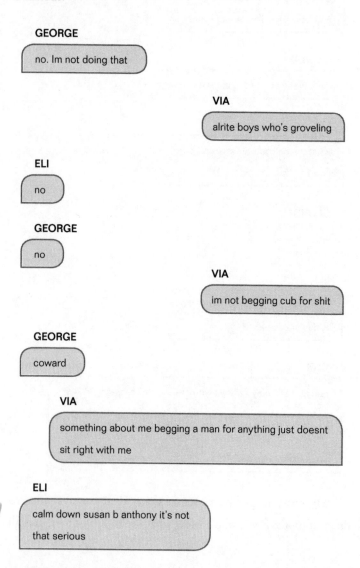

GEORGE
no. Im not doing that

VIA
alrite boys who's groveling

ELI
no

GEORGE
no

VIA
im not begging cub for shit

GEORGE
coward

VIA
something about me begging a man for anything just doesnt
sit right with me

ELI
calm down susan b anthony it's not
that serious

GEORGE

eli you do it

ELI

no u

GEORGE

i would rather eat dirt

ELI

ok. you all owe me for this

Commotion percolates in the first group chat, where Eli's written up an apology.

ELI

cub, we need you. you're really funny and we'll fall apart without you. please come back, we'll give you more respect. you're the best, dude.

CUB

alright. I'll stay in the group

VIA

thank god

CUB

but fuck your jacks

GEORGE

fuck em

CUB

and you guys gotta stop taking me for granite.

It could've been autocorrect. I pray it's autocorrect. I wait a minute. Then another. But Cub doesn't correct himself.

CUB

hello? are you seriously ignoring me after all this

VIA

did u mean to send that

CUB

yeah, no duh. ive been taken for granite since day one

GEORGE

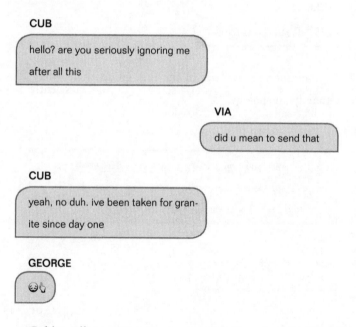

Cub's spelling error is a great cruelty. Few times in life will a punchline ever lay itself out so gracefully. It's a real *water, water, everywhere* type of situation. We've just talked him off the ledge—we can't undo it all for the sake of a joke. I pray that George and Eli are making the same decision, wherever they are.

SUPPRESS UR INSTINCTS, I send to the second group chat. Nobody responds.

And then my doorbell rings. It's George and Eli, their arms full with recording equipment. They don't say anything. They just walk right past me and into my kitchen.

"Where's Birnwick?" asks George.

"Not here yet," I say. They take seats at my dining table. There is an undeniably mischievous gleam in George's eye. "Don't," I warn.

"Olivia," George says, "what in heaven's name are you talking about?"

And then I hear it: the telltale lock beep of a Honda Civic. Cub's walking up my driveway. Eli perks up. "I know what you're thinking," I hiss through my teeth. He shrugs innocently. Cub raps his knuckles on my front door.

"He's here, V," Eli says.

"Yeah, I know."

"Aren't you gonna let him in?"

"Yeah," I say, narrowing my eyes. I see Cub's outline through the frosted windows of my front door. His Air Jordans. His Snapback, positioned at the very top of his head. I turn the doorknob and let him in. "Really glad you changed your mind," I offer.

"Yeah, well, you begged me, so."

We pull out our scripts and Eli sets up the camera on a tripod. Cub runs through his lines, rehearsing them over and over with emphasis on a different word each time like a true *artiste.* And then we start rolling.

It soon becomes clear that something's off. Our script is terrible. Our acting is atrocious. Every joke falls flat. The scene makes

no sense. There's no chemistry. Eli and George are uncharacter-
istically wordless, and Cub is still basking in his own righteousness. Halfway through, George leans back in his chair and tosses
his script aside. "I'm thirsty," he says. "Need a refreshment."

"Same," I say. "I'll grab some water."

I head to the sink, paying close attention to the table in my
periphery. *Please don't provoke Cub,* I try to communicate tele-
pathically.

I come back in the room, arms full of cups. Cub's playing
Flappy Bird on his phone (after the game was removed from the
App Store, Cub refused to delete it, swearing he could make big
bucks selling his device on eBay). Eli and George stare at each
other from across the table. There's something going on. I hand
the waters out.

George takes a long slurp, then wipes his mouth with the
back of his hand. He speaks: "You know, once again, Birnwick, I
want to give you an apology."

"Thanks, man," Cub says.

"Yeah," Eli says, smiling. "I'm sorry that we took you for
granite."

I close my eyes. Here it comes.

"You know," George begins, his face still and grave, "that
thing that you put on countertops for a sleek modern touch to
your kitchen decor?"

And so, Cub quits. This time, we don't push for him to stay. Com-
patibility is an important factor in all relationships, including professional ones, so we know that this conscious un-quadrupling is
better for us in the long run. And it is. We finish our audition

tape, all ten minutes of it, and it's a sight to behold. Eli did the editing. It looks professional. It starts with a reenactment of the *Saturday Night Live* opening, only it's the three of us offering sly grins from Calabasas hotspots: there I am, in front of the movie theater in the Commons. There's George, leaning against his vintage Chevy in a parking lot outside Golden Spoon. And then Eli, walking through the automatic doors of the Gelson's down the street from school. The remainder of the video is a perfect balance of comedy sketches and montages of goings-on at the school. It's a great tape. It's far, far better than the ones uploaded to YouTube from past years. We've got it in the bag. All we need to do is ace the interview.

In the hours before the meeting, the three of us journey to George's house, skipping class once again for the sweet sanctitude of the Chevy's classic interior. He swerves into the driveway. "Pardon the mess," George says, opening his front door. "My castle."

His house, a small one-story near the middle school, has an open floor plan. Very modern. There isn't much furniture, and hardly any art, except for a giant mural of a naked woman above his sofa. He leads us to his dining room. "Let's discuss," he says, cleaning off the kitchen table. He rummages through a cabinet and procures a sack off flour. "Move your hands."

Eli and I step back and he dumps the flour onto the table. Then he cracks an egg in the center of the pile. Eli and I watch quietly. "There's one less of us but I say we're better off in the long run. He was a heavyweight," George says.

"You mean a deadweight," I correct.

"That too," he says, and I cringe.

George adds salt to the mixture and begins to knead. It

becomes apparent that this concoction will soon develop into homemade pasta. We watch him slap the dough. "Did you wash your hands?" Eli asks.

"Fuck off," George says.

"Okay," Eli says, and swallows.

He cuts the dough into thin strips and we ask where his parents are. "Dead," he says, serious. I don't answer. For all we know, George could very well be an orphan, or an alien, or an undercover cop. "I'm just kidding." He continues the process, with a series of flamboyant, sweeping gestures. "You oughta see me make a pizza," he says, disappearing into the pantry to grab sauce ingredients. "Can spin a whole crust on my finger like I'm in the NBA or something."

He stands at the stove with his back to us, so we miss this part of the recipe. It doesn't matter, though. I have a feeling that the best part of the show is the pasta itself. "You ready?" he says after a while. Eli and I share a side-eye as he slides a steaming dish of fettuccine Alfredo across the table to us.

"C'mon, this is so romantic," George says. "Don't act like the two of you haven't had your *Lady and the Tramp* moment before." He pops a hand-rolled cigarette into his mouth and attempts to form rings of smoke, instead looking very much like a beached salmon.

"We haven't," I say, very serious. "Eli is like a brother to me."

"Yeah," Eli adds, "we're like *brothers*."

"We could never be attracted to each other."

"Never in a million years."

"Not even if we were the last people on Earth."

"Not even if, like, somebody said we had to procreate or else, like, our parents would die. Not even then." Eli gags.

George looks back and forth between the two of us. "Okay, relax, I was just kidding. Christ." He raises his eyebrows. "Try it though, it's good."

I take the first bite. Rich. Creamy. Decadent. Butter and cheese, and a slight herbal undertone. It's the best pasta I've ever had. "George," I say, "you're gifted."

"That's what I'm saying," he says. "Eli. Please. Humor me."

Eli enacts a perfect pasta twirl and inspects his fork. He shrugs and puts it in his mouth. Chews. His eyes widen, AWOOGA-style. "George," he says.

"Right?" says George.

"Incredible."

We share more of the pasta and talk about what we'll do as KYOTV. We'll throw parties. Probably at George's house, since his parents are never around. We'll continue the tradition that Valentino started our sophomore year, passing out donuts in the mornings. We'll buy a grill and make burgers. We'll use filming as an excuse to skip class, and we'll implement secret messages into our videos. As we discuss, Eli and I share more and more of George's fettuccine until it's almost all gone. Eli leans back in his chair and checks his watch. "We should get back to campus," he says. "Interview."

"It's so good, though, George, really."

"It's 'cuz of my special ingredient." He reaches into his pocket and pulls out something small and brown. I pick it up between two fingers and examine it carefully. It's a mushroom. No. It's a *shroom*.

"You fucker," Eli says, "you did not. Tell me you did not."

He smiles, wide and psychotic. "Guess you'll find out sooner or later," he says, and then he stands. "We oughta get back to school, kids. Don't wanna be late."

The interview's in the black box theater. Principal Stack waits for us outside. "One at a time," she instructs. "Who's up?"

I'm on my phone, googling how long it takes for shrooms to kick in. Eli's face is white, and I know he's considering making himself throw up. George looks at the both of us, bemused, and raises his hand. "I'll go," he says, chipper. He shakes Stack's hand and disappears into the theater.

"Do you feel weird?" I ask Eli, as soon as they're gone.

"No. Do you?"

"I don't think so," I say.

"He's probably bluffing."

"Yeah, he's gotta be fucking with us."

"'Cuz I feel fine."

"Yeah. I feel fine. We feel fine. It's all good."

"Although it would just suck if . . ." He shakes his head. "Never mind."

"Say it."

"I was just thinking that it would suck if we started tripping balls in that meeting right now."

I sit on the curb and tuck my knees into my chest. "Yeah, but it's not gonna happen. We're fine."

He sits down next to me and we wait for George to finish. Five minutes pass, then ten. The parking lot empties; cheer practice starts on the football field across the way. My brain works a mile a minute. I've never done a psychedelic before. I wouldn't know what to expect. I stare at the pavement, searching for a sign. Something like what I've seen in movies, maybe. Moving sky. Patterns in the dirt. I don't know. Something strange. I open my eyes wide and examine a sprig of dandelion erupting from a crack in the pavement. The little yellow flower is just beginning to bloom. I marvel at its leaves, at the pop of gold surviving between heaps of stone and concrete. Life is amazing. It's beautiful, really. Here I am, a living thing on this great big planet. I'm no different than this dandelion. In fact, the two of us are more similar than we are different, and—

"Wait." Eli looks ill. "Dude. I, uh."

"What?"

"I think I'm fine, but like . . ."

"Like *what?*"

"It's just that the trees look really green. Or something. I could be wrong."

I turn around and stare at the eucalyptus, its boughs thick with springy verdant foliage. "That tree *is* green," I agree. Before I can begin to comprehend what this could mean, George barges from the back door of the theater and grins.

"Warmed 'em up for you," he says, rubbing his hands together. "Who's up?"

Eli and I look at each other. I shake my head. "Via is," he volunteers.

"Come *on.*"

"Sorry V," he says, and then: "Good luck, though."

I start up the ramp to the door. Though it's maybe two yards,

I'm taking the longest walk of my life. I look at the palms of my hands and steady my breath. If I'm about to peak, panicking will only make it worse. I know that much. I take a deep breath and enter the black box.

Here's the setup. There's one chair in the middle of the room. That's for me. Then there's eight or so chairs across the way, at a line of tables. Sitting at these tables are the ASB officials and Mr. Purcell. The lights are dimmed, except for a single bright spot above my chair, like I'm under interrogation.

"Hi, Via," Purcell says, and flashes me a smile. The lighting makes his features look warped and demonic. Deep breaths.

"Hey. Happy to be here." I swallow. "I'm, like, super digging the illuminati vibe in here."

He clears his throat.

"Sorry. Dumb," I say.

"We're just going to ask you some questions so we can get a better idea of your ability to fill a leadership position. Super easy, not a big deal at all."

"We're all rooting for you," says the ASB president. He's in my grade, a fixture in all the AP classes. A know-it-all. We once clashed over Chaucer in English class.

I fold my hands and answer the routine questions. Yes, I'm planning on attending all future pep rallies. No, I don't have experience with Final Cut, but Eli does. Yes, I think that I'm equipped for this position and here's why.

I take long pauses before I respond to each inquiry. I ground myself carefully, willing myself sober. I've heard urban legends about the powers of adrenaline, about small women hefting entire cars to save their children, or out-of-shape fugitives becoming track stars when outrunning police. I'm banking on *that* mystery chemical to combat the *other* mystery chemicals that may or may not be coursing through my body. I fixate on the shadowy members of ASB. They don't speak, only bobbing their heads and taking notes when I give my response.

"Well, Via, everything sounds great," Mr. President says. "We'll review your audition tape and get back to you by the end of next week."

Home free. I stand up.

"Hold on, actually, for one minute," Purcell says. "I have one more question, if you don't mind."

"Of course," I say.

"If we felt it was right, would you be okay with splitting up the group?"

He leans forward, the shadows forming a Rorschach test on his forehead. The room is moving. Am I moving? My spit catches in my throat and I cough.

"You mean, like, some of us make it, some don't?"

"Sure," he says. "Just like that."

Somewhere deep inside the building, a door slams. I jump.

"Everything alright?" he asks.

"Yeah," I say. And oh man, here it comes. It must be the drugs talking, because I find myself saying: "And yeah, it's fine with me if we split."

I stumble into the light. Eli brushes past me, rushes into the black box without saying a single word. George leans against his car, arms folded, cigarette in his mouth. "Well?" he says.

"You asshole."

"What?"

"You drugged us," I say, "and I'm having a bad trip. What's your problem? You could go to jail for this, George. This is *illegal.* And beyond fucked up." I close my eyes and repeat: "I'm having a bad trip."

"Are you now."

"Yeah," I say. "And I freaked out in there, too. They totally knew something was off, dude."

"You freaked out."

"Yeah, George, I did. Do you wanna hear all the lurid details? Dickhead? This is sabotage. What's the ulterior motive here, McCloskey? Who're you working for? *Cub?*"

"How'd you *freak out,*" he says, using air quotes.

"I dunno. I just did. They asked me a question and I fritzed."

"What question?"

"I, like, can't, uh, remember." I'm lying, of course. I remember perfectly. I just sold out.

"You're a serious dumbass, Via," he says. "I was just fucking with you."

"No way. I was like *seeing stuff,*" I say. "Stuff was *moving.* You're not gonna get out of trouble just by lying about it. I might press charges, because—"

"You stared in the face of authority and got nauseated. Happens to the best of us." He drops the cigarette and steps it into the ground. "There's the other dumbass."

Eli speeds toward us, the theater door slamming behind him. "George, you asshole."

"I didn't do anything, if that's what you're on about." He shakes his head. "Neither of you idiots can hang, that's for sure."

"This is gaslighting," says Eli.

"The secret ingredient to my fettuccine is pure love, baby," he says. "Get over yourselves. I'm going home." He puts on his sunglasses. "Better drink *fluids*. Since your *trip* is so extreme, you know."

"Shouldn't we talk about what happened in there?" I say, guilty. "Like, unpack?"

"What's there to unpack? It was easy. We're a shoo-in," George says.

"Didn't they ask you guys anything weird?" I say.

"Not really," George says. "I mean, they asked about splitting us up but that's all. I said no, obviously. We all did. So let's just all chill until we hear the results."

"Yeah, since we all said no," I say. "Because it would be so messed up if, like, only some of us got put in the group and others didn't." I fold and unfold my arms.

George narrows his eyes. "Did you say yes?"

"No, of course not," I say.

"She's lying," Eli says. "I can tell."

George smacks his hand over his eyes and shakes his head. "What the fuck? What the *fuck*," he says. "Via. Do you know what this means? Since Birnwick left, we're a person short. They're gonna tack on some ASB nerd and we'll be supervised by a narc the entire time. No van. No drugs. No fun. They're gonna make us do *work*. Actual *work*."

"It's not that big a deal. Especially if you guys said no. Two against one, right?"

"Um." Eli swallows hard. "Listen. I wasn't thinking, and—" He stops himself and looks at me. "V, I mean, you get it. That was a stressful situation, and I didn't know what else to say."

"Don't tell me. Don't say it," says George. "I let you into my house. I cooked for you. And this is how you twats say thanks." He looks up at the sky intently. Perhaps he's seeing God. "By stabbing me in the back and splitting us up."

"Why do you assume you're the one they'll kick out?"

"Why? Because they hate me, that's why. Because I snuck tequila into the spring formal and I say *fuck* during class presentations, that's why. Because I don't *subscribe* to their BS."

"We can fix this," I say. "It's fine. We'll figure something out. We'll send a letter, or . . ."

"Yeah, you're gonna fix this alright," George says. He gets into his car, leans out the window, and he gives us a look. "You're gonna fix it."

We watch as he bolts out of the parking lot. "He's gonna kill us," Eli says.

"Oh, absolutely."

"He has that look in his eye, dude. He might be batshit insane."

"I've always thought so."

"We all have," he says. "So. What's the plan?"

"I'll draft an email, or something," I say.

The thing about email is that it's out of my wheelhouse. Though it's a product of the Internet, email doesn't belong to Gen Z—it's strictly the property of millennials and Gen X.

That's not to say that I fit cleanly into the Gen Z box. The Internet's been around for as long as I've been alive, but when I try to picture its presence in my childhood, I draw a blank. I think the mark of a true Gen Z-er is absolute immersion in online culture since the dawn of memory. Which I didn't have. I missed the cutoff by a handful of years. And yet, I don't identify with millennials either. People born between 1997 and 2004 exist as outliers. We're miscellaneous. Sure, I remember the early days of YouTube. Omegle. The rage comic. But you lost me at dial-up.

I'd rank email etiquette somewhere between HTML code and .gov resources in terms of my own Internet literacy. When I send an email, I feel like I'm barging in on an age-old tradition. I struggle with the greeting. Hi? Hello? Do I begin with *Dear So-and-so*? It's hard to gauge formality when my in-progress draft is right next to a spam email from an old Moshi Monsters account. It only gets more complicated when I'm addressing an authority figure, as I am now. Worse, I'm trying to negotiate with some nonexistent leverage. I slap a speedy draft into the body of an email and send it to Eli for approval. And then I forward it to Mr. Purcell and we wait.

A single sheet of paper flaps on the door of the main office on Friday afternoon. I stand between George and Eli.

George kicks at the pavement. "Man," he says.

Eli and I nod in agreement.

"This is messed up," he says again.

We did not get the position. Instead, they've given it to two others: Zoe Melton and a girl in the junior class. A junior! As KYOTV. It's unheard of. They hadn't even auditioned. "I don't understand," I say. "Was there something wrong with the email?"

"I thought it was good," Eli says.

"Lemme see it again." George snatches my phone from me

and opens my Gmail. "*We would prefer that you consider us as-is, without taking any new additions, or not at all.*'" He looks back up at us, his face pained. "Well, it says it right there."

"What?"

"You said, 'or not at all.' So they're saying, Okay, fine. Not at all." He tips his head back and lets out a sigh. "They hate having their authority questioned. They all do."

"This sucks," says Eli.

George shakes his head. "No, you know what? We're not giving up. This isn't the end." He grabs Eli's shoulder. "Leak the audition tape. Tweet about it. Leak it to the school. They'll love us so much, Purcell and Stack will be begging for us to come back. And if not, I'll deliver my Big Fuck You."

It's against ASB policy for KYOTV candidates to release their audition tapes without faculty permission. "You sure?" I ask.

"Stack's gonna call us in and they're gonna be like: 'We're so sorry, the school clearly needs you, we were wrong to give it to a *junior*, for Chrissakes, you three have the students on your side and their opinions matter most.' And then you wanna know what we're gonna say?"

"What?"

"We're gonna say, 'No thank you.' And then she's gonna say pretty please and then *maybe* we'll think about it. But we're gonna make them beg first," he says. "And, like I said, worse comes to worst, I'll give 'em a Big Fuck You."

"That sounds so ominous," I say.

"Yeah, maybe you should stop saying that. Before someone overhears and calls the police," says Eli.

"I'm a wholesome guy. Don't get it twisted," he says.

"Via, what do you think?" Eli asks.

I think it's a shit plan, and I think it'll get us nowhere. I think George McCloskey's a wild card and I think he's leading us down a path that could easily turn sour at any minute. I think the best plan of action would be to cut our losses and move on. But I'm bored. "Yeah, release the video," I say.

It's Monday when Eli uploads our audition tape to YouTube; within seconds it's been shared on Facebook and Twitter and Snapchat. I'm in my English class. My phone is blowing up.

Everyone's outside watching, Eli texts in the group chat, and so I lean over and look out the window. Sure enough, there's a scattering of truants, all with headphones in. The view count climbs with each page refresh.

My teacher's playing the tape for my whole class, George texts.

The kid behind me nudges my back. I turn around. "Watching it now," he says. "Killer tape."

That's only the beginning. People recognize me. I'm stopped in the hallways. "Robbery," they say, between classes, during lunch. "Fuck Stack."

Teachers, clueless to the drama, play it in their classes. I receive texts from people I've only met once before, in classes I took freshman year. Our audition tape spreads, as do our names; we're the basis for many a subtweet. The whole grade is outraged that we're being represented by someone younger than us. Some people get mean on Twitter but I figure it's not a big deal since I'm not the one doing it.

"I didn't ask for this, you know," Zoe says to me, when we run into each other during lunch. "Everyone's shitting on me but it's not like I stole KYOTV from you. I didn't want the position either. I wanted to be pep commissioner."

"I'm not attacking you. I haven't done anything," I answer.

"Right." She shrugs. "Look, I know you and Eli have your thing or whatever, but it's not cool to throw me under the bus," she says.

"What thing?"

She rolls her eyes. "Okay, sure. Whatever. I'm just saying we've known each other since middle school and you're . . . you're choosing a guy over being decent."

"Eli's not a *guy*," I say, "and I don't know what you're insinuating."

She shrugs. "I'm just saying," she says.

George and Eli and I meet at the Calabasas Lake. The sky is a clear blue, and the man-made lake bubbles with baby ducks and lily pads and the odd paddleboat. We're fishing without a permit. Very illegal, but George insists we're fine; he's apparently got a connection with the lake security.

"Plan's working," George says. "Any second they'll be begging for us back."

"You think so?" I say. Inside, I'm doubtful. Faculty higher-ups have been eerily quiet since our video dropped, and I'm starting to get uneasy. I was at least expecting a slap on the wrist. Maybe a detention. But we've heard nothing.

George lights a cigarette. He's wearing reflective sport sunglasses and a green dad shirt buttoned all the way up to his chin. He turns his head toward me slowly. "Ye of little faith," he says.

Eli tosses a piece of bread to a goose. "We're gonna get in so much trouble. Someone started a petition," he says, shaking his head. "I bet faculty's pissed."

"A petition?"

"Yeah, to get us installed as KYOTV."

"Well shit!" says George. "That's just what we need. You *have* to follow a petition. That's like, the law."

I stare at the end of my fishing pole. "Pretty sure it's not."

"They hate the others. What're their names again?"

"Zoe's one of them," I say. "She's cool. We ding-dong-ditched Kylie Jenner together."

"Zoe's the *enemy*," George says. "She's in the way of our *van*."

"Your smoke's scaring away the fish," Eli says.

"Your negativity's scaring them away, dumbass," George says. "What happened to you guys?"

"People are being kind of mean about it is all," I say. "Zoe came up to me today and I felt kind of weird. Bad. I felt bad."

"Listen. It's nothing personal. I don't have a problem with her. It's faculty I have an issue with. Zoe didn't even audition for KYOTV. She wanted to be, what? Pep? So this situation sucks for everyone." He blows a perfect O in smoke, then pokes a hole through it. "I've been practicing." He grins.

Eli lets out a bitter laugh. "Might as well just cut out the middle man and make videos anyway."

"Call it KYOTZ," I joke.

George snaps his fingers. "Now we're talking," he says.

Vice Principal Monroe's office sits behind tinted windows. "Young ladies love to come and fix their hair in the reflection," she says. "You don't even know I'm right here."

She probably eats children.

George and Eli are on either side of me. The three of us are in deep shit. Per George's idea, we continued filming at assemblies, during sports practices, at events. We even conducted interviews with students and staff. We aggravated the situation so much that the petition circulated—widely enough to attract faculty attention. I'm not sure what I'd expected out of senior year, but it sure wasn't going rogue. George squirms in his seat.

"What's going on?" Eli says, the bravest out of the three of us.

"What's going *on*?" she repeats, smiling so hard her eyes could pop out of her head.

Eli nods and swallows hard. Ms. Monroe is a new kind of supervillain. She's so normal looking that I can't help but wonder if she saves this special kind of evil just for us. Maybe she goes home after work and drinks iced tea and browses Pinterest and watches *Grey's Anatomy*. Maybe she shops at Target and cooks spaghetti. There is nothing more perplexing to the developing mind than the concept of a teacher going home, doing perfectly normal things. Having dinner. Wearing *pajamas*.

"Well, since you asked, here's what I'm thinking," she says, cheerful, her fingertips tap-tap-tapping the top of her desk. Her manicure is dark blue. I'm almost positive that that particular shade is called Midnight and I have the very same one in my cabinet at home. I don't like knowing the name of her nail polish. It's far too much information for me to handle.

"Did you hear me, Via?" she says.

I snap out of my head and meet her eyes. "Sorry," I say, "I, um. I missed that."

She folds her hands. She doesn't reveal any signs of impatience. "I said that I'm thinking that the best way to handle this would be . . . perhaps . . . to use the Internet to our advantage."

Eli physically cringes when she says *Internet*. She pronounces the word deliberately, stressing the first syllable. It's an audible capitalization.

"The student body clearly looks up to you," she says. "Whether you asked for it or not. So. Here's the deal. One tweet. One Instagram. One Facebook post. I think it would be helpful for you three to declare your public support for this year's KYOTV group."

"I don't give shout-outs. Doesn't fit my brand," George says.

Eli kicks him under the table.

"And what exactly is your brand, Mr. McCloskey?" Monroe asks. She tilts her head. There's a sudden chill in the room.

"Nothing, ma'am," George says, confidence evaporating.

"So we have an understanding?"

The three of us offer frenzied nods.

"I think it's the right thing to do," she says. "And if this continues to be an issue, we'll have to reconsider your senior activities."

George cups his head in his hands. "Shit," he says. It's Calabasas senior tradition to make trips to various LA hotspots: Zuma Beach, Disneyland, Six Flags.

"Language."

"Sorry, Ms. Monroe," he says. "Just sucks, is all."

"Doesn't have to be this way. Just think of the others. You've put them in quite an uncomfortable position."

"It just doesn't make sense. Like, I'm sorry to talk back and all, but we thought the whole problem was 'cuz we were too small of a group and you wanted to add people. But there's only two of them, and there's three of us."

Monroe sits back in her chair and looks at George coolly. I've never seen him look so unsure of himself before. For once, he's a teenager, and not an ageless mystery man. "We are currently seeing new auditioners, George," she says. "We're open to adding others to their group. You can apply if you like. Separately."

"So it's just us you don't like," Eli says. "Because everyone's saying they love our tape. Best in years."

We've heard rumors about the things she's said behind our backs. Words like *slackers* and *troublemakers*. Or *bad for the CHS image*.

"There's a lot of different factors that go into the decision." She looks out the window. "You can go."

We shuffle out of her office like humiliated dogs. "I might play their little game. For now," says George, "but I'm still having my Big Fuck You."

"Just lay low. And don't be weird," I say. "If they keep us from senior activities because of you I'll kill you."

"Yeah, I believe it. You give off closet psycho vibes, Via, no offense."

"You give off dumbass vibes."

"I will cop to that."

Eli rolls his eyes. "Come on," he says. "It's over."

"Where are you guys headed?" George asks.

"Math."

George makes a pouty face and holds up his car keys. "Are we never gonna hang out again?"

"Aww, shit," says Eli. "Look, he likes us."

"Let's go to Fatburger," he says. "Or I could see about getting us a free pizza from work?"

"Can't," I say. "If I miss another class I drop a letter grade."

"I'm supposed to get lunch with someone," Eli says, and looks at me. "Cassie, actually."

"A lady friend," George says. "Alrighty then, I guess."

We watch him go: the wild card, the Hawaiian shirt, and the vintage Chevrolet.

In the end, we concede. We give the shout-outs we were asked for, these bogus shots of us all standing around like dweebs, giving thumbs-ups to the camera. We attend senior activities—most notably Six Flags, and the three of us meet up to ride Goliath together.

Of course, we do receive our karmic comeuppance. It's Cub. He's added to this year's KYOTV group with the special assignment of covering team sports. He's a total dick about it, strutting around campus with a cameraman and a press pass. "Listen, I'll feature you guys if you want," he offers, but it's condescending, and we wouldn't want to sell out anyway.

In time, Eli and I forget about George's Big Fuck You. He doesn't mention it to us again. We figure he must've gotten tired of the whole thing. He's college bound, committed to Arizona State. He parties. He sells the Chevy.

I make up with Zoe. We sit on the curb outside school and I apologize. I tell her I'm sorry about the petition, for being a bad friend. "You like him," she says coolly.

"George? No way."

"Eli." She hugs her knees to herself. "It's cool, you can admit it. You like each other and that's why you guys were so pissed. You couldn't do this stupid TV thing together."

I shake my head and tell her no. "I wanted to do drugs in a van," I say.

On the last week of school, the yearbook committee distributes copies of the hardback across campus. The culture of the yearbook message has developed far past a HAGS and an autograph. Close friends are expected to pen miniature letters. Eli and I have set aside entire pages for one another. We meet in the morning to switch our books and flip through the senior quotes together. Mine is something Millie Bobby Brown said; it's a dull inside joke with some friends. Eli forgot to turn his in on time, so there's nothing. We go to check George's photo. And there it is.

The Big Fuck You.

In the ensuing days, someone will post a photo of his quote and it will go viral on Twitter, racking up thousands of retweets. It'll be shared by one of the biggest meme accounts on Instagram. Faculty will catch wind and the entire institution of senior quotes will be questioned—there'll be new safeguards, new approvals required in the coming years. But the damage has already been done. George's Fuck You will go down in Calabasas history, a perfect representation of the high school's "image."

Eli and I stare at his quote in disbelief.

"He really did it," I say.

"The psycho," Eli agrees.

We read it out loud, in unison, our voices careful and deliberate:

"I Can And I Will."—*Barry McCockiner*

Valley Girls

I've spent my life in the shadow of the Valley Girl.

Who she is, I'm not sure. Of course, Frank Zappa gave us a brief rundown with the release of his 1982 single, "Valley Girl." I know she loves going into, like, clothing stores and stuff. That much is clear. But still, she remains a vague character in my understanding of West Coast generalizations. What makes the Valley Girl, exactly? And how does she stack up against Katy Perry's "California Gurls," for example, or Beck's "Hollywood Freaks," or Jim Morrison's "L.A. Woman"?

It could be the way she talks. "I will give you twenty dollars if you can make the entire weekend without saying 'like' once," my parents once challenged me. I didn't last three hours. I've heard similar criticisms about *upspeak*, when the tone of voice rises at the end of a sentence, and *vocal fry*, the slowed-down, gravelly texture that you've probably heard Britney Spears slip into across every track of her discography. It's an accessory I bear with pride.

It could be how she shops. Once upon a time, the Valley Girl maintained an exclusive relationship with the mall. She took to boutiques with an enthusiasm typically reserved for Christmas mornings; she slung department store bags across her shoulders and tucked Abercrombie receipts into the pockets of her True Religions. Now, I'd say that if I were to ascribe a specific shopping experience to the Valley Girl, I'd point to the Melrose Trading Post, where it's common to spot spare members of Brockhampton and minor Internet celebrities browsing vintage windbreakers. It's the Instagram Explore page come to life. Or Goodwill. Or shoplifting ("borrowing") from Brandy Melville.

Maybe it's the way she handles her social media. Never will you find a Valley Girl with her phone's auto-capitalization setting turned on: she wants to appear cool, collected, and unconcerned. Her photos will be edited in secondary apps and her grid will appear sleek and color-coordinated. Her tagged photos will be vetted with care and her following list trimmed like an Omaha steak. Before you even *touch* her phone, she will have cleared her search history, because she's already looked you up: on Twitter (you're not funny), on Instagram (you're not hot), on Spotify (you follow the Teen Party playlist, ok), and on Venmo (all your transactions are thinly veiled beer buys). Social media is a way to make a reputation for yourself without actually having to *do* anything, and the Valley Girl takes this opportunity seriously. Dead seriously.

Not any one of these things seal the deal, though. It's the combination of it all. I suppose you could argue that the only defining characteristic of the Valley Girl is, well, her being from the Valley. But there's something else at play. A state of mind, perhaps. I struggle to put my finger on it, but I know it when I see it.

Gina Ricketson, fellow Calabasas High senior, takes whatever this special ingredient is and overdoses on it. She transcends the label. Gina uses Snapchat and Instagram more than anyone I've ever met, and that's saying a lot. Her story is updated at a near hourly rate, and she posts OOTDs (outfits of the day, duh) on her grid biweekly, with each article of clothing tagged with the store she bought it from. Whenever she wants to buy a new bikini, she consults with her loyal followers and takes a poll. The two voting options always mean the same thing but with slight variation, like: "SUPES CUTE 🔥 or TOTALLY HOT 😊." Maybe she'll add some commentary here and there: "this Bikini (always capitalized, the Bikini is God) is adjustable in the back, so it makes space for my DD girlies. So fire."

She's confident. So confident, in fact, that she's not afraid to verbally berate those she deems as her subordinates. I once asked her if she could move her backpack off a desk so I could see the whiteboard. "Shut the fuck up," she responded, her voice harsh and throaty. And you know what? I did.

Zoe Melton and I share a fascination with Gina. We stalk her socials together, pulling one another aside during rehearsals to analyze her updates. We're both involved with Calabasas High's Murder Mystery Night, a three-act dinner theater run entirely by the students. Now, Zoe and I sit on the edge of the stage and tap through her Snapchat story, where she's posted a #TBT of her long-distance boyfriend, a cheerful-looking guy she's publicly nicknamed Blakeypoo.

Zoe pulls her phone closer to her face. "I'm trying to see if there are any secret messages in this photo," she says, and tilts her head. "Like a secret code. Maybe he's a hostage, and he needs our help."

"I wonder if she's nice to him," I say.

"I doubt it." Zoe stretches her arms and leans back on the stage. "Freshman year she walked up to me in the locker room and straight-up called me the F-slur. And I'd spoken, like, maybe three words to her. So I can't imagine how she'd act toward someone she *does* know."

Max, the student director of the show, interrupts our discussion and claps his hands. "Alright people, break's over," he shouts. Zoe and I separate. She's in the cast, I'm on the production team. Eli and I, shortly after parting ways with George, wrote the script together. It's about the murder of a rising starlet on "Wizzney Channel," and Zoe is our lead. She's perfect, of course; after all, she has experience with the same network that our show is based on. If you watch enough Disney Channel, you'll come to recognize that there's a specific acting style that Disney stars employ. Exaggerated, facial, and beat-heavy. Zoe's got it down to a science. She's also assumed the position of honorary consultant. "Table reads aren't usually like this," she says, as we block the scene of the crime. (Zoe's character is murdered by a Wizzney Channel wand when the lights go out during a table read.) "Usually, the director would sit here, then the actors over *here,* and finally, the writers here."

We're one week away from opening night, and things are hectic. Eli and I still aren't completely done writing the final act.

Entire scenes have yet to be staged. And Mr. Purcell, despite approving our show, still hasn't read the whole script.

Actually, that's speculation. Maybe he did. But something tells me that if he had, we would've heard from him by now. The bulk of the script was penned in the hours between one and three in the morning, when Eli and I were delirious with exhaustion and eager to see what we could get away with. For example, a major plot point revolves around a child pretending to be chronically ill so he can exploit the Make-A-Wish Foundation and meet his celebrity crush. And that's only scratching the surface; the show is filled with stupid jokes and innuendos and general bouts of immaturity.

It's a cast of thirtysomething kids and they're all devoted to the cause. Because the show is student-run, it draws participants from all different social spheres. Whenever Purcell enters the room to check on us, the actors adjust the scene, glossing over certain lines so we don't get into trouble. Nothing brings an eclectic group of seventeen-year-olds together more than eluding authority. We're like *The Breakfast Club,* only instead of smoking weed and contemplating social expectations, we smoke weed and make questionable jokes about children's television.

As if summoned by my thoughts, Mr. Purcell opens the door and stops rehearsal. "Where's Eli?" he says.

"I don't know, actually," I say. "I can call him, though."

"That's fine. I just need his paperwork for the playbills. Let him know when you see him next, okay?" He leaves, and the scene resumes.

Truth is, things have been weird between Eli and me lately. Most of the time, I don't know where we stand. It started with minor creative differences, but now it seems we argue about everything. I consider texting him to let him know Purcell was looking for him, but I can't remember if we're on speaking terms today.

Max runs the scene over again because someone keeps forgetting their lines. I open my backpack. At home, my parents and I aren't talking much. My dad has become increasingly conservative, and we argue at every turn. My mother and I are at odds, too, but for different reasons: she found out I'd been taking remedial math all last year and took the news about how you'd expect. She says to get my act together, but I say my grades are so average already that it feels useless to try.

I pull out my composition notebook and visit a dog-eared page near the back, where I've scribbled some sentences down. My chicken scratch is starting to build into a personal essay about an abandoned house on my grandmother's street in Old Saybrook. When I should be studying to appease my mother, I instead find myself returning to this page, crossing words out, rewriting, adding new ones. I know I should be getting my priorities into order. But writing this essay *feels* like a priority.

My parents own a collection called *Smiling Through the Apocalypse: Esquire's History of the Sixties*. Several months ago, I noticed it eyeing me from the shelf, its spine an offensive orange color. Inside, I was introduced to Gay Talese. Stokely Carmichael. James Baldwin. Roger Kahn lumped imperialism and passé liberalism together and called them "bad vibrations." I developed a crush on Jacob Brackman, the twenty-five-year-old who said normality is a disease. How wild it is, I thought, reading Gina Berriault, that someone could write about tits and ass so matter-of-fact. How sick it is that Tom Wolfe can make the exclamation point seem less like a bastardization of the whole punctuation thing and more like a brushstroke.

The collection was great but I wanted more. I delved deeper into Truman Capote's backlist. I liked how he said Marilyn Monroe's voice sounded the way bananas taste. I read John Waters and I was overwhelmed with a love for the tacky and grotesque. I turned to the Internet, where I was directed to Zadie Smith. Jia Tolentino. I read essays by Toni Morrison, poems by Louise Erdrich, stories by Lucia Berlin. I ransacked my mother's nightstand and stole what would soon become my favorite of all: *The White Album*, by Joan Didion. "Oh, shit," I said, when I finished. I found that I was out of breath. Then I turned back to the title page and read it all over again.

I've since started wearing oval sunglasses. If I had easy access to cigarettes, ones besides George's hand-rolled disasters, I would smoke them.

In school, I'm taught the specific and precise beats of a five-paragraph essay. I follow a strict set of rules, clearly delineated in a rubric handout: hook, then topic sentence. Claims, supporting evidence, conclusion. I'm expected to read Shakespeare, but only in the specific way that the classroom allows—not for the story, but to highlight quotes that fit into the assigned essay topic. There's no room for anything else. It's abysmal. There's no use in thinking within the confines of one-inch margins and MLA citations and Times New Roman. I want to consume things that make me realize that I have no business living a comfortable life in an uncomfortable world. I'm beginning to understand that I've been lied to about a great many things. About sex, and about drugs. About art and music and God and California. I've grown distrustful of the adults around me.

"What's that?" I hear from behind me. Instinctually, I slam the notebook shut. It's Eli, risen from the dead. "Calm down, I'm not spying," he says. "Jesus."

"Purcell was looking for you," I say.

"Yeah, I just ran into him." He sits down next to me. "Well."

"Well." I'm not sure what else to say.

"Alright. Well, I'll leave," he says. "Don't want to distract you from whatever you were doing."

"It's not that serious."

"Whatever." He gets up.

"What's wrong with you?"

"What's wrong?"

"Yeah, you're constantly weird."

"I'm not the weird one," he says. "You're the one that thinks that, like, you're better than everyone."

Zoe clears her throat. The actors have taken a pause; they're watching us in stunned silence.

"I don't think that at all. What are you even saying?"

He shrugs. "Whatever, Via. I just think it's fucked that, like, I just come over there and you close your notebook like you're some kind of . . . I don't know. It's just weird and defensive." He turns toward the stage. "Can you guys stop watching us?"

"Take your beef outside, you two," says Max.

"There's no *beef.* We're fine," I say.

Eli glares at me and takes a seat on the other side of the room. When our script was first picked a month or so after the KYOTV debacle, I'd thought we'd designed the perfect senior year for ourselves. Not so. He's been picking fights with me so often that I know there's no use in trying to mend things because we'll only have another falling out in the next few days. I don't text him, he doesn't text me. The weekend arrives and we're still at odds.

Zoe and I meet at the Westfield Topanga mall. I know I said the Valley Girl isn't tied to the shopping center like she once was, but Zoe and I stalk the Westfield for an alternate purpose: to people-watch. In the Valley, you don't get many opportunities to feel lost in a crowd. Our sidewalks are empty. But here, at the Westfield Topanga, there are always too many people. It's a daunting kind of comfort, knowing that everyone in line for Wetzel's Pretzels is living their own separate lives, wearing outfits they picked out that morning, window-shopping in their own special way.

We're inside Claire's, a store that I'd normally gloss over, but that Zoe insists on browsing every time. She examines a pair of earrings that look like tiny donuts and asks me what the deal is between Eli and me.

"No clue. It's just been weird."

She puts the donut studs down and picks up a pack of rainbow hair clips. "Maybe it's the whole senior year thing," she says. "You're going to college, right?"

"Hopefully," I say.

Just last month, I submitted the last of my college applications. With plenty of despondence, I might add. My grade-point average hovers just around a 3.0, deeming nearly all my schools reaches. My only hope is my writing. Over the summer I learned about a creative writing program at UC Santa Barbara, so most of my efforts went toward that: I'd submitted two short stories, a letter of intent, and a personal essay. But I'm not delusional. My chances are slim to none. I'm prepared to enroll at the local community college. I just haven't told anyone about that yet. Not that I hold anything against junior colleges—it's just that I'd always pictured myself moving away to a college town, living in a dorm, studying late night in library armchairs.

"And he's not," she says, "so maybe he feels weird about that. I mean, you guys have been inseparable for years, so it's gonna be weird when you leave him behind."

"I guess," I say. Eli's not applying anywhere, at least that I know of. He doesn't like to talk about plans.

"Or maybe you're just growing apart. It happens." She moves across the store to a shelf of glittery stationery. "I'm glad I don't have to worry about college shit. Seems stressful."

Zoe's going to act full-time. She's not interested in college. It always seemed like she had one foot in high school and the other in the real world. Now, it's practically true—she misses class all the time, applies herself just enough to maintain the minimum GPA required to participate in extracurriculars. It's not like she's slacking off; actually, she's been working nonstop ever since I've known her, only her efforts are spared for the screen.

"I only do homework for Mr. Barclay," she says, "and even then, like, not really."

Mr. Barclay teaches English to seniors and I can tell he enjoys it. Where I might disregard certain classics as dry and outdated,

Mr. Barclay finds scandal, edge, and drama: *Hamlet,* Dante's *Inferno, Oedipus Rex, Crime and Punishment.* His is the only class I won't skip. Zoe's in a different English period than I am, but I know she avoids skipping, too, unless she has a casting call.

"I actually got cast in a pilot," she says casually. "I haven't told many people yet."

"No way," I say.

"Yeah. Starring [XXXXX]. It's already been greenlit."

"That's insane," I say. Zoe's been cast in a few pilots before, but they never received approval to air on TV. A show getting the green light in advance is a huge deal. And [XXXXX] is a major star, too. "He's from the eighties, right? My mom loves him."

"All moms do."

"Was he at the audition?"

"No, auditions are usually with casting directors. Maybe a producer."

"Do you still get nervous for those?"

"Not really. Depends, though. But for the most part they're all the same." She shrugs. "I'm excited for this new thing, though. I'm usually typecast as the quirky best friend. Never the main girl. Which hurt, at first, but now it's like, whatever, you know? That's the industry. I look young. That's how they all *think.* But this part isn't the goofy BFF character. Or a little kid. I'm a love interest. New to me. So, like, that's exciting."

As she speaks, her eyes flit across a wall of scrunchies. I'd always thought Zoe was cool because she gave zero fucks. But that's not true. Everyone cares. It's just that she's put all of her caring into who's shuffling her headshots and calling her to auditions, instead of whether or not a high school sophomore thinks her Lisa Frank tee hits the mark. She's cool because she cares about the right things.

"By the way," she says, as we leave, "Purcell has definitely not read your script. It's been in the same spot on his desk since you first got picked by the Theater Arts Club."

"I figured. He's gonna freak out," I say.

"Who cares?"

"He could make us change it last second."

"*I'm* not changing anything. I already memorized my lines," she says. "Besides, it's funny."

Zoe and I sit on a bench across from the carousel and watch three little kids squeeze inside a giant teacup. I bite on my straw. "I want Gina to come to our show," I say. "For the bit."

"I'd ask her, but she'd call me a you-know-what."

"Maybe it's worth it," I say.

"They should update the serial killer warning signs. Clothing hauls on Instagram, hurting small animals, and setting fires.

"Tell me the story about her and Cub again," she says. It's a favorite of ours.

It was two weeks ago. We were in economics class. Gina kept staring at Cub with bizarre intensity. "Cub," she said finally, "there's rumors going around that I'm into you."

"Oh?" he said. "I'm not, don't worry."

"I just wanted to make it *very* clear that I have a boyfriend," she said. "I'm taken."

"Okay?"

"So don't go and try to flirt with me, or anything."

Cub blinked. "Um."

"Thank you," she said, and bent down to unzip her backpack. As she fished in the front pocket for a pencil, she glanced back up at him coyly. I reenact this scene beat-by-beat for Zoe, imitating the way she batted her eyelashes and puckered her lips.

"That's so good," she says. "You look just like her."

"But the best part was right after. When Nicole Guinn was like, 'Gina, your makeup looks really good,' and she was like, 'Thanks, I had a party on Friday.' But it was Monday *afternoon*."

"You should've told her that's bad for her skin," Zoe says.

"She'd have told me to shut the fuck up," I argue.

"True," Zoe says. "I wish I had the guts to just tell people to shut up like that."

"I guess there's something to be learned from her."

"There's something to be learned from everybody," Zoe says, and stirs her tea with the straw. She fishes around the bottom for a tapioca ball. "Apparently."

Of course, Eli and I are called into Mr. Purcell's office.

"Dysentery?" he says, and drops our script on the top of his desk. "You have a character die of *dysentery*?"

"She's a plumber, so it makes sense," says Eli.

"Narratively," I say.

"Come on, guys," he says. "And what's with this part? Are you insinuating this character is attracted to his mother?"

"It's an homage to *Oedipus Rex*," I say. "Which we read in English class."

"There's stuff in here that we can't put onstage."

"What's wrong with it?" Eli folds his arms. "It's just jokes."

"We're going to get complaints," he says. "Come on, you two. You know better. Fix it."

"The show's in five days. That's not fair."

"Fix it," he says.

Purcell's timing couldn't be worse. Everyone's already memorized their parts. Eli and I leave his office, muttering curses under our breaths like cartoon characters. "Who does he think he is?" Eli says.

"A dictator."

"We don't have time to change anything," he says. "We haven't even finished the last scene."

"I know. It's fucked."

"I guess we could work on it tonight. Yours or mine?"

My phone dings. "Hold on a minute," I say.

It's an email from a school I've applied to. I stop walking.

I stare at the subject line and I immediately know. There's no congratulations, no word of welcome. I don't feel sad, but I do feel useless. Maybe it would be easier if I'd worked harder, if I could accuse a faceless admissions officer of shortchanging me. But I can't be disappointed because I haven't really earned it. I probably wouldn't have accepted me either.

"Hey," Eli says softly, "is everything okay?"

"Yeah, everything's cool," I say.

"Did you just get a weird text or something?"

"It's not really your business."

He frowns, but I don't apologize. I pick up my pace and leave him behind for the refuge of the girls' bathroom, where I splash cool water on my face and run through the platitudes: everyone fails sometimes, if it wasn't meant to be it wasn't meant to be.

I sit on the lid of a closed toilet. I consider texting my mother. Instead, I check Gina's socials.

"I didn't make it into FIDM," her story says. She's been vocal about her desire to rush sororities at the Fashion Institute of Design & Merchandising (interesting, because FIDM doesn't have Greek life). "But it's A-OK because I'll just transfer. It's my dream to write for *Vogue* one day." I tap to the next picture and it's a photo of a Fashion Nova bodysuit. "The boyf is gonna luuuuuuvvvv this one-piece."

I shove my phone into my backpack and kick the stall door, over and over again, until I get tired of it.

I sit in the back of Mr. Barclay's classroom before school. I don't talk to anyone. I've checked out a laptop from the library and I peck at the keyboard until my head hurts. My phone vibrates. It's another text from Eli, which I will ignore, just like the previous six. I'll see him after school and I'm sure we'll have a blowout argument in front of everyone. I don't care. My Old Saybrook essay has a continuity error that I'd like to fix before I place it on submission.

I open my composition notebook to the dog-eared page and I scratch out parts of the outline—and not without aggression, I might add. The tip of the pencil snaps.

"You good?" Mr. Barclay says, from his place at the front of the room.

I freeze and set down my pencil. "Yeah."

"Need to talk?"

I hesitate. "Probably."

He gestures to a chair across from his desk, and I close the laptop. He has a nice desk. Never trust an organized teacher. There's a haphazard stack of books here, a mess of essays there. He has a photo of his little girl in a picture frame and two cans of lime La Croix.

"What's up, Via?" he says.

"I'm bombing life," I say, and then I launch into the whole thing: I haven't talked to my mom in two weeks, I'm doing awful in school, I'm in a fight with my best friend, I'm supposed to patch up an entire play before opening night in oh, four days. But worst of all, I thought my writing was going to save me and it didn't. Like my parents said, I'm drifting. And when I think about it, I mean *really* think about it, I'm not happy. I'm not sad, either. It seems the only things I feel anything for at all are writing and reading. But even that seems silly, when apparently I'm not good enough at that to get into college. And I feel lonely, but I'm not sure if that's just a normal part of growing up, and sometimes I worry that I'm missing out on something, and I don't know what it is exactly. And it sucks, because I feel like everyone else at least *kind* of understands who they are—even this girl, Gina, who's unapologetically herself to a fault. I'm just freaking out all the time, and high school is moving too fast for me, and I think I'm going to be left behind.

I trail off. "Sorry," I say.

"Don't apologize," he says. "School isn't everything, you know. Life is hard. Growing up is hard, and everyone your age is just as confused as you are. They're only hiding it. I'm sure there are people out there who see you writing a play and assume that *your* whole life is put together. Everyone's scared, but that's normal. This is the time in your life where you're supposed to be questioning the world around you.

"You're a writer. That's what you love. What I've gotten from all of this is that you are, above all things, passionate about something. If you hold onto that thing you love, and you keep writing, Via, you'll be okay."

When I walk into the theater in time for dress rehearsal, I'm relieved. The stage has come together since I last saw it. It's an explosion of primary colors, like a real school set on a Disney show. Zoe catches my eye and waves. She's in a denim miniskirt and cheetah-print leggings, though I'm not sure if it's her costume or her outfit. "Three steps to your left, Zoe," Max says. "Cory, stand up straight. You're playing Skrillex. Do you think Skrillex slouches?"

"What's my motivation," Cory says dryly. He's in a long black wig and fingerless gloves.

Daniel Summers raises his hand. "Someone moved my prop from the prop table," he says. Daniel's playing one-half of the writer duo on the show-within-a-show, an obvious self-insert for Eli and me.

Max cups his face in his hand. "How many times do I have to say it? Don't touch props that aren't yours, people. Let's take five." He turns to me. "Got you guys' latest update this morning, printed it and passed it out."

"Oh," I say. I don't have the heart to tell him I haven't read the additions. "Where's Eli?"

"Right here, *Olivia*," Eli answers. He's right behind me. Max detects the tension and darts away, pretending to look for Daniel's stolen prop. "What happened to *you*? I had to finish the third act all by myself last night. I didn't even have time to make the changes Purcell wanted, so we'll probably get in trouble; thanks for that. You haven't answered any texts all day."

"I had stuff going on."

"Right. You had stuff going *on*. We both have stuff *going on*. Like a show. This week."

"I put in most of the work at the beginning, Eli. So God forbid I miss one day."

"Are you serious right now?"

"I wrote, like, most of the first and second act. You're playing the victim here. Ever since Alice left, you've been so weird. Like you're obsessed with arguing, and you have to make everything about yourself. You're, like, a textbook narcissist."

"*I'm* a . . ." He stops, and restarts. "Are you on your period or something?"

"Did you seriously just ask me that?"

"You know what, Olivia? Fuck you."

"Excuse me?"

"I *said,* fuck you. You're the most selfish person I've ever met. And sorry for saying the period thing or whatever, but, like, you suck. You wanna know why I've been upset?" He lowers his voice. "I used to call you my best friend, until I realized, hey, you know what's crazy? I don't know *anything* about you. I tell you everything. You know about Alice, about my family, about school. But like. I have no clue who you even *are*."

"What's that supposed to even *mean*?"

"And at first I was sad. Because I thought you, like, replaced me with Daniel, or something. So I was kind of butthurt. But then I realized I don't care. Because he doesn't know anything about you, either. At all. Right? Does he know anything? Does anyone know anything about you? Why don't you tell me anything? Why can't you be serious about anything?"

"I *am* serious."

"You're not. You know you're not. Everything's a joke or a bit or something. And that's nice, but how do you think I feel when you slam your notebook shut when I'm around, or, like, refuse to tell me why you're upset? And I get that maybe it's a writing thing, and you wanna be a journalist, so you listen to people a lot. But this is your life. I'm your *friend*."

"Places," Max shouts. The room's beginning to quiet down now, and we shuffle out of earshot.

"I said I love you, and stuff," he says quietly. "Does that even mean anything to you?"

"Eli? Via? Can we get you guys to watch this scene?" Max asks.

"Whatever. Just forget it. I'm giving up," he says. "Let's just get this stupid shit over with." He sits at a chair across the black box, as far away from me as possible.

Max calls action and the scene plays out smoothly. Nobody forgets any blocking. It's come together since we last convened—call it a theater miracle, I guess, because twenty-four hours ago I was positive we were headed straight for disaster. Daniel Summers and Arizona, the actors playing Eli's and my characters, fumble their lines a bit. "Hold," Max calls. "Daniel. Arizona. You guys are playing best friends. Like, conjoined-at-the-hip, tell-each-other-everything kind of friends. Your banter should be smooth and easy. Like these two," he says, nodding toward Eli and me. "You're Eli and Via," he says.

"They're not," says Eli. "Their characters have nothing to do with us."

Word spreads of Murder Mystery Night's added edge, and we sell out every evening. Alumni return, including Norbert Cox and Logan Ahmadi, formerly known as Valentino. (Mr. Purcell pretends not to notice him.) Lines reach all the way through campus. We squeeze audience members into folding chairs. Some even stand in the back. Somehow, Mr. Purcell doesn't think dysentery is so bad anymore. "You two make a great duo," he admits. Eli and I exchange tight-lipped smiles. We don't talk to each other unless we have to.

We're passed around like minor celebrities once the show is over. Our friends congratulate us, parents pinch our cheeks. Daniel's Disney and Nickelodeon friends tell us how much they liked it. Zoe's the real star, however. Her comedic timing was so good it made everyone else fade into the background. She and I stand outside the theater and search for Gina, but unfortunately, she's a no-show.

"I'm sad she missed it," I confess to Zoe, several weeks after closing night. We're at the mall again. Our friendship took a bit of a hiatus after the show ended—she got caught up with KYOTV responsibilities, I started hunkering down on my schoolwork. That's the nature of extracurriculars, I guess.

"She would've hated it," Zoe says. "She hates everything."

"I'm obsessed with her. I think she's a character." I take a sip of my drink. "Like Borat."

We run over the basic catch-ups. Things are going well between her and a girl she's into. I've been listening to some new albums. Our respective siblings say hi.

"When do you start filming for that show you were cast in? Are you gonna have to take time off from school?"

She glances down at her cup and fusses with the straw. "I, uh, well. Actually, they recast me."

"What?"

"Yeah. I made it to the table read and everything. And then they decided that I look too young. So they recast me."

"I'm so sorry," I say.

"It's not a big deal, though. I was sad at first, but now, I'm like, whatever. Onto the next thing." She smiles and shrugs. Zoe's positive, always calm and collected, but a rejection like that would be a blow to anyone. Hollywood is cruel. Especially to girls. "It does suck, though. I was so close, you know?"

"Yeah," I say. "I'm sorry. They're stupid."

"Yeah, well."

I decide that now maybe isn't the best time to share my news—my Old Saybrook essay was accepted by the website, and I'm going to be published. I've been rejected from three more schools, but it doesn't hurt as much because my writing is out there in the world.

"How's Eli?"

"We haven't talked since Murder Mystery Night," I say.

"That sucks," she says.

Quiet, we watch the Topanga mall crowd. It's a Friday, so it's more claustrophobic in here than normal. A group of sixth-grade boys walk by with bags from Hot Topic.

"I have this idea, you know," I say, "that Gina's the ultimate Valley Girl."

One of the sixth graders gives Zoe a painfully obvious up-and-down. She shoos him away. "Yeah, right, for sure," she says. "There's no way. Two things. First off, Valley Girls are cool. Like us. We're Valley Girls. Gina's just mean. And, like, nuts."

"I guess you're right. It's an important title."

"Valley Girls write plays," she says.

"And they get TV roles," I answer.

"A true Valley Girl would *not* do what Gina did on the Disneyland bus," she notes. (At Calabasas High's Grad Night, she forced the entire bus to pull over at 4 a.m. so she could pee in a random gas station in the city.) "A Valley Girl would piss in a water bottle." She shakes her head. "No, Gina does *not* possess any of the Valley Girl's admirable traits."

"What's the second thing?" I ask. I fiddle with the handle of my shopping bag (two pairs of bobby socks and the neatest miniskirt).

"Well," Zoe says, and smiles. "I don't think she even lives in the Valley."

Lipvirgin in a New Dress

Kanye West wants my high school.

I walk across the quad in the afternoon, hall pass pressed in my palm. It's quiet. There's a boy playing guitar outside the music room, a stoner lying down on the lawn. A member of the year-book committee passes by with copies of the water polo spread. A couple sneaks off to the football field. And there's a few stray reporters in the parking lot, microphones cocked, cameras propped up on tripods to film B-roll for tonight's news. I avoid the scope of the camera; I've been there before. Nobody acknowledges the setup. We're used to it by now.

Calabasas High School was born in the olden days: 1975. A photograph of the first-ever graduating class hangs in the hallway of the main building: a grainy, saturated mess of bell-bottom jeans and feathered bangs. Freshman and sophomore year, the photo's a schoolwide joke; we zoom in on faces and jeer at the ponchos and paisley prints and dagger collars. Junior year, Free

People starts selling peasant tops, and suddenly the artifact hanging in the hall is a piece of retro decor.

It's an outdoor campus. Split into two quads, Calabasas High is thirty-nine beautiful acres of pure Californian scenery. Take a look around. Those rolling hills are the Santa Monica Mountains, coastal chaparral, home to oak and sycamore and bay laurel. Close your eyes and you'll hear running water, echoes from the nearby Calabasas Creek. Have a deep breath and you might catch a whiff of Malibu's ocean air, if the breeze is right. Rosebushes frame the outdoor staircase, tended to at regular intervals by a dedicated gardening staff. The academic buildings are a little run-down, true, but what CHS lacks in architectural presentation it makes up for in its library of Mac desktops and designer water vending machines.

Calabasas High has sixteen Advanced Placement courses offered for college credit. The graduation rate is 95 percent. There are around eighty active clubs on campus. It's a Blue Ribbon School, which means it ranks highly in standardized testing. The school is largely homogenous. Eighty percent of the student body identifies as white. It falls in the top 10 percent of California schools when it comes to familial income. Parents are mostly neoliberals.

And Kanye West wants us. He wants to donate millions of dollars. Revamp the sports facilities. Redesign the football uniforms. Change the mascot from the Calabasas Coyotes to the Calabasas Wolves. Kanye West would like to effectively turn Calabasas High School into the first-ever Yeezy institution.

Celebrities dipping their toes—and dollars-—into education isn't new. In fact, it's even happened in Calabasas before, when

Will and Jada Pinkett Smith founded the New Village Leadership Academy back in 2008. It wasn't long lived, and closed its doors in 2013 after parents accused the school of indoctrinating students with Scientology-slanted curriculum. Of course, there have been wildly successful instances of celebrities giving back, too. Take Chance the Rapper, for example, who has donated millions of dollars to underfunded schools in his hometown of Chicago. Perhaps Kanye, after receiving copious backlash for his endorsement of Donald Trump, hoped that by following Chance's example he could gain similar favor in the press. Perhaps. The only thing is, Calabasas High's parking lot could be mistaken for an Audi dealership.

But hey, Calabasas High isn't going to complain. The second half of my senior year is overshadowed by the attention. Where we'd usually be discussing prom after-parties and college acceptances, we debate the ramifications of Kanye's offer. It's a divisive topic. Loyalists can't fathom leaving the coyote school mascot behind. And after all, West has been known for his outspokenness. One ill-thought-out comment could tarnish the reputation of the entire school. But Kanye fans push back. He is, after all, a musical genius. There is no denying his talent. Plus, it would be hilarious.

We joke about his curriculum. Maybe he'll add more electives. An esthetician class on asshole-bleaching. Film lectures on the art of the *home movie*. And as for uniforms, why stop with the sports teams? Maybe he'll introduce us to a whole new dress code: bike shorts. Eyewear with tiny lenses. A large portion of the student body already wears Fashion Nova, so why not go the full nine yards?

I glance back at the reporters, who are now beginning to pack up their gear. In my hand I have a check for five dollars. I'm ordering an official transcript for my community college application. I've received notice of rejection from all but one school—my top school, the College of Creative Studies at UC Santa Barbara. And things aren't looking too good there either. The average GPA for accepted students is 4.1. I'd spent hours haunting online forums for a shred of hope, maybe a single anomaly. But I saw nothing but students with far better academic records than mine getting denied.

In the main office, I see one of the campus overachievers. I offer a smile.

"Transcripts?" he asks.

"You know how it is," I say.

"Isn't it such crap that we have to pay for this?"

"Yeah," I say, placing my envelope into a basket on the counter.

"No offense, of course, Ms. Brungardt," he says to the receptionist. "Anyway, see you around, Via."

In a few months it'll be revealed that he applied early decision to multiple universities, a big no-no in the college system. But it won't matter all that much. He ends up at an Ivy League anyway.

Calabasas suffers from a false sense of consequence. For many students, college isn't a matter of if, but when. People like Zoe and Eli are exceptions to the rule, and even they are often on the receiving end of more than a couple raised eyebrows.

But of course, there are some obstacles. Grades, for example. If you want to go to a good college, you have to study. But Calabasas High students have found some workarounds. Super rich kids enroll in AP courses online or at phony tutoring services. If they're *very* rich and lazy, they might hire someone to take their exams in their place. I heard about someone who received acceptances from all the top UCs via this method. They're CHS students through a technicality, attending campus for only a bare minimum of hours. Not everyone has this option, though, so others are pushed to find academic successes through simpler (but still nefarious) means. I once took a math midterm with a particularly unpopular teacher. At the start of the testing period, a boy handed out blank pieces of scrap paper to the whole class. "It's composted paper," he explained, "so it's good for the environment." As I leaned back in my chair, prepared to fail, something glinted on the sheet before me—this was trick paper, and when held at just the right angle to the light, I could detect invisible type. Every formula we'd been taught was printed into the paper. A man of the people. More commonplace methods include test questions smuggled onto Quizlet, or programming answers into calculators, or sneaking prewritten responses into in-class essays.

As decisions roll out, I notice more and more tears on campus. Doors slammed halfway through lecture, urgent sprints to the bathrooms: these are the sounds of springtime. "Where'd you get in?" is the new "What's up?" I dodge these questions at all costs. I've learned how to flee a lunch table as soon as someone mentions a UC. I've mastered the art of the subject change. I'd rather nobody ask me about college ever again. The exchange is always painful. *Nowhere, thanks for asking.* And then: *Oh, sorry. I'm sure it'll work out. Community college is a smarter investment anyways.* And that all might be true, but still—there's condescension in their tone.

And then, UC Santa Barbara releases its decisions. In my science class I see others sneaking into a different Internet tab, stalking the online portals. Huffs of disappointment. Abrupt exits to the bathroom. I shouldn't look, it'll only upset me. "It's okay," I hear one student console another. "Even the valedictorian was wait-listed."

On a whim, I check the admissions portal. I conceal my phone behind my leg and slump in my seat. The website loads slowly. But when it finally does, I feel my arm raising, hear my own voice ask to please be excused. Then I'm outside, and I'm leaning against the wall, and I'm calling my mother, and I'm crying.

"Are you okay? Olivia? Are you hurt?"

"I'm fine," I say. I can't remember the last time I've called my mother just to talk. But she's still in my reflexes. "Everything's okay. Sorry. I didn't mean to freak you out."

"What's going on? Olivia?"

"I just got accepted to the writing program at UCSB."

As soon as I say it, it's real. I google pictures of campus, marvel at the little yellow building where my writing classes will be held. I read course lists, stalk current students on Instagram. I don't freeze up at the future tense.

I wish I could tell Eli, but we're not like that anymore.

Calabasas' senior prom is a big deal. Past locations include: an airplane hangar, the Jim Henson Soundstage, and the Malibu arches. Girls in my grade start comparing dresses in the autumn. I haven't put much thought into it yet. Haven't even looked for a dress online. It's not that I think I'm above it or anything, it's just that the whole premise makes me kind of nervous.

The prom announcements are at the end of a pep rally in spring. It's the only one I don't skip. It's packed—I have trouble finding a seat, so I squeeze into the bleachers next to some classroom acquaintances. We're in the early stages of friendship, which means everything is still slightly awkward, and when we're prompted to cheer, we just kind of sit there.

Paisley Henderson and Parker Judge sit in front of us. They're both shoo-ins for prom court. I hesitate to use the word *popular* because there seems to be an implication of bitchiness there. They're both friendly, and it makes sense that everyone likes them.

I take a look around me to see if there's anyone else I know nearby. There's George, and over there that's Cub, and a couple of rows away I notice Cory and Paige. Zoe sits crisscross applesauce on the floor of the gym with the rest of the dance team. I wonder if Eli's skipping again.

He's not. In time for the pep rally game, in which representatives from each grade compete on an obstacle course, Eli emerges from the sidelines to play for the seniors.

"Fuckable," Paisley says.

"Yeah," says Parker. "Would you?"

There's a roar of teenage yelps as a freshman is smacked in the head with a water balloon.

". . . know him that well," Paisley says. I've missed the first half of whatever she's said.

"Talk to him, then," says Parker.

"Maybe," says Paisley. "But I won't go for it unless he talks to me first."

Eli's a great guy. And Paisley's cool. She's asked me for book recommendations before. She and Eli would make sense together. But there was a lilt in the way she said it, the way she called him *fuckable*. If you're gonna like Eli, like him for his sense of humor, or the fact that he once stopped the car to save a runaway baby turtle and bring it back to the pond, or because when he played the lead in the fall play, he cried for real during his monologues, or how he never used to call me Via, just "V." Maybe I'm thinking too much into it, I don't know. But I wonder if I should tell Eli that Paisley's into him. I mean, on the one hand, I shouldn't try to deny him a potential love interest. But on the other hand, well. From a technical standpoint, she probably wouldn't have said anything had she known I was right behind her. It's not even my business. And besides, it would be strange for me to approach him out of the blue, after we've avoided each other for this long. I decide to pretend like I didn't hear anything. I won't say a word. Because it's the right thing to do. For Paisley. I can't betray her trust like that. Satisfied, I fold my arms.

The prom theme is announced and it's something bland and forgettable, like "A Night of Magic" or "Starlight Romance." I'm not really paying attention. The main driving force for my prom attendance is my mother. I can't begin to count how many family dinners have been derailed by my anti-prom speeches and my mother's insistence that I go anyway. "What, do you think you're too cool or something?" she always asks.

"Yes," I answer. But it's not the truth. While sure, I'd rather sulk at home in my Doc Martens listening to, like, Peter Ivers or the Modern Lovers or something else way pretentious, it's not because of my edge complex. Instead, I'm scared by the prospect. In the last couple of weeks, all my boy-space-friends have stumbled into relationships or casual associations: Cub's seeing resident cool-girl Amy Shin, George McCloskey's taking April Stewart. Daniel's got a girlfriend. Cory's already been asked by a friend from another school. And all this prom pressure reminds me of the tenth circle of Hell—the eighth-grade dance.

The theme was "Masquerade Ball" and I'd worn a lime-green high-low dress from Forever 21 and Maybelline mascara in the pink bottle. You know. The works. We were still infatuated with *Jersey Shore*; hence, the night was filled with fist pumps and Bumpits. The DJ played censored versions of all the hits: CeeLo Green's "Forget You," Cher Lloyd's "Want U Back," and of course, generational anthem "Like a G6."

The chaperones allowed our parents to come in to watch the slow dance, the first I'd ever taken part in. "A Thousand Years" by Christina Perri—the crown jewel of the *Twilight* franchise soundtrack. I stood on the outskirts of the crowd, pretending to be preoccupied with the candy buffet.

"Wanna dance, Olivia?" Chris Hines appeared from thin air as I shoved a gummy bear into my mouth. And I was about to say yes, until I realized his friends were behind him, stifling laughs.

"I'm good," I said, and turned back to the snack table.

"Lipvirgin," one of the boys muttered.

Lipvirgin. That's the chip on my shoulder keeping me from prom. *Lipvirgin.* Stupid. But still.

As prom comes closer, so do logistical discussions. I'm asked who I'm going with, if I've got a dress. Which bus will I be on? Everyone's booking hotel rooms for afterward, so we have to make sure everyone's rooms are close to one another. I shrug off these questions.

"Let's go get you a dress," my mother says. We're parked outside a Macy's. "Come on."

"I don't wanna go."

"I'm not going to have my daughter miss out on prom."

"I don't care, actually, so there's that."

"You're going to look back and regret it," she says. "All your friends are going."

"What if all my friends jumped off a bridge?"

"Twenty minutes. Just look around," she says. "For me."

Already, we're late to the game. The formal section of the store is a wreck. A third of the racks are empty. Every girl in the store has a pained expression on her face. Hell is a Macy's at three o'clock in the middle of prom season. My mother and I take in the scene, then grab whatever's left in my size from the sales racks.

We reconvene in the dressing room. I wear a full skirted, floor-length pink dress. I run my fingers over the bodice. Bedazzled. "I look like a birthday cake," I tell my mom.

"You look great," she says. "I like this one."

"I look ridiculous." I strip myself of this bubblegum monstrosity and try on the next one: blue, way too small. And then the next: green, atrocious. "I hate all of these," I say. "The strife is not worth the experience, I'll tell you that."

"*Strife,*" she repeats.

"Yeah, strife."

"You're gonna be sad you didn't go."

"I'll be fine."

"You need to get out of your comfort zone. You were fine going to your homecoming dances."

I button my jeans. "Homecoming's different. It's way more casual."

"You should be doing everything you can in high school," my mother says. "Do you want to look back and think: Gee, I wish I'd done that? No, you don't. You don't want to have any regrets in life. Stop taking the easy way out." She passes me my T-shirt, and I pull it over my head. "Think like a writer."

"Wait. So she falls in love with Skrillex and then dies of dysentery. I get that. But I think we're missing a transition or something here. It happens too abruptly."

"Shh," Eli said. It was pitch black, but from the blue light emanating from his laptop I could make out his hand lifting a finger to his lips. "You're being way too loud."

"Right," I whispered back.

"Okay," he said softly, "so what were you saying?"

This was back in the fall, when Eli and I were just starting to write the script for Murder Mystery Night. Fresh from our KYOTV rejection, we'd met several times before, outlining our draft, building a cast of characters. Now, the due date was impending nearer and nearer. Six days left to come up with two complete acts. Tonight, we'd converged in a dark crevice of the theater, one we deemed most unlikely to be stumbled upon by a grown-up. Several rooms over, Mr. Purcell was moderating a PTA meeting—so we had to stay quiet.

"Snack?" I said. We'd packed a supply of Hostess cakes in advance.

He reached into his backpack and tossed me a Twinkie, the official snack of our friendship. "We can rework that part if it's confusing," he said.

"I dunno," I said. "I feel like we've been staring at this for so long that nothing makes sense anymore."

"Well, look," he said. I moved closer and leaned in to look at his computer screen. He smelled nice. "We could take this," he said, highlighting a block of text, "and we could put it here, if that makes more sense."

"Hm. Yeah, I guess," I said, unwrapping the Twinkie. "I'm so tired."

"I'm tired too, but we gotta finish this," he said.

"Maybe we should resume tomorrow."

"V," he said, his voice raising in volume, "we have to finish this. If we don't, someone else's script will get picked, and it'll be shit, and then Murder Mystery Night will suck and it'll be our fault for not giving them our genius. Well. Your genius," he said.

"No way," I said. "You came up with the whole plotline about the Top Ramen heist. Inspired."

"This should be a breeze, right? If Sharon McGill could do it last year, we should be fine."

As he spoke, I heard sounds coming near. "Shh," I said, stuffing the Twinkie into his mouth before he could protest. The footsteps moved closer. I closed the laptop and lay back behind a row of chairs, yanking Eli down next to me by the shoulder.

"Ow," he said, muffled.

A light turned on. "Hello?" It's Mr. Purcell. "I heard voices," Purcell said. "Show yourselves or I'll have to check security cams, and you'll be in twice as much trouble for wasting my time."

I met Eli's eyes. He swallowed the last of the Twinkie and shrugged. "Just, uh, me and V," he said, standing up and brushing crumbs off his T-shirt. He offered a smile. Of course. I should've known. In no conceivable universe could Eli ever get in actual trouble. Adults love him.

Mr. Purcell shook his head. "Get out of here," he said. "I don't even want to know what you two are up to."

We moved to the parking lot. We squinted at our notes in the dark before it got too cold and we decided to go home. "Fuck," he said. "I wanted to get more done tonight."

"It's okay. Worst-case scenario, we don't finish in time and we take our mischief elsewhere. We'll find a new project."

"Like what?"

I thought about it for a second. "The Scientology Celebrity Centre," I said finally, "in downtown LA."

Although Los Angeles is supposedly littered with them, I've never actually met a Scientologist. Of if I have, I wasn't aware of it at the time. The organization is shrouded in mystery; for the curious teenager, it's the neighborhood boogeyman, or the haunted house on the end of the block. It's the inspiration for many empty threats at dinner tables: Well, one day I'll join Scientology and

I'll cut everybody off. L. Ron Hubbard is especially fascinating because he's only recently dead. There's plenty of debate over whether or not Jesus Christ really existed, or Buddha, or Zoroaster. But L. Ron Hubbard, executive director of the Church of Scientology, was a real person, one who lived long enough to see the release of Kate Bush's fifth studio album. That blows my mind. And his legacy, the Church, is splattered all over LA. The command base sits on Fountain Avenue, its big blue facade looking out over the rest of the world like the breast of a haunted ship, a cerulean chunk of evidence for "the cult of personality." And only a little ways away, eight stories high, looms the Celebrity Centre, the Church's largest recruitment tactic. I've heard plenty of rumors about what happens inside, all deeply horrifying.

"You wanna die," he said.

"I wanna write about it," I said.

"You wanna get framed for a murder," he said.

"It'll be fun. There's a restaurant inside. Maybe we'll see Tom Cruise."

"Infiltrate the Scientologists if our script flops," he said. "Good plan. I like it." He spat in the palm of his hand. "Thinking like a writer."

"No," I said.

"Don't be a dick." He shrugged. "Come on."

I shook his hand.

At the time, it didn't feel like it meant much. But now, I feel like I've broken a pact. The handshake wasn't about writing a play or investigating a cult—it was about staying friends, even if we weren't bound together by something school-related. Of course, we never went to the Scientology Centre because our script did get chosen, but maybe we'd have been better off losing. Because we haven't talked in weeks. I wonder if my mother's right, and I'll come to regret different parts of high school. Ones unrelated to prom.

I think about the two of us, skipping class to hang out behind the dumpsters. Going to his house after school and making grilled cheese sandwiches. The time we visited the Leonis Adobe Museum and fed the goats until closing time. Or when we went to Starbucks and he got up to go to the bathroom, and while he was gone an old lady at the table next to us told me it was so wonderful to see young love, and I was like, "No, it's not like that," and she was all like, "Suure."

"What's going on?" my mother asks. We've left the dressing room for the midday glare of the Macy's parking lot. My hand hovers over the passenger's side door handle.

"Huh?"

"You look out of it," she says.

I open the door and get inside. "It's nothing," I say.

I think about asking Eli to prom but I don't, because I don't care about things like prom, and I don't like him like that anyway. I know I'm supposed to think like a writer, but at the end of the day I'm going to think like a teenage girl who's been saturated in seventeen-year-old suburban apathy, one who cares too much about seeming affected or involved and would much rather maintain a tight image of carelessness. I smoke weed and I skip class and I don't want to care about fancy dresses or slow dances.

And besides, when I do talk to him—for the first time in a long while—he's got his arm around Cassie. She congratulates me for getting into college, I congratulate her for making things official with Eli.

"I miss hanging out. A lot. This is all so dumb, you know?" he says to me.

"No, yeah, I was thinking the exact same thing, actually," I say. "Fighting's stupid."

"You both just had a lot on your plate, I think," Cassie says.

"We should hang out again sometime," Eli says.

"Yeah. Maybe we could still visit the Scientology Centre. For this thing I'm writing."

"Yeah, that'd be sick," Eli says.

"All of us could go," I offer, and nod at Cassie. "Could be a fun thing, I don't know."

"For sure," says Cassie. "Let's do it."

But we won't, and I think we all know it.

Prom's at the Hummingbird Nest Ranch, a venue in Simi Valley that's usually reserved for weddings or movie shoots. Someone at CHS was able to pull a few strings, as usual.

The biggest part of prom isn't the actual event, of course—it's the photos everyone takes at the park for an hour before. It's a maze of mothers, all armed with DSLRs and pocket combs. Then the buses come and take us to the ranch, 123 acres of sprawling lawn and white tablecloths. I'm wearing a dress I found for thirty dollars. It's long, with pink flowers, and it's the kind of dress I could wear to dinner if I wanted. I like that about it. It's not sacred to anything.

Tristan Laypalm, one of last year's graduates, is my date. Of course, it's a formality. We're acquaintances, he's seeing a guy at his university. We arrive to the venue separately.

Eli catches me filling up a little plastic cup with water. "Hey, V," he says. "You look really pretty."

"Thanks. You too. Not pretty. Good, I guess. You look good," I say.

"Who're you here with?"

"Tristan," I say. "Your favorite."

"Cool," he says, "maybe I can get him to finally write that Every Fifteen Minutes letter."

I start filling my plate with french fries. "I gotta go, but I'll see you at the after-party?" he says, and I nod. And then I watch him walk away. I'm not sure if I'm sad. I'm not sure how I feel at all. I zone off into the crowd, taking lazy bites from my plate.

"Via," Cub says. He's in a gray tuxedo. He takes a seat across from me.

"Hey," I say. I nudge my fries over to him.

"I think things happen if they're supposed to happen," he says. "I hope I'm not overstepping anything, but maybe in the end it's better you ended up as friends. You know?"

I shrug.

"And I hope you don't let anything make you feel bad about yourself," he adds. "And seriously. I think you're cool. So, you know, don't forget who you are."

I smile at him. "So wise," I say.

Prom is uneventful. Parker Judge doesn't win prom queen, but she doesn't care anyway. One of the band kids requests "Party Rock Anthem" three times in a row. The slow song is "A

Thousand Years." I guess not much has changed since 2013. But by that time, Tristan's long gone—he's left to pick up alcohol for the after-party. I visit the bathroom and lock myself into a stall and I wait for it to be over.

I sit on the closed lid of the toilet and prop my heels against the stall door. Outside, Christina Perri croons. I ponder a glittering Robert Pattinson.

My phone buzzes. It's Tristan.

TRISTAN

peach or mango ciroc?

Ghosts of prom-parties past have granted Calabasas High a permanent ban from most hotels in the Valley. Each year, the seniors have to migrate farther and farther downtown. Tonight, the only hotel that will have us is all the way at LAX.

The bus ride is almost an hour long, and the playlist is bizarre. "Sister Christian" repeats twice. Someone in the back threatens to vomit into someone else's clutch purse; everyone freaks out for a second, but it's just a false alarm. Eli and Cassie sit across from me. Nobody's drunk enough to have an excessive amount of fun. There's the occasional burst of energy, a joke peppered in here and there, but the bus is otherwise quiet. I lean back in my seat. Out the window, there's a stream of other cars headed downtown. It's late at night, but it's still June. We're overrun with tourists, probably returning to their hotels, or going to a late showing of *La La Land,* maybe visiting a celebrity's grave. All of LA flickers behind a chain-link fence.

There's the promise of stardom somewhere out there, wedged between the Os of the Hollywood sign, or on a balcony of the Griffith Observatory. It's being sold at a kiosk on the Walk of Fame. You can get a little plastic Oscar engraved with whatever you want.

I think I see the silhouette of the Scientology Celebrity Centre protruding over the highway's retaining wall. I look over at Eli but I don't say anything. Next year, he'll move to Hollywood and I won't see him much. Sometimes he'll text me a memory from high school, an old inside joke. He'll go on auditions but he won't have a big break, at least as far as I know. I'll hear he's doing production work somewhere, editing videos for YouTube influencers, fetching coffees on sets. Cassie will get into Stanford and they'll break up. One day, not too far in the future, we'll all become near strangers. But that's just high school.

The hotel is run amuck with the drunk and the horny. Instead of one big party, there's dozens of little ones in all the different rooms. You play roulette, knock on any door, and hope it's someone you know. The elevator is on a constant bounce between floors 2–6. It reeks of weed and alcohol and post-prom BO. The carpeting in this place is stained and the overhead lights flicker. In anticipation, the hotel's hired security guards, posted on every floor.

We get drunk and order Subway sandwiches at two-thirty a.m. Cub's kicked out of his room for belligerence and sleeps in his car. I crack my phone screen in a bathtub. When I wake up in the morning, I have three fidget spinners on my nightstand and my shoes are missing, so I buy a pair of flip-flops from a bodega next door and we all meet for waffles at a diner back in Calabasas.

"Well. That's over," Cub says, and then he passes me the coffee.

Graduation day arrives hand-in-hand with a record-breaking wave of hundred-degree heat. We're seated in collapsible chairs on the football field. The smart kids bring handheld battery-powered fans. The slightly less-smart kids bring bottles of Dasani. But most of us just sit there and sweat.

In this extreme heat, the last few weeks have gone by in slow motion. Interest in Kanye's pursuit of our school title has dwindled. It's hard to think about anything besides the sun. I've already said my goodbyes, counting each time I close my locker or walk across the quad. Yesterday I stood on the edge of the lawn and thought long and hard about how I will probably never stand in this exact spot ever again. When I lifted my foot, I felt like I was officially grown up.

Some students tried to shove in some last-minute hijinks. There was the senior prank, when hordes of kids snuck into the humanities building in the middle of the night to glue slices of bologna to the portraits of former class presidents. A student body officer tried knocking on Kanye's door to ask him to perform at our prom. Someone was caught watching porn in the computer lab.

When Kanye's representatives walked on campus for the last time, nobody tried heckling. Nobody stood outside Stack's door with a glass to the ear. We glanced nonchalantly and didn't move from our lunch tables. Because we'd all arrived at the same conclusion: it does not matter if Kanye West buys our school or not.

To the rest of the world, Calabasas isn't a place so much as it is a Snapchat geotag.

I have no school spirit. I just want to wrap this up and lie down under an air-conditioning vent. I look through the crowd and make eye contact with a familiar face: it's Connor Nesbitt from Catholic school. He must've transferred, and I never even knew until now.

Ms. Stack takes the podium to give her big speech. She's brought a giant bottle of electrolyte water onstage with her, of course. This is her moment. She clears her throat, taps the mic, rambles on for fifteen minutes about how we're such a great and wonderful class. I tune out for most of it and stare instead at her water bottle. Beads of condensation collect around the label. It's ice cold. I've never wanted to storm a stage as much as I do right now. I want to yank the bottle off of the podium and spray it into the crowd of graduates.

"And finally," Mrs. Stack says, wrapping up, "finally, I would like to give my warmest congratulations to the class of two thousand and seventeen. We are proud to be—"

She takes a dramatic pause.

". . . the Calabasas Coyotes. Not WOLVES. Never WOLVES. Sorry, Kanye, but we are Coyotes, and we will always be Coyotes. Valiance, nobility, grace, and courage. That's what the coyote represents. And that is what we are, and what we forever will be."

The class erupts in cheers. Five hundred arms, fist pumping the air.

* * *

And then, just like that, I hardly know anybody anymore.

That's the funny thing about high school. Everything's so important. Then it's over.

The months between graduation and freshman year of college go by like I'm on autopilot. There's no summer work. Late May, I make trips to retail hellscape Bed Bath & Beyond and buy the same green shower caddy that every other first-year gets. In June, I take a plane to my grandmother's house in Old Saybrook. She's recently moved into an independent living facility in Maryland. We're staying at her Connecticut place for most of the summer, packing up her things, donating old furniture. In rooms I'm not allowed to go, in phone calls I'm exempt from, the adults talk about selling. Market value. Zillow. Remodels. Open houses.

Jackie and I pretend like we don't hear it. This house is as much a part of my childhood as my real home. Maybe more so. I can count back my life in household inventories: serving spoons, baskets of potpourri, bedroom wallpaper. Cheap orange bars of soap that sting.

So I lean into the meantime. Summer is in full swing, and Junes in Old Saybrook feel different than they do at home. For breakfast we sit on the front stoop and watch the early risers tug their fishing gear toward the Long Island Sound. For lunch we have tuna sandwiches and we eat them barefoot in the backyard. For dinner we order pizzas from the restaurant near the train station, or my mother cooks pasta, or we have a big family meal at the English pub on Boston Post Road. And for the in-betweens, I ride my bike to the used bookshop. Or the grocery. Or the ice cream stand. I keep a mass-market paperback in my back pocket and a pencil in my shoe. My sister sells cups of lemonade from the driveway at twenty-five cents each.

July brings rain. The marsh droops heavy with mosquito and sludge. We sit by the screen doors and play cards. Pools of water and sidewalk chalk mix in little purple moons at the park across the street. The public tennis court sags in the middle, like paper folding into itself.

We don't have WiFi or television, and cell connection is spotty. We read books, play board games, take walks. I don't know what's happening in the world. I don't know what's happening with my classmates. I'm sure there are parties. Vacations to five-star resorts. European tours. But there's no way to know for sure, so I don't care.

August arrives with a sweep of humidity. I take showers. Maybe even twice a day. Sometimes I shampoo, sometimes I just stand there, pressing my fingers into the glass, drawing pictures in the steam. Most of the house has been cleared out now. I pace the living room over and over again; there's no coffee table to stop me. My grandmother's collection of Waterford crystal is in piles on the floor. It's worthless now. Even the Salvation Army won't take it. I pick up the crystal grapes and hide them in my backpack.

When it's time to leave, we do so slowly. We have a long breakfast. I have a bagel and a soft-boiled egg and I chew them thoughtfully. I pull the crystal grapes from my backpack and return them to a shelf.

My father narrates as we drive out of the Old Saybrook town limits like he's reading us a picture book. Jackie and I point out our favorite parts. Flagpoles. Hydrangea bushes. That old white dog we always see sleeping on our neighbor's front lawn. The future is unsure for the Old Saybrook house, so we might as well say goodbye in case it's our last time.

We take Route 66 home. We stop at Graceland, barbed wire museums, sixty-six-foot tall soda bottles and Panhandle ghost towns. I like the kitsch. Every town in the world is famous for something or other, whether it's an Eagles song (Winslow, Arizona) or the second-largest cross in the western hemisphere (Groom, Texas). Calabasas isn't unique, in fact, it's all the marketing with none of the originality that makes a small town so special.

In September, I move to Santa Barbara. I'm going to be living in the Santa Catalina dorms, about a mile from the campus. I can see the ocean from my room. My new roommate strings fairy lights above her head. "Where are you from?" I ask.

"Nebraska," she says, pinning a Polaroid to the wall. "What about you?"

I watch her sort through her photographs, all of friends of hers from home. They stand in front of foreign landscapes, smiling next to trees I've never seen and likely never will. There are graduation photos, too. They look the same as mine. My mouth acts before my brain does. "I'm from Calabasas," I say.

She hops down from her bed and looks at me curiously.

"Calabasas," she repeats. "Where's that?"

Epilogue

NO MORE SMALL TALK

Maybe it's because I'm in the middle of a midlife crisis (something that my housemate Katie says is entirely plausible, considering climate change will wipe us out in twenty years) that I am so desperate to make sense of things, that I feel a compulsive need to cling to a specific place in time where I can say I grew up and became someone else—someone whole and sound and altogether unconfused. But a midlife crisis implies ennui, and I don't feel bored or hung up on life. It's more of a creeping discombobulation. To cope, I've started taking three to six walks a day. I've made a game of counting the lawn chairs in my neighborhood. Twenty-seven yesterday evening, twenty-five today. I hope it means something.

The truth is that I'm looking for an epiphany. The search is extensive. I read books with terrible covers. I order something new off the menu. I try drugs and I talk to strangers. But none of these things brings me any closer to a definitive resolution, and in fact they only tie me up in a million new ways. "Don't be a dope," my father says over the phone, but interesting stories don't come from taking advice. And besides, I live in Isla Vista. It's a college town of 23,000 subpar decision makers, all crammed into a single square mile between ocean bluffs and a couple dozen grease pits. The specter haunting UCSB is a pillar of smoke in the strain Grandaddy Purp, or perhaps the sudden ubiquity of ketamine at house parties. Our sidewalks glitter with emptied whippits. We aren't exactly grounded in decorum. When I write my name in wet cement or crash my bike into someone's garage or vomit into a manzanita bush, I'm only doing as the Romans do.

My epiphany was supposed to come over a year ago, when I first signed the book deal. It arrived by email, thirty pages of legal jargon wedged between a discount code for 1-800-FLOWERS and a gallery of B-horror movie recommendations from Amazon Prime. I was sure that once I submitted the e-signature, my life would split into pre and post. I'd grow a cup size and win the lottery. But what actually happened was this: The little white bar in my Gmail inbox turned gray, and I closed my laptop.

I spent the whole day waiting for it. I took a walk on the beach. I warmed up frozen dumplings. Read a book. I went with a boy to see a local band play at a house show. Maybe the epiphany would come there, I hoped. But as we stood on the balcony, swaying to a disjointed bass line, passing joints and cigarettes and whatever else to darting silhouettes, I only felt like I was missing the point. I couldn't find it in myself to wax nostalgic about the poetic value of a college party, to euphemize the state of being a stranger, or the funny, friendly lightness of getting drunk. Parties in IV can feel hopeless sometimes. You make best friends with a girl one night and she tells you about her ex from high school, about her GPA, about how the copper IUD really fucking hurt. In the morning you'll maybe follow each other on Instagram and that's it. It's happened dozens of times before. "It's cool you got close with so-and-so," the boy I was with said, after seeing me talk to someone for fifteen minutes. I nodded, bit the cigarette filter, and changed the subject. At house shows I tried to maintain a certain degree of unaffectedness, but really, I found it entirely alarming that people could have such varying definitions of closeness. I took a step back from the crowd. Of course, faking coolness is a trap. I've caught myself saying things that ascribe to the way I imagine others characterize me, rather than things I really mean. Conversation feels distantly familiar, like we're repeating things we've heard on TV or seen on Twitter. It's fun to dance, but then what?

I glanced back at him—he was entertaining a group of his friends, recanting a sexual escapade he'd shared with a girl that wasn't me—and I leaned over the embankment so I could watch the ocean gurgle against the rocks. It was too dark to see anything. Somewhere down below, there were tide pools, entire countries of shrimp and minnows and snails who'd never felt lonely while holding somebody's hand, who'd never thrown up five shots of Kirkland into an unknown toilet and then gone home to wish that things could be neatly tied into a personal essay. I thought about the hermit crab. He's never had any expectations. Neither has the sea star, the jellyfish, the barnacle. In a tide pool, you don't have to do party work and you don't have to learn lessons. You just eat seaweed and tiny worms and that's all.

I turned around and rejoined the crowd. Poured one out for

the sake of lost causes: I was jealous of a crab, which is about as far from enlightenment as someone can get. I figured I should stop looking for signs. If an epiphany was on its way, it wouldn't reveal itself on the balcony of a house on Del Playa Drive, nor would it happen while I was losing feeling in my face, and I seriously doubt it would come to me while a DIY cover of a Tyler song was playing.

Then came the third-act bombshell. Midway through my junior year, the coronavirus pandemic confiscated Isla Vista of all its hedonisms and indignities and sent me back to the Valley. I'd never seen Los Angeles so still and gray. My first night back, I lay down in the middle of my street and let the Santa Ana winds roll over my body. There were no cars to worry about. I'd tripped over a pause button. Life wasn't real, and neither was time. I stopped turning pages in my calendar. Months came and went; it was March, then April, then May, but my walls still read March 12 and my mind was still set on March 12 and in my bones I could swear it was still March 12, and the worst part was that my confusion didn't even seem worth writing about, since everyone else was already doing it. I didn't know how to explain to my parents that no, I couldn't wake up early because I wasn't keeping up with time, and I couldn't bring myself to feign dinner-table enthusiasm when I'd forgotten what it felt like to stand close to somebody. That was another thing—I was living with my parents for the longest period since high school, and it didn't take much time for me to see that things had changed. I wasn't a kid anymore. And my parents weren't an infallible authority—they were people, ones I disagreed with often, especially when we talked about the world. I love them, but for the first time I understood the distinctly individual nature of adulthood. But that wasn't the epiphany I'd been looking for, just something everyone has to notice eventually.

Then June came. I caved to my vices and ordered a discreet Puff Bar off of Depop. Didn't even dome, just felt massive amounts of shame, because I felt like such a zoomer tool, squirreling away in the family bathroom to suck off something flavored "Lush Ice." I sat on the floor and glared at the nic stick. I was in suspension. I missed my housemates, and I couldn't focus on my classes online. But most of all, my search for enlightenment had plateaued. Isla Vista was to me now what Calabasas High once was: a place to fuck up, or discover something new, or both. Probably both. I shoved the Puff into my sock. It was time to go back.

In Isla Vista, my epiphany was long overdue. And while I'd stopped reading into balconies, my listlessness manifested in odd ways: the fixation on walking, for example, or the way I sometimes kept the lights off when I showered, because fumbling in the dark, flinging my palms at the wall, was the simplest and most available form of catharsis. I shared one of my walks with a boy who had a mullet and worked in the campus greenhouse; he showed me the pindo palm, whose little orange fruit tastes exactly like piña colada. "There's so much fruit to eat if you pay attention," he told me. "You just have to know where to look." I thought about the killer oranges back home.

My housemates and I became a unit. We took up new hobbies. Katie got into cooking, Rachelle bought a Venus flytrap, and

I got weirdly competitive about playing Smash. On the downside, our nicotine habits turned to full-blown dependencies. "Can I hit your JUUL?" I asked Rachelle. I was sitting on the kitchen counter, eating baby carrots out of the bag.

"No, rat," she said.

"Eat your carrots," Katie added.

I admired Katie because it seemed like her epiphany had already come. She'd started keeping crystals on her windowsill, pulled tarot cards. Said "thank you" to the moon. "It's totally working," she said. "I'm pretty sure I'm gonna stop having diarrhea soon."

"That's huge," I said. For the last year or so, Katie's identity had been closely tied to the fact that she was always in serious gastrointestinal distress. Other facets of character include: sleeping on an upright futon, drinking moonshine, and attending a threesome while keeping her beanie on the whole time.

"That has nothing to do with the moon," Rachelle said, "and everything to do with the fact that you stopped with the 7-Eleven pizza."

"No way, dude. TikTok keeps recommending me these videos about, like, how to manifest good things into your life. You just have to give off the right vibes. So, I've been trying to manifest not shitting my pants every day. It should start working any second now, 'cause my vibes have been, like, crazy good."

"Can confirm," I said. "Just look at her. She's, like, in tune with her higher consciousness."

Katie nodded in agreement and choked on a piece of pickle.

"Placebo," Rachelle said.

"I manifested you to come out of your room just now, so."

"I'm going to manifest myself leaving," Rach said.

"Long as I get to watch you walk away," says Katie. "I manifested that, too."

I stood up. "Going on another walk?" Rachelle said. It was long past midnight.

"Yeah," I answered, and pocketed a canister of pepper spray. "You have my location."

Isla Vista doesn't have a bedtime. I ran into people I knew, only now it was perfectly fine if I crossed to the other side of the street, one of the few benefits of the pandemic being the obsolescence of small talk. I saw a kid from the school newspaper. A member of the radio club. I even thought I saw the boy from the house show skate by, though of course we didn't acknowledge each other. I kept walking. I stood outside 7-Eleven, took laps around the block, visited the cliffs. I homaged Katie with a thank-you to the moon, hoping that I'd summon a mystic sign or a sense of closure. Anything. I was sick of the gray areas, of being grown-up but not really, of feeling like I was missing out on some existential truth that every adult has filed away with their auto-shop receipts and tax returns.

Somehow, morning had arrived. I sat on the cliffs and watched the sun climb over the ocean. The seagulls cawed at each other, skimming the water for breakfast in wide, lounging scoops. I squinted at the early morning surfers, perhaps the most relaxed population in Isla Vista. I know quite a few; they all claim that surfing is an exercise in tranquility. "But if you eat shit, the water's so cold," I'd always said back, but maybe there's something to it after all, something about the air being yanked from your throat, about your body temperature being double-shocked, bubbles rolling and bumping toward the sun in big fat plumes. I imagine it must feel like an epiphany.

I hugged my knees to my chest and braced myself. It had to be coming. It was here now, gliding through the air along with the brine and the sea tar, and surely, I was about to realize something big; I was going to raise my arms to the sky and say "aha," I was going to understand the world and I was going to grow up. Right now.

But nothing happened. Because of course it didn't. That's life.

An important part of selling a book is knowing your audience. At the beginning, when I was first pitching my idea, I suggested there'd be reader overlap with books similar to mine, with viewers of this TV show or that movie. But when I wrote, I only ever addressed an amorphous blob. Maybe my reader would be someone like me, who liked pop culture and knew too much about the Internet. Or it'd be someone totally different, a technophobe maybe, who'd never even seen *Twilight*. But somewhere along the way, the amorphous blob took shape—into a young girl, one with questions and a pointed way of looking at things—and I realized I'd been writing for Jackie, even if I didn't know it.

She's sixteen now, a sophomore in high school. I hadn't realized how much she'd grown until I came back for quarantine. I remember going with her to pick up salads from Health Nut. She didn't even copy my order. She got her own thing. Like, I'm pretty sure it had seeds on it, which I found entirely mind-boggling, because I would never, ever think to order seeds on a salad. "That's pretty grown up," I believe I said to her.

We sat in the backyard and I watched her curiously. I'd been so absorbed in my own life that I hadn't noticed how much she'd changed. She was taller than me, and so beautiful, and she had her own style and hobbies and way of looking at the world. She listened to Janis Joplin and kept a morning routine. Boys slid into her DMs. All of this was evidence of something I'd never really thought about before, something equal parts horrifying and wonderful: she wasn't a little girl anymore. And as we sat there, catching up on small, insignificant things like school drama and TV, I suddenly felt the immense gravity of being someone's big sister.

I think the reason I've been looking for a revelation is because I'm hoping there's a shortcut that I can pass along to her, a shred of wisdom that will save her hundreds of beers and thousands of walks. But now, I've come to suspect that there is no epiphany. I think confusion is a fact of life. Even if there is some grand moral to everything, I wonder if it would matter. She's sixteen years old. I didn't take advice when I was her age, and I hardly take advice now. I get it. There are some things you're just supposed to figure out on your own. And sometimes the most important parts of getting older are the ones that feel the most frustrating: the pandemonium of a high school friend group, or the zillions of questions that might get answered but also might not, or the odd, displaced feeling that summons you to a bathroom stall at your senior prom. The whole point of everything is that there is no real point. As far as I know, of course. I'm only twenty-one.

Acknowledgments

There are so many people to whom I owe a huge thank-you for their help and support throughout my entire journey.

Thank you to the College of Creative Studies. To Caroline Allen. It was in your creative nonfiction class where this book began to take shape. To mentor Nick Neely. To my cohorts at CCS whose thoughts, opinions, and zoomer insights pushed me to think harder and write better: Emma Demorest, Vianna Mabang, Talia White, Hannah Morley, and Mattie Jones. And to my advisor, professor, and friend, Kara Mae Brown: your wisdom and guidance changed my life.

To Isla Vista. To that one girl who walked me home in January 2020: I hope you dumped your boyfriend. To the house on 66 Sabado whose toilet I threw up in in August 2019: I apologize. And to Katie Mathieu and Rachelle Winters. Thank you for four years of friendship, advice, and degeneracy.

To BJ Robbins, for taking a chance on me.

To everyone at Flatiron, especially Cat Kenney, Jordan Forney, and Sydney Jeon. Thank you for your wonderful brains. And to Sarah Barley, my incredible editor, who always asked the right questions and shaped this book into what it is today.

And to my mom and dad, for everything.

About the Author

Via Bleidner is studying writing and literature at the University of California, Santa Barbara. She lives in Isla Vista. When she's not writing, she's shotgunning Bang Energy, dodging the debt collector, and badgering her professors for homework extensions. *If You Lived Here You'd Be Famous by Now* is her debut.